SOCIAL WORK IN
PRIVATE
PRACTICE

SOCIAL WORK IN PRIVATE PRACTICE

BY
ROBERT L. BARKER

2ND
EDITION

NASW PRESS

NATIONAL ASSOCIATION OF SOCIAL WORKERS
750 FIRST STREET, NE
WASHINGTON, DC 20002

Library of Congress Cataloging-in-Publication Data

Barker, Robert L.
    Social work in private practice / by Robert L. Barker.—2nd. ed.
    p.   cm.
    Includes bibliographical references and index.
    ISBN 0-87101-198-0
    1. Private practice social work—United States. 2. Social
workers—Professional ethics—United States.   I. Title.
HV10.5.B34   1991
361.3'2—dc20   91-35705
                                                                      CIP

Printed in the United States of America
Cover and interior design by The Graphic Issue

CONTENTS

4 GETTING AND STAYING QUALIFIED   40

5 PLANNING AND ORGANIZING THE PRACTICE   57

6 CHOOSING THE PRACTICE SETTING   70

7 MANAGING THE FINANCES 84

8 LEGAL AND ETHICAL ISSUES 104

9 WORKER–CLIENT CONTRACTING 116

10 MARKETING AND BUILDING A CLIENTELE 123

FOREWORD

Is private practice social work? Can one be an entrepreneur and still uphold the values of the profession? Since Mary Richmond predicted a role for private practitioners in 1922, social workers have debated these questions.

The National Association of Social Workers (NASW) officially deemed private practice an appropriate social work role in 1958. NASW established standards for private practice in 1962, the year that the Academy of Certified Social Workers (ACSW) was initiated. To augment the ACSW credential, which is a generic national credential for master's-level social workers with two or more years of experience, NASW developed the *NASW Register of Clinical Social Workers* to specifically identify clinicians who are qualified at the master's level.

The Association's efforts to develop credentials and licensing laws that protect the consumer have benefited private practitioners. Private practitioners are accountable to the public because they do not have agency or supervisor rules to follow. Therefore, credentials and licensing laws that regulate social workers enhance their ability to practice.

In addition to credentials and vigorous lobbying for licensing bills, NASW has offered private practitioners other tools for practice. Following the formation of the Council on Private Practice in 1964, the Association issued the *Handbook on the Private Practice of Social Work* in 1974. The *Handbook* was used by the profession until NASW released Robert Barker's *Social Work in Private Practice* 10 years later. Now we are pleased to offer a completely updated second edition of this excellent guide to developing and managing a private practice.

The number of private practitioners is growing. NASW estimated that there were about 8,000 social workers in private practice when the *Handbook* was published in 1974. Today, we estimate that there may be 30,000 private practitioners. The percentage of NASW members who report full-time or part-time private practice has grown from 11 percent in 1982 to over 17 percent in 1991.

The numbers are growing, and the nature of the practice is changing. As the costs of health care have escalated, practice in health and
mental health settings has changed. Private practice does not entail only
sitting in an office and working alone with a single client or a group.
Managed care and other forms of cost containment are a reality. Patterns
of reimbursement for services have been altered significantly. Conse-
quently, private practitioners work with a much wider range of agencies
and other providers; multidisciplinary work is the norm, rather than the
exception. Managed care, health maintenance organizations, employee
assistance programs, and other such entities are part of the fabric of the
private practitioner's work.

At one time, students viewed private practice as nirvana, a profession
in its own right through which they could expect to earn substantial
salaries, be autonomous, and select their own clients. Barker describes
the realities—and the rewards—of private practice very clearly. It is
possible to be a "genuine" social worker, a private practitioner, and a
successful entrepreneur; however, doing so requires substantial knowledge, hard work, and strong support from the profession. NASW offers
the support. Social work education and experience equip the social
worker with knowledge of social work. And this second edition of
Barker's *Social Work in Private Practice* provides the sound guidance that
aspiring as well as experienced private practitioners need. We highly
recommend it.

— BARBARA WHITE, PhD, ACSW
NASW President
— MARK G. BATTLE, ACSW
NASW Executive Director

PREFACE

Private social work practice has grown considerably since the first edition of this book was published in 1984. The number of its practitioners has almost doubled since then. According to available directories, about 18,000 social workers now identify themselves as private practitioners. In addition, there are far more than 10,000 social workers who identify themselves by their agency jobs who also see some clients privately.

Several other changes have occurred since 1984. Licensing or some form of public regulation of social work practice now exists in every state, and these credentials have become essential for a worker entering private practice. Managed health care and other third-party programs have generally granted vendorship status to qualified private social work practitioners. All sectors of the public, including the disadvantaged, are increasingly willing to pay for the services of private social work practitioners. And more people with mental health problems now go to social workers than to any other professional group.

The antipathy that many private practitioners once felt from their professional associations and agency-based colleagues now seems to have largely passed. Private practitioners have achieved leadership roles in the professional associations far out of proportion to their numbers, from national board members and presidents to local chapter officerships in most states. Fewer speeches and articles are now written against private practice, and more endorse it. Applications to schools of social work are reported to be increasing, and an increasing proportion of social work students is interested in private practice. Surveys in social work schools show that at least 22 percent of the students plan on careers in private social work practice.

In such a climate it is understandable that there would be heightened interest in private social work practice. Scholars and researchers seek information about the development and norms of the field. Experienced private practitioners want to know what their colleagues are doing to develop their practices. Those who want to enter private practice want to know about its potential hazards and the qualifications needed. Other social workers and professionals from other disciplines want to learn the reasons for the increasing success of social work private practice.

Providing this information is the goal of this second edition of *Social Work in Private Practice*. The book has been completely revised and updated to account for the trends of the past decade. It is greatly enlarged and now includes much more information about topical issues such as legal and ethical problems, marketing techniques, financial concerns, and contracting. There are two new appendixes. Appendix A contains sample contracts for the various client groups most likely to see private social workers. Appendix B lists the state licensing boards for social work and the state chapter offices of the National Association of Social Workers.

The information found in this book comes primarily from two sources: the growing literature on private social work practice, and personal interviews and polls of hundreds of private practitioners and those interested in joining the field. The literature cited in the bibliography includes the latest research and thinking about this field.

The interviews and polls were conducted mostly during my seminars on private practice. Largely because of the first edition of this book, I was invited to dozens of meetings where private practice was the theme. Many of these meetings were conducted with my friend and private practice colleague, Dr. Phil Brown, now a faculty member at Tulane University School of Social Work. During our presentations we asked members of the audience for their oral and written input about experiences, opinions, and useful tips on practice management. Their ideas have been included here, too.

It is to these social workers and their private practice colleagues that this book is dedicated. They have had to overcome many hurdles on their ways to private practice, and they have been generous in sharing their ideas with others. I also want to thank the editorial staff at NASW, Linda Beebe, Nancy Winchester, and Hyde Loomis, who deserve enormous credit for producing this book. I am grateful to Jacqueline M. Atkins and Susan H. Llewellyn for their editorial help on the first edition and to Roseanne Price, who edited this edition with such competence. Finally, my wife, Mary Elizabeth, deserves many thanks for her patience and valuable assistance.

1 THE EVOLUTION OF PRIVATE PRACTICE

She was just 29, with little education. Her only experience to speak of was office work. But her biggest problem was that she was female. It was 1891, and women were never considered for positions of authority. Especially not in a rough, bawdy port city like Baltimore.

But she was good with people. She had a knack for organizing them. And she was a very capable teacher and public speaker. Most important, she was honest. The men who had founded the local Charity Organization Society (COS) several years before had no doubt about that. They had hired her as their bookkeeper and were very pleased with her work. They had promoted her to assistant treasurer just the year before. Now they needed a new director, and they wondered if they should offer such a demanding job to this young lady. Mary Richmond was her name.

The men were ambivalent. The job would be challenging, even for a man, even for someone with experience. Poverty was everywhere, and there was no public money to help people in need. Only private philanthropy was keeping thousands from the almshouse. The COS had been established to solicit funds and distribute money and advice to the needy. Mary Richmond did a lot of this work herself when she could get away from her bookkeeping duties (Deutch, 1987). Always eager to learn, she spent most of her free time studying and talking with people about how to be an effective helper. The men realized she had already proved herself. They decided to offer her the job.

As the chief executive officer of the Baltimore COS, young Mary Richmond found herself working harder than ever with the poor and the rich, with volunteers and employees, with drunken sailors and respectable merchants who were down on their luck because of the recent depression. The Baltimore COS, like the others around the nation, was staffed primarily by volunteers. Most of these people were affluent, concerned socialites who had some spare time on their hands. They came to be known as "friendly visitors," and they talked with the needy and decided whom they would help (Richmond, 1899). But their work was unsystematic, and they were uncertain about how to do it well. Mary Richmond was often the only person in the office they could consult. They appreciated her taking time to teach them. She taught them that people often needed more than money, that they also needed encouragement and advice on where to get jobs or education, where to find affordable homes, how to get landlords to make repairs, and how to unite the neighbors to help one another.

Before long, many of the contributors and volunteers recognized the worth of Mary Richmond's advice and its applicability to themselves, as well as to their clients. She was bright, understanding, a good listener. Many shared their problems with her: "Miss Richmond, please don't utter a word about this, but my daughter is in the family way." "Miss Richmond, could you come talk with my wife tonight? She is becoming insufferable and I shan't be able to tolerate it much longer." "Miss Richmond, I think my husband is possessed by Demon Rum and I wish you could help him overcome this affliction."

One evening after the office was closed for the day, Mary Richmond was in her office catching up on her correspondence. There was a knock on the door, and it turned out to be one of the volunteers. The woman said she had personal problems and wanted Mary Richmond's help. After the talk, the grateful woman offered three dollars. Mary Richmond was perplexed. Should she take money for her services? Would it be proper? Ethical? She was on salary with COS. But the money was offered for her private work, not for the usual services of the organization. The woman who offered the money was not a COS client. Three dollars was half a week's pay! Mary Richmond could use the money to help other clients. So, in 1895, Mary Richmond, one of the major founders of professional social work, accepted money for private practice (Levenstein, 1964).

Years later, after she had trained countless social workers and formulated the first comprehensive statement of the principles of direct social work practice (Longres, 1987) and helped establish many of the principles and values that are now inherent in the profession (Richmond, 1917), she wrote this about private practice (Richmond, 1922):

> How rapidly social casework will develop a private practice of its own cannot be predicted, but it should be evident from the examples given in this book that the skill here described can be utilized quite as well in the homes of the rich as in those of the poor, that in the one as in the other, personality can be thwarted and retarded, developed and enriched. (p. 22)

THE 40-YEAR DEBATE

When a leader of an organization or movement practices and condones an activity, the followers tend to embrace, sustain, nurture, and encourage its evolution from insignificance to maturity. After Mary Richmond was gone, however, much of social work seemed antipathetic toward private practice. It was treated almost as an illegitimate child, a bastard to ignore and disavow, lest acknowledgment disgrace its parents.

For the next 40 years, from the 1920s through the 1950s, the "parents" bickered about what to do with this little creature, scarcely noticing that it was becoming larger and more independent on its own without much support or encouragement (Barker, 1987c). By the 1960s, it had become too large to ignore.

Not everyone in social work wanted to disown private practice, but the advocates were sparse and the opponents persuasive. Besides, everyone agreed that far more important issues faced the profession. Public help for the disadvantaged was virtually nonexistent, and the needy had little choice but to turn to private agencies. Before 1930, there was an efflorescence of social services agencies and a severe shortage of trained workers for the many new facilities. Nevertheless, membership in the nascent social work profession was increasing dramatically in all sections of the country (Lubove, 1965). Professional schools were being created; new ideas and techniques were being discovered and used. The profession had little time to develop private practice systematically and little attention to pay to those who might have wanted to provide their services outside the agencies.

Some Early Pioneers

Nevertheless, some would not be ignored. In 1926 a Philadelphia social worker decided to enter private practice. Seeking encouragement and ideas from her colleagues before embarking on the venture, she went to her professional organization, the Philadelphia chapter of the American Association of Social Workers (AASW). The members listened to her idea, pondered its implications, and debated its merits. Finally, the group decided not to endorse her entry into private practice. There were no criteria, no norms, and no qualifications to use as a basis for taking such a step. The members declared that there could be no such thing as private practice until standards and qualifications could be established by the profession.

The social worker was unhappy with the decision and persistent in keeping the issue alive at subsequent meetings. At her continued behest, the chapter contacted AASW national headquarters for an opinion. AASW agreed with the chapter and would not sanction anyone as a private practitioner until more facts were obtained. A memo, which is still on file in the archives of the National Association of Social Workers (NASW), was sent to the Philadelphia chapter saying that the private practice of social work was a contradiction and that, without auspices, what was being practiced was something other than social work (AASW, 1926). Private practice would have to wait.

But many social workers did not want to wait. NASW files contain numerous references to the activities of private social work practitioners in the 1930s (Levenstein, 1964). Some workers requested guidance on how much to charge. Some asked what they should do to get more referrals, what their relationship with social services agencies should be, or how they could get professional approval. Some writers wanted to know what they should call themselves. A Seattle private practitioner wondered if it was acceptable to be known as a "consultant on human relationships."

The Tribulations of Lee Steiner

The first person known to publish anything about her personal experiences in private practice was Lee Steiner (1936). In 1934 she "hung out her shingle" to establish a private social work practice. She wanted to indicate her master of social work (MSW) degree along with a designation of "social worker" on her signs, but her landlord forbade it. He pictured his building being filled with derelicts and impoverished beggars seeking her services. He believed the other tenants would not want to share the building with a social worker. He finally consented to lease space to her only if she deleted any reference to her profession.

Lee Steiner also had problems with her professional organization. AASW had still not sanctioned private practice, and her local colleagues disapproved of her plan to charge fees for her services. Ironically, her landlord and fellow tenants held her in higher esteem and were less reluctant to lease space when they learned of her fee-charging plans. It must be remembered that fee charging by agencies and agency social workers was almost unknown at the time (Goodman, 1971). The Jewish Family Services of New York City was one of the first social services agencies to charge fees, and it did not do so until 1943.

Among other obstacles Lee Steiner faced was the problem of acquiring clients. Potential referral sources were not accustomed to recommending social workers. There was no listing for social workers in the telephone book, and the state had no certification or licensing for the profession. Advertising was considered unethical. Most of Lee Steiner's referrals came from her professional colleagues in social services agencies—but not as many as she would have liked.

Admitting that the experience resulted in financial insecurity, she abandoned the project after two difficult years. "One person cannot set precedents for an entire profession," she wrote. "She might attempt a few experiments but the profession itself would have to decide upon the validity of those experiments" (Steiner, 1938, p. 196).

Lee Steiner returned to agency work for a brief time, but, still determined to work as a private practitioner, she left social work, returned to school, and became a certified psychologist. She eventually established her own successful private practice but in a different profession.

A Self-fulfilling Prophecy

There were still only a handful of social workers in private practice before World War II, and they tended to be secretive about it (Rockmore, 1948). Some gradually moved away from social work and into professions more hospitable to their private practices. Those who retained social work identities continued to ask their professional association for guidelines, sanctions, standards, and recognition.

What they got was disparagement. Most of the profession's leaders continued to criticize the private practice movement and declare that it was inappropriate for the field of social work. This view remained strong through the 1950s. Helen Harris Perlman, for example, wrote, "As a private practitioner without an institutional connection, [a social worker] can make no formalized contribution to the development of social casework" (Perlman, 1955, p. 430). Another leader in the profession, Ruth Smalley, stated categorically, "social work, as I understand it, is always practiced under some agency auspice" (Smalley, 1954, p. 214).

Without the approbation of their profession, the small number of private practitioners faced many difficulties. They were not unified and thus had little influence to obtain credentials within the profession. It is not surprising that many followed Lee Steiner's example and moved to other professions. Ironically, many opponents of private practice used this exodus as a major justification for their efforts to push the movement out of the profession, saying that private practitioners had no social work identity or interest. Private practice was caught in a self-fulfilling prophecy.

An Underground Movement

In spite of the difficulties, some practitioners were finding success in private work, and in some cities they were unifying their forces. Ruth Fizdale organized a large and successful private practice group in New York in the early 1950s, and she documented the organization's experiences in articles in the professional literature (Fizdale, 1959).

In other cities, some private practitioners began meeting regularly to discuss their common concerns. They were not yet recognized by their professional associations, but their influence in some local jurisdictions began to increase. The first public licensing of social work practice took place in San Diego in 1952, largely through the efforts of one such informal group. Several other municipalities and states followed suit in the next few years, primarily because of the influence of similar private practice groups.

Systematic analyses of private practice began to appear in the late 1940s (Ryerson & Weller, 1947). The first studies confirmed the prevailing impression that private practitioners usually identified with professions other than social work, had more education and experience than their agency-based counterparts, and claimed they were practicing psychotherapy rather than social work (Peek & Plotkin, 1951). They usually called their clients "patients," and most of their referrals came from psychiatrists.

Even though such findings did not lead to much sympathy for private practice on the part of agency-based social workers, the findings were crucial to the movement. They described what private practitioners were doing and what kind of workers were doing it. This description was an essential step toward establishing norms and standards for private practice.

PROFESSIONAL RECOGNITION

The growing number of workers entering private practice by the mid-1950s and their increasing visibility gave hope to those who had long been frustrated in their efforts to obtain professional recognition. In 1955 the seven major social work organizations* merged to form NASW. Many practitioners hoped this new organization would include private practice under its auspices. But that dream faded when the new president, Nathan Cohen, made his inaugural statement to the membership. Commenting on the growing interest in private practice, he said he doubted whether private practitioners were any longer engaged in doing social work (N. Cohen, 1956).

Many members disagreed. Several local NASW chapters and individuals immediately began calling for the Association to accept and de-

---

*The organizations that merged to form NASW in 1955 were the American Association of Social Workers, the American Association of Psychiatric Social Workers, the American Association of Group Workers, the Association for the Study of Community Organization, the American Association of Medical Social Workers, the National Association of School Social Workers, and the Social Work Research Group.

velop standards for private social work practice. The Association was still in its infancy, however, and more concerned with reorganizing its historical fields of practice. Besides, NASW replied, it could not determine if private work was a legitimate part of social work practice until social work practice itself was formally defined (Briggs, 1961). This working definition of social work practice—priority of the new organization—was developed within the year (Bartlett, 1958). The definition enabled the profession to finally recognize private social work practice officially in 1958 and to acknowledge formally that private practice was an appropriate part of social work practice (NASW, 1974).

In 1961 NASW formally endorsed the following definition of private practice (NASW, 1974):

> A private practitioner is a social worker who, wholly or in part, practices his profession outside the aegis of a governmental or duly incorporated voluntary agency, who has responsibility for his own practice and sets up his own conditions of exchange with his clients and identifies himself as a social work practitioner in offering his services. (p. 40)

The sexist language of the statement did not raise as many questions as did the meaning of the definition. Thus, NASW soon issued a policy statement to elaborate on private practice. It stated in part that "practice within socially sponsored organizational structures must remain the primary avenue for the implementation of the goals of the profession. . . . NASW avoids any action that will set apart or establish a special status, negative or positive, for private practice" (NASW, 1974, p. 41).

Private practitioners might well have breathed a collective sigh of relief with these developments. At last they existed! They were finally acknowledged and sanctioned by their profession, albeit reservedly. Of course, there was some dissatisfaction with both the definition and the subsequent policy statement. Many workers believed that the definition was inconsistent with the policy. For example, the policy stressed that private workers would have no status apart from the profession, yet the tone of the definition seemed to say that the private practitioner was an outsider. By definition, the practitioner was "outside" a government or private agency. Many also questioned the necessity of identifing themselves as social workers to be a part of the profession. Because numerous private practitioners had not previously referred to themselves as social workers, the issue was important and controversial. In any event, many practitioners took a "beggars can't be choosers" stance, and this official NASW definition and the policy statement have remained essentially unchanged to date.

NASW's minimum standards for a social worker's entry into private practice were ratified in 1962. To become a professionally sanctioned private practitioner, one had to have a master's degree from an accredited school of social work; be professionally certified by the Academy of Certified Social Workers (ACSW); and have five years of acceptable, full-time, supervised agency employment. The supervision and experience had to be in the specialty of one's private practice. These standards have been modified slightly since their inception, but ACSW membership has been the basic professional standard since 1971.

THE DEBATE INTENSIFIES

Professional sanction and standards raised the consciousness of those who were opposed to private practice, and in the early 1960s the debate became more intense than at any time before or since. Ruth Fizdale, by then the preeminent private practitioner–writer, declared to the National Conference on Social Welfare in 1961 that there was an increasing demand for private practitioners in social work (Fizdale, 1961). She said this demand required the profession to develop systematic and enforced standards. Max Siporin, in an influential study about the roles of private practice, determined that social work could be practiced equally well in an agency or a private setting (Siporin, 1961).

The arguments against private practice tended to emphasize five points, which were summarized by Sherman Merle in the article "Some Arguments against Private Practice" (Merle, 1962). He suggested that private practice may be anathema to social work values because (1) it discriminates against the less affluent; (2) it does not provide services to those who are in need but unable to pay; (3) it is so ill-defined that it needs agency auspices to provide norms and standards for the workers; and (4) it encourages workers to leave agencies, resulting in a shortage of personnel where the services are most needed. Fifth, he contended that the problem could be seen even in the term *"private* practice of *social* work"* itself, which is an oxymoron, using words and concepts that are mutually exclusive. The arguments have been restated in the social work literature many times since then (Howe, 1980; Karger, 1989).

IN DEFENSE OF PRIVATE PRACTICE

Of course, private practitioners continue to dispute these arguments. They point out that private practitioners need not be in agencies to have clearly defined roles and activities. Anyone offering a service for fee must be specific about what is being offered and what the credentials are.

Private practitioners, possibly even more than agency social workers, find it imperative to define their roles to each potential consumer of their services, or the consumer will not purchase those services.

Private practitioners also defend themselves against the charge that private practice is discriminatory. If discrimination means that only certain segments of the population would be eligible for services, they point out, then agency workers also discriminate. Most agencies charge fees for client services, and the amount can be as high as any charged by private practitioners. When fees are flexible enough for all clients to pay, the social services agency must then subject the applicant to a "means test" to determine the client's resources. Most social workers have long felt that the means test is a highly questionable, discriminatory, and undesirable practice (Bentrup, 1964).

There are many established social services agencies oriented to serving ethnic or religious groups; many other agencies specialize in work with select segments of the population such as the aged, those with specific disabilities, the young, or those who live within certain geographic boundaries. These social services agencies are also discriminatory, private practitioners claim, but their criteria of discrimination have, with tradition, become acceptable.

Still, most private practitioners acknowledge the fundamental validity of the charge that many poor people simply do not have geographic, social, or financial access to their services. This is true despite some practitioners' assertions and rationalizations that agencies also charge high fees, that insurance companies cover much of the cost of services, and that fees tend to be based on sliding scales.

Private practitioners also find it hard to refute the contention that the terms "private" and "social" are contradictory. Many practitioners, for that reason, call themselves "autonomous" or "independent" social work practitioners instead. These terms, however, have not caught on among social workers, probably because the other helping professions have used the private practice designation.

The argument that the private practice movement would draw needed social workers away from already understaffed agencies has not been borne out. Such a concern may have been warranted during the rapid expansion of social services in the 1960s, but it is not now. Although some social work personnel shortages temporarily exist in areas of rapid population growth or where there are newly emerging social problems, overall there is a balance between supply and demand in social services agency employment (Williams & Hopps, 1990, p. 291). At present, there are few social services agencies in the government or the private sector that are unable to find well-educated, highly competent employees from among their many applicants.

GRUDGING TOLERANCE

As the private practice movement has grown since the 1960s, the debate has diminished but not ended. Nor does it seem likely to end in the foreseeable future. Social work's history and heritage, its values and aspirations for society, and its methods for reaching these goals place the private practice model of delivering social services at the center of a complex and possibly irreconcilable conflict. Social work is and has always been ambivalent about two systems inherent in private social work practice: the entrepreneurial or business approach to helping and the clinical or "residual" model of delivering social services.

Private practice is a business, and the social work profession has mixed feelings about business and its practices, goals, and consequences. Many social workers see the proponents of business as the enemy, the perpetrator of social disadvantage. If the system were more equitable, social workers frequently say, if people had greater protection from capitalistic exploitation or business upheavals, then there would be far less suffering. The language of business—terms such as "free enterprise," "rugged individualism," "competition in the marketplace," and "profit motive"—is seen by many social workers as shibboleths. Many social workers are convinced that those who use such terms subscribe to the philosophy known as "social Darwinism," or survival of the economic fittest, and have proclivity for exploiting, or at least are indifferent to, the needy.

The other source of the profession's ambivalence about private practice grows from the perennial conflict about the profession's social function. Social workers have long debated whether to serve society by helping individuals cope more effectively with the unavoidable problems of society or by seeking to bring about institutional changes in society so individuals will not have to face those problems. The debate has had many different names through the decades—"cause versus function," "social activism versus individual therapy," "developmental versus residual intervention," "primary versus tertiary prevention," "macro versus micro perspectives"—but the substantive issue remains the same.

Most social workers, regardless of what they do in practice, believe that achieving institutional change is the fairest, most efficient, and most logical way to achieve professional objectives. Yet private social work practice is, or seems to be, primarily a residual approach to problem solving. In other words, the private practitioner enables the client to cope with or adjust to a condition in society that caused the problem.

Of course, there is considerable merit in this view. At best, private practice can be only one of many ways to ameliorate problems. It is not and does not pretend to be a cure-all. It will never have more than a minor impact on the entire social welfare process. Major emphasis may properly be placed on bringing about institutional rather than residual improvements in the social welfare system, but it is grandiose and naive to expect that there will not always be a need for both.

It is not valid, however, to imply that because private practice has its limitations it should not be a part of social work. Neither agency-based practice nor the broader approach of social work advocacy and policy development is without limitations. These models also have their critics.

The proponents of private practice ask what is wrong with peaceful coexistence and mutual support. The delivery of social services is a vastly complicated, ever-changing process that requires a wide variety of people who use an array of different techniques in heterogeneous settings. A variegated approach leads to innovation, creativity, and greater efficacy, all sorely needed commodities, especially in the much-beleaguered profession of social work. Employing the best elements of agency-based and private practice is in the best interests of the client, the profession, and society.

NUMBERS OF PRIVATE PRACTITIONERS

Those who are unenthusiastic about private practice may not be swayed by the arguments above, but today they are confronted by another compelling factor. Whatever merits or demerits independent social work may have, it is too large to be ignored and too influential to be wished away (Wallace, 1982). It took four decades for the movement to grow from a handful to a few hundred, but today thousands of social workers are hanging out their private practice shingles.

The exact figure has always been hard to calculate. Obtaining accurate statistics is impeded by two factors. One is that the definition of private practice does not precisely distinguish between who is and who is not a private practitioner. Is one considered a private practitioner or an employee when he or she is hired by another private practitioner to treat the overload of clients and is paid a percentage of the income from those clients? Is a social worker who is salaried by a for-profit group of private practitioners also considered a private practitioner? Why is a person who maintains a consulting firm and, for fees, advises businesses on the social services needs of employees not considered a private practitioner? The number of social workers said to be in private practice has varied depending on which of the many possible definitions and criteria are used.

The other factor is that private practitioners have tended to be independent, and therefore they are not easy to count. Many are not affiliated with any social work organization or group and thus are not included in statistical records.

Many private practitioners do not list themselves as social workers but identify themselves with other psychotherapy-providing professions. Some belong to social work organizations other than NASW, organizations whose focus is on clinical work and private practice. The most influential of these organizations have been the International Conference for the Advancement of Private Practice (I-CAPP) and the National Federation of Societies for Clinical Social Work (NFSCSW), publisher of the journal *Clinical Social Work*. Many have joined these groups because of the perceived antipathy toward private and clinical social work practiced by the social work "establishment."

Other social workers in private practice join non–social work organizations such as the American Association for Marriage and Family Therapy (AAMFT), the International Group Psychotherapy Association, and the American Psychotherapy Association. These and many other organizations are open to several professional groups in mental health services, and, in some cases, their membership rolls have a high percentage of social workers. In addition, some private practitioners belong to more than one of these organizations and are possibly being counted more than once.

Therefore, whenever estimates of the numbers of private practitioners are given, they must be scrutinized carefully. The numbers have varied widely and sometimes can reflect the bias of the estimator. Proponents of private practice have tended to assume the numbers are high, and opponents have suggested the numbers are minuscule. In 1954, for example, Ruth Smalley estimated that there were fewer than 100 private social work practitioners (Smalley, 1954). In 1962, when the profession reluctantly sanctioned private practice, it was estimated that between 1,700 and 2,000 practitioners were at work full- or part-time across the nation (Levenstein, 1964). In 1967 the NASW Committee on Private Practice calculated that 3,000 to 4,000 practitioners were so engaged (Golton, 1971). Nine years later, the NASW executive director testified that there were between 8,500 and 10,000 social workers in part-time and full-time private practice (C. Alexander, 1976).

Such figures are important clues about the growth of private practice but cannot be taken as conclusive statements about the number of practitioners. More recent estimates are not exact but show continued growth. One NASW survey indicated that 15.3 percent of the sampled social workers were in private practice (Williams & Hopps, 1990). Another study indicated that 31 percent of all social workers in clinical social work are involved in private practice, either part- or full-time (Mackey, Burek, & Charkoudin, 1987).

As of 1991, the author estimates that many more than 28,000 social workers are in private practice, of whom about 18,000 are in full-time practice. This figure is based on an actual count of the social workers found in available directories who indicated that they were in private practice. These directories include the 1991 *NASW Register of Clinical Social Workers* (NASW, 1991a); the *1989/90 Diplomate Directory* (American Board of Examiners in Clinical Social Work [ABE], 1989); directories of other groups such as I-CAPP, NFSCSW, and AAMFT; and the Yellow Pages listings in major U.S. cities.

In making this count I tried to eliminate all duplications as well as social workers who could not be identified for certain as having private practices. For example, I excluded from my count social workers employed in such places as the Chicago Guidance Center and the Montgomery County Psychosocial Services Center. I did include workers whose affiliations clearly sounded like private practices (for example, Marital and Family Stress Center and Jones Counseling Center) even if they did not list themselves as private practitioners. I believe this estimate is very conservative because it does not include the many social workers who may have part-time or full-time practices who were not specifically listed as such in the directories available to me. It is likely that there are more than 28,000 social workers in private practice.

In addition, private social work practice is growing not only in the United States, but also in many other countries. Australia, India, Israel, Great Britain, and Canada have significant numbers of private social work practitioners, and social workers from other countries are showing increased interest (Levin & Leginsky, 1990; Pinker, 1990; Rosenman, 1989).

ACTIVITIES OF PRIVATE PRACTITIONERS

What are today's social workers doing in private practice? For many years they have been providing more services to more low-income clients than most people realize (Drucker & King, 1973). They are seeing about 10 percent of their clients for reduced fees or for free. Most use flexible fee scales to accommodate clients with lower incomes.

Their activities are even more diverse than those of their agency-based colleagues. They have been highly involved in the movement toward managed health care and provision of services to prepaid groups in the community (Bailis, Stone, & Bailis, 1990). They are providing services to industrial organizations to provide for their employee assistance programs (Cunningham, 1990). They are serving on boards of social services agencies (Goldmeier, 1986). They are engaged in social activism at least as commonly as other social workers, and more than others on some issues (Reeser, 1988). They have led the struggle to get licensing for social work practice in nearly every state.

They are identifying themselves as social workers and developing recognition for having unique expertise. To the general public, which has proved its willingness to pay for social work services through the private practice model, the profession of social work is seen as a worthy profession—worthy of their patronage, and not just for the poor.

2 DEFINING PRIVATE PRACTICE

What is and what is not private practice in social work? To be considered a private practitioner, must one be a clinician? Must one be a licensed professional? Can someone be a private social work practitioner without an advanced degree?

The term "private practice" has been so value laden, controversial, and ill-defined over the years of its existence that there is considerable disagreement about what it actually is. For example, social workers themselves are not always enlightening when they are asked if they are private practitioners: one might say yes and another no, even though they are doing identical work in identical settings.

Some social workers identify themselves as private practitioners even when they are salaried by agencies, because their agencies are funded through private contributions. Some see themselves as private practitioners even though they are salaried social workers employed by other private practitioners. Some identify themselves as such, whether or not they have any clients, simply because they have not been able to find agency employment. Some social workers who are employed by social services agencies consider themselves private practitioners because the agency pays them on a fee-for-service basis like independent contractors. Some do not consider themselves to be in private practice, even though they receive fees for service, because they do not work in a clinical setting. Some social workers are completely self-employed but work as management consultants or community organizers. Others say they are not private practitioners because they work primarily in social work agencies and see only a few clients on their own time just to keep in touch with that kind of therapy.

The variations in practice models seem endless and add to the difficulty in specifying what is and what is not private practice. The situation is reminiscent of the case confronting the U.S. Supreme Court about pornography that led Justice Potter Stewart to say, "I may not be able to define it, but I sure know it when I see it."

Nevertheless, a formal definition of the term can be found in *The Social Work Dictionary* (Barker, 1991):

private practice: In social work, the process in which the values, knowledge and skills of social work, which were acquired through sufficient education and experience, are used to deliver social services autonomously to clients in exchange for mutually agreed payment. (p. 181)

TEN CRITERIA FOR PRIVATE PRACTICE

Any definition is merely a skeleton. Considerable filling out must take place before one can grasp what private social work practice is. Criteria must be established to state who is and who is not in private practice. According to the 10 criteria, or norms, used in this book, the private practitioner

- has the client as the primary obligation
- determines who the client will be
- determines the techniques to be used in service to this client
- determines practice professionally, not bureaucratically
- receives a fee for service directly from or in behalf of the client
- is educated as a social worker
- is a sufficiently experienced social worker
- adheres to social work values, standards, and ethics
- is licensed, certified, and registered, where applicable, to engage in private practice
- is professionally responsible.

Each of these norms is discussed below. Comparisons are made between the agency worker and the private practitioner for each norm. Making these comparisons does not imply that one or the other model of delivering social services is necessarily better. It is a fundamental premise of this book that both private and agency-based forms of practice have value as well as limitations; there is a place for both.

Primary Obligation to the Client

The NASW *Code of Ethics* (1990b, p. 4) states that "the social worker's primary responsibility is to clients." That principle is more difficult to follow than it seems. Employees of any organization are obliged to fulfill the conditions of employment; it is unreasonable to expect most employees, whatever the standards of their profession, to place something else above this obligation. As Piliavin (1968) pointed out, the agency employee will generally conform to the policies and work requirements of the agency rather than the needs of a given client if there is conflict over whose interests have precedence.

Many agency-based workers would dispute this contention if it is made in the abstract. The issue is rarely tested, fortunately, because agency requirements and those of clients are generally compatible. However, in actual practice, there can be conflicts. An agency policy, for example, might be to maintain a waiting list for potential clients; but suppose that one person could not wait. Workers who know their services are needed, but also know that their agency is firm, have to make choices. In another example, an agency's policy is to provide short-term treatment for emergency clients; this permits it to serve as many clients as possible. When one client reaches the time limit and wants to continue with the worker to acquire further insights, what is the worker likely to do?

Certainly, in these examples, there would be some flexibility in agency policy, but if the flexibility became so great that the policy was widely ignored, the agency would have to begin to tighten up. Eventually, there would be enough pressure put on the workers who kept taking advantage of the flexibility to ensure subsequent conformity to agency policy above all other considerations; otherwise the worker would not be able to remain at the agency. As Noll (1974) wrote,

> Whenever the mental health professional is employed by an agency or by an institution, the institution's needs will almost invariably supersede those of the patient. There is a basic, usually unacknowledged, antagonistic relationship between the individual and the institutional professional. (p. 3)

In the private practice model of delivering social services, there is less of a problem than in agency-based practice with this dilemma. The principle of client precedence is unquestionable for the private social work practitioner except in very rare and highly unusual circumstances. The first and foremost distinguishing characteristic of private practice is that the practitioner is an employee of the client. The practitioner may be fired or replaced at any time, for any reason, if the work is not satisfactory to the client. The agency-based worker is fired only if the work is unsatisfactory to the agency. The client has much the same authority over the private practitioner as would any other employer, so the worker is faced with fewer conflicts about divided loyalties.

The client–private practitioner relationship is implemented, or the worker is hired, when a mutually satisfactory agreement is reached. This agreement or contract may be implicit or explicit (see chapter 9 and appendix A), but both parties come to it without manifest responsibility to other auspices (Kutchins, 1991). It must be noted, however, that there may be some risks in private practice that are less serious or nonexistent in agency practice. The major threat to the client's interest would be the private practitioner's personal motivation to exploit or otherwise let per-

ɔ predominate over the client's. The agency structure has
. ʌ ɔnecks and balances than private work, and these help decrease the
likelihood of such occurrences.

Selection of Clientele

In the agency-based model of social work practice, the worker typically is assigned clients, and the typical client has little choice about the
worker he or she will see. An intake worker might determine which staff
member would be most appropriate for the client, or the decision might
be made at random, depending on which worker is next on the list. In
smaller agencies, where there may be only one or two workers, it is still
agency policy that determines which worker sees a given client. F. J.
Turner (1978) suggested that the client's relative lack of choice may be
due in part to social work's primary emphasis on serving society's objectives first, with "client self-determination of only secondary importance"
(p. 178).

Many agencies, but certainly not most, have recognized the importance of effective matching and have learned that worker-client interactions are significantly improved when care is taken. *Matching* refers to
the exclusive or preferential assignment of certain types of clients to
specific types of agency personnel. The matching process in many agencies, if it exists at all, often leaves much to be desired.

In private practice, the matching process is carried out by the social
worker and the client; the practitioners themselves decide what type of
client they work best with and target their practices to this type of
clientele. The practitioner may pursue more knowledge about a given
type of client or a given type of technique but makes the decision freely.

The risks inherent in this approach are readily apparent, however.
Workers are not always able to judge their own competence. Most private
practitioners cannot be objective about the clientele to exclude. Moreover, in a competitive marketplace, some practitioners are inclined to take
any client who seeks their services, regardless of whether they are capable of providing the needed services. This circumstance would be less
likely to occur in the social services agency, where the worker most
capable of providing the service is more likely to be given the assignment.

Choice of Service Method

Agency policy often predetermines the methods to be employed in
providing services. Agency supervisors, because of the agency require-

ments, often require that the worker provide a specific and limited type of service or method of service delivery. For example, some agencies are oriented to long-term, insight-oriented treatments, whereas others provide short-term crisis intervention. Some specialize in helping people get jobs or financial support; others specialize in group therapy techniques, transactional analysis methods, or behavioral training programs. The agency worker is thus restricted in the type of method that can be used, no matter what the worker personally believes is best for the client.

In private practice there are fewer restrictions about method. As a professional person who has the education, experience, skill, and knowledge to make decisions about the best approach and best treatment for any given problem, the private practitioner decides which method to use. The method is then explained by the worker to obtain the client's consent or refusal. For example, a private practitioner could make house calls if work with a rigid family was not progressing well in the office (Whittington, 1985), but an agency might not permit it.

There are controls on the private practitioner, but not immediate and direct ones as in the case of agency rules. The private practitioner's controls are the threat of malpractice suits from clients, grievance committees within the professional association, and competition in the marketplace.

Professional, Not Bureaucratic, Service

Social services agencies and other organizations use bureaucratic principles as their mode of operation. Division of labor, specialization, delegation of responsibility, and definition of roles to prevent overlap are among the essential components of bureaucracy and of any social work organization (Holland & Petchers, 1987).

Unlike most private practitioners, most agency social workers are bureaucrats. As such, "the social worker is required to negotiate the stresses, opportunities, and constraints that permeate organizational life, regardless of what his position is in the organization" (Pruger, 1973, p. 26).

It is the nature of any organization to state what the expected behavior of its members is to be and to enforce conformity; this helps the organization to coordinate its activities and avoid disorganization. Thus the agency worker's ability to make professional decisions is circumscribed.

In sum, agency practice is essentially determined bureaucratically rather than professionally. Professionalism and bureaucracy are not mutually exclusive, however, and there is ample opportunity for effective professional behavior within organizational limits.

Private practice is essentially nonorganizational. The independent practitioner does not spend a large portion of time engaged in organizational prerogatives, and behavior is limited only by professional requirements and personal judgments. Decisions affecting practice are circumscribed by the practitioner's professional organization and public statute. However, a private practitioner who chooses to ignore professional mores (which is, unfortunately, more easily done in private practice because of the lack of bureaucratic controls) can provide a disservice to those in need of help.

Income through Fees for Service

The client pays the private practitioner to perform a specific service. The payment is related to that particular service; payment is not made for activities that do not directly benefit the client. For example, when the worker takes a special course to improve skills that can help the client, the client does not pay the worker directly for that training. The worker's income depends on the service provided, for which there is an agreement about payment.

In contrast, in the agency-based model, payment is not based on service delivered but on conformity to the agency's expectations. The agency might require the worker to maintain regular hours, provide service for all assigned clients, attend workshops, and engage in administrative duties as part of the conditions of employment. In exchange for this conformity, the agency pays the worker a salary, money to which the worker is entitled regardless of how often any one client is seen.

One exception is the case in which an agency pays its employees on a per capita contractual basis. The amount paid is based on the number of clients seen. The worker receives fees for service, but the amount of the fee or the conditions of payment are set by the agency rather than the worker. The contractual worker is not engaged in private practice, despite fees for service, because the worker does not fulfill the first three criteria.

Many social workers consider themselves private practitioners when they work on a contractual basis for a private practitioner. Actually, they are employees of the private practitioner, just as a nurse works for a private practice physician or a legal research assistant is employed by a private attorney. Usually, the employer is a well-established private practitioner who has more clients and referrals than can be seen by one person. This person may be a social worker or a member of another profession who recognizes the value of social services delivery to clients. The practitioner usually provides the office space and clients for the social worker and maintains overall responsibility for each case by reviewing and supervising the social worker's direct treatment of clients. The social worker is paid only a percentage of the amount paid by or in behalf of the client; the rest goes to the employing private practitioner. Less commonly, the social worker is paid a predetermined annual or monthly salary for providing services prescribed by the practitioner. This system is becoming popular as a way to increase the practice and income of an established private practitioner, and it provides some social workers with jobs.

To some, however, this activity borders on the dubious practice of "fee splitting" (Barker, 1986a), which is discussed in chapter 7. Government peer review organizations and third-party payers have been challenging the practice with increasing regularity and success. The social worker as well as the client is possibly being exploited. In any event, the contractual worker in this circumstance is not a private practitioner.

Education as a Social Worker

Private practice is very demanding. It requires the worker to make frequent, rapid, and independent judgments without much help from others. There are no supervisors to add ideas to the decision-making process. No agency or clinic policies exist to predetermine what kind of client to serve or what methods to use. The private practitioner is more visible as an individual to the public than is the worker employed in an agency. Thus knowledge at ready command to make these judgments is crucial, and the social worker's professional education provides both the theoretical and the practical foundations for being able to make such independent judgments.

Social work education does make a difference, as recent studies demonstrate (Dhooper, Royse, & Wolfe, 1990). It is practical as well as conceptual, qualities most important for private work. Engaging in private practice with only a theoretical foundation could be hazardous to the client as well as to the worker. It would be like playing on a professional basketball team after having read books on how the game should be played but never having played it. It also takes practice, trial and error, and a considerable amount of coaching to be able to carry out the right plays.

The amount and kind of social work education necessary to engage in private practice are the subject of debate. Most states that license social workers for independent practice specify that the practitioners must possess at least a master's-level degree in social work from an accredited graduate school. NASW and other professional social work organizations that sanction private practice also require the MSW as the minimum educational standard. But whether a two-year graduate program is enough formal education for private social work practice is being debated by social workers, government funding organizations, and third-party financers (Barker, 1990a). The question is also being raised by other mental health care professions, largely because they consider a two-year program unfairly advantageous to social workers. It is a fast track to private practice (Karger, 1989). These critics also point out that the doctorate is their minimum requirement and that it takes this level of education to provide adequate services (Lesse, 1990).

Some schools of social work have been considering awarding doctorates for practice that are distinct from research doctorates. It is possible that the practice doctorate will eventually become the minimum educational requirement for social work, too.

Social Work Experience

Regardless of the quality and extent of the social worker's education, substantial practical experience is required to consolidate and integrate that training. The profession of social work has long recognized that the master's degree is only a beginning step toward providing professional social services. Supervised practice in an agency is an important aspect of the worker's continuing education. This supervision provides a safeguard for clients and makes it possible to assure them that they are, directly or indirectly, in the hands of competent professionals. Professional ethics and personal consideration for the client's well-being should dictate that the social worker acquire substantial agency-based supervision in the beginning practice years.

Many practitioners believe that the supervision requirement has been overdone in agency settings. In private practice, however, it is rarely overdone and is in considerable danger of being underdone.

There seems to be a trend toward relaxing this requirement in agency work. One study revealed that 75 percent of the social workers sampled who had graduated from schools of social work since 1967 had not met the requirement for supervision (Borenzweig, 1981). But without benefit of objective professional observation, the relatively inexperienced private practitioner is more vulnerable to developing bad professional habits and blind spots.

It must be remembered that the practitioner represents the profession to the public, and mistakes could be viewed by consumers of services as representative of the profession. This is not to suggest that a recent social work graduate could not work under supervision in a private practitioner's office. In this instance, the graduate would not be working autonomously but would be gathering the necessary experience to eventually work independently.

How long must a social worker be supervised before being considered capable of practicing autonomously? The NASW professional standard, operationalized in its Academy of Certified Social Workers and Qualified Clinical Social Worker (QCSW) qualification, is two years of paid social work employment or 3,000 hours of paid part-time experience (NASW, 1991a). The profession considers it desirable, but not required, for this work to be done under the direct supervision of an ACSW social worker. Also expected for ACSW and QCSW certification are professional references, with one from the worker's present immediate supervisor.

State licensing laws that have supervisory requirements have, for the most part, duplicated the NASW recommendations as to the amount of required experience. Nevertheless, some state licensing requirements include no provisions for experience, although several others require more than two years of experience before sanctioning private practice. The social worker obviously will need to conform to the state legal regulations before considering entry into private practice.

Social Work Values and Ethics

The NASW *Code of Ethics* is "based on the fundamental values of the social work profession that include the worth, dignity, and uniqueness of all persons as well as their rights and opportunities. It is also based on the nature of social work, which fosters conditions that promote these values" (NASW, 1990b, p. iii). Thus ethics and values are so integral to the nature of the profession that the profession is meaningless without them. The profession's values and ethics are designed to enhance the client's well-being.

The *Code of Ethics* represents to the public and to consumers of private social work services a standard of behavior to which the practitioner must adhere; without such a commitment, the practitioner cannot lay claim to membership within the field.

NASW's *Code of Ethics* is not the only ethical code for social workers. Other codes have been developed by NFSCSW, AAMFT, the National Institute for Clinical Social Work Advancement, and numerous special interest professional associations such as the National Association of Black Social Workers and the American Association of Industrial Social Workers. Is a social worker in violation of some principle by choosing to adhere to one of these codes over another? In fact, all are similar to NASW's code, and compliance with any one of them is essentially compliance with any other (Barker, 1988b).

Licensing and Certification

A license is a credential awarded to an individual who meets certain qualifications established by law. The purpose of a license, in theory, at least, is to protect the public. It is assumed that the applicant for the license engages in complex activities that are difficult for a potential consumer to evaluate independently. The state thus provides this as an a priori evaluation for the consumer. The state says that the license holder has met its standards and accordingly is qualified to provide the service. It is therefore in the interest of the profession, its clients, and its members to have licensing wherever social work practice exists.

Certification is the credential awarded to individuals who meet the explicit standards of a professional organization. The purpose, although not usually stated as such, is to protect the profession as well as the client. Certification protects the title "certified social worker" and demonstrates to the public that anyone with that designation has fulfilled the requirements inherent in that title. The most important certifications are NASW's Academy of Certified Social Workers for all experienced social work professionals and the Qualified Clinical Social Worker credential for those ACSW members with clinical specializations. Another credential is the Board Certified Diplomate (BCD), which is authorized by the American Board of Examiners in Clinical Social Work.

There are considerable problems with social work licenses and certificates. Hardcastle (1990) evaluated the existing licensing regulations and found many deficiencies. In most cases, he wrote, they are so unspecific and imprecise that they have little potential for protecting the public from the professional. Substantial strengthening is needed.

This shortcoming is due not to legislative indecisiveness but to the difficulty of defining with precision what it is that social workers do and what skills are required to do it. That being the case, many social workers might wonder what difference it makes whether or not they have a license or certification. Whatever the deficiencies in the statutes, it would be illegal to practice social work without the relevant credential. And most private practitioners in social work believe that licensing criteria can be refined and strengthened once some statute is in place on which to build.

Professional Responsibility and Accountability

That professional responsibility and the maintenance of social work's high standards are important is implicit in all the above criteria, but it also needs to be made explicit. The private practitioner, in making independent judgments and in implementing decisions about practice, is primarily responsible for those actions and accountable for their success. The private practitioner does not have the protective blanket that often covers the agency-based worker, who shares responsibility with colleagues, supervisors, agency administrators, and agency policy. Accordingly, the private worker must answer to the public and the profession for any actions that are below standard or not in keeping with the best interest of the client. The private practitioner's ability, knowledge, and behavior are put on the line with every contact made with a client. Responsible action requires diligence and a high commitment to the standards of social work practice. The agency-based worker is typically expected to behave according to those same standards, but the enforcement of those behaviors comes from agency policy, supervisors, and administrators rather than from only the practitioner.

Social workers—whether they are employed in agencies or in private practice, whether their primary orientation is clinical treatment or prevention and institutional development—share a common purpose. According to NASW, it is "to promote or restore a mutually beneficial interaction between individuals and society in order to improve the quality of life for everyone." Private practitioners are not excused from this obligation, even though they may not be reminded of it as often as someone in an agency. Private practice social workers have at least as much of an opportunity, and probably more than most other social workers, to uphold this purpose. Freed from the constraints of cautious employers and the restraints against political activism imposed on some government employees, they are in a good position to work toward this objective. It is not necessary for a private practitioner either to be a clinician, or, if the practitioner is a clinician, to limit activity to clinical work. As a citizen and a social worker, the practitioner has the opportunity to get outside the office and work to achieve the values to which the profession subscribes.

PRIVATE PRACTICE AS A BUSINESS

The 10 norms of private social work practice outlined earlier refer to professional issues. Another element, which is also significant, is the nature of private practice as a business enterprise. To succeed in such a venture, the social worker must be more than a competent professional. Knowing the principles of sound business, implementing them appropriately, and reconciling them with the values of the profession are also essential.

As a business enterprise, the private practice model of delivering social services has always had more in common with social services agency service delivery than has been generally realized. There are and will always be significant differences, but of late the differences have been greatly reduced. The services of private practitioners have become available to people from a much wider portion of the economic spectrum than is generally realized, and agency services are becoming less accessible to many of those in need.

Because of severe financial pressures, many social work agencies have found themselves struggling (Reynolds, 1987). They are charging much higher fees and serving more affluent, well-insured clients. The fees charged the more affluent are often as high as those charged by private practitioners. Agencies are not doing this because they lack compassion for the needy but because many of them could not survive otherwise. The costs of running an agency have become so great, and governmental and philanthropic contributions have been so reduced, that there is no alternative but to get funds from those served. Agency spokespeople point out, with ample justification, that they would be unable to serve even the smaller number of needy clients if they had to cease their operations due to lack of resources.

Private practice has experienced the opposite trend. Third-party financial involvement through increased insurance coverage and governmental subsidization has made services provided by private practitioners more accessible. The United States has more than 1,200 private health insurance companies, 626 health maintenance organizations, and 78 Blue Cross/Blue Shield plans (Leon, 1990). Most of these pay for the services of independent practitioners.

Of course, it may be unfair to compare the cost-effectiveness of agency and private practice. Even though the differences are getting smaller, there are still significant differences in populations served, in treatment modalities used, and in economic incentives operating in each. Overhead may be less and direct service will be proportionately more in private work because of the greater economic incentive to keep the hours filled in direct service to clients. In public agencies, more time is presumably spent on improving the social conditions that lead to the problems as well as on providing unmeasurable and unchargeable services that only indirectly benefit the clients.

In any event, financially hard-pressed agency directors who have been seeking cost savings in service delivery are looking more carefully at private social work practice. Many of the private practitioners' methods are being emulated in agencies, and some agencies are contracting with private practitioners to provide agency services through a purchase of service agreement (Kettner & Martin, 1988). Agencies have found not only that this system provides services for clients who otherwise might be placed on waiting lists, but also that the productivity and effectiveness of private practitioners have been high and provide an economical way of meeting service needs.

3 THE REWARDS AND RISKS OF PRIVATE PRACTICE

Many people, especially overworked and underpaid agency social workers, think private practice is a "bed of roses." They are right. It is often a nice place to be, but it is also full of thorns, bees, frost warnings, and manure (Roth, 1983).

Why do social workers want to enter private practice? It is, after all, a venture filled with numerous everyday burdens and the potential for serious financial and professional risks. The rewards are never guaranteed and rarely are as generous as anticipated. The hazards are guaranteed and are often more serious than expected (Freudenberger, 1983; Hines, 1988). Thus, the first thing a social worker who is thinking about going into private practice should do is objectively weigh the pros and cons, the rewards and risks, of this challenging venture.

MOTIVATIONS FOR ENTERING PRIVATE PRACTICE

Despite the many obstacles to success in private practice, there are enough rewards, or perceived rewards, to make it the fastest-growing setting for social work practice. Many experienced social workers, perhaps up to 30 percent, have decided to establish private practices to supplement or replace their agency jobs (Pawlak & Bays, 1988). Many adults with established careers have been applying for admission to graduate schools of social work in the hope of establishing private practice careers (Magner, 1989). An estimated 22 percent of the MSW class of 1990 indicated their intention to go into private practice eventually (Abell & McDonell, 1990).

There are many reasons why so many aspire to social work in private practice. No doubt some people want to become social workers because it is the fastest way to become a legitimate professional private practitioner (Karger, 1989). Some seem destined to enter private practice even before becoming social workers because of factors in their own backgrounds and experiences (Flanzraich, 1985). Others gravitate to it because it seems healthier than agency employment: Studies indicate that private practice is less stressful and more satisfying than agency-based practice (Jayaratne, Davis-Sacks, & Chess, 1991).

Still others become private practitioners not as a matter of choice, but because traditional social services agency jobs are not available. Even though the need for social work services continues to grow, funding and job openings in the past decade have not; the social work labor force is currently geared to replacement rather than expansion (Williams & Hopps, 1990). Thus, private practice might be viewed by some as a temporary expedient to be tolerated until agency employment is found.

Most of those who enter private practice, however, do so after they have carefully weighed the advantages and disadvantages (A. M. Levin, 1988). For them, the potential rewards seem great enough to make the risks worth taking.

Various studies about the incentives and motivations for private practice have achieved consistent conclusions (M. P. Alexander, 1987; Brown, 1990b; Hardcastle & Brownstein, 1989; Morris, 1991; Smaller, 1987). Although many critics of private social work practice claim that the primary incentive is to make more money (Feldman, 1977), several other considerations actually carry more weight. In order of stated importance, the actual and anticipated rewards are (1) freedom from the bureaucratic limitations found in agency employment, (2) flexibility in work, (3) the opportunity to remain in direct practice, (4) financial considerations, (5) the challenge, (6) the opportunity to work with more motivated clients, and (7) greater control over one's own work environment.

Freedom from Bureaucratic Controls

For many social workers, especially those with considerable professional experience working for social services agencies, the primary appeal of private practice is an escape from bureaucracy. Most social workers are employed in state, municipal, or federal government jobs or in large personnel-intensive organizations such as medical centers (Williams & Hopps, 1990). Agencies and large organizations, like all bureaucracies, have established work rules, lines of authority, supervision requirements, and many other controls on their employees.

Social workers, like all professionals, devote a considerable part of their lives to acquiring the skills, knowledge, and experience necessary to serve their clients effectively. Many of them feel that the many controls in government or large private organizations prevent them from using these skills. They are supervised closely, given little power or opportunity to make professional judgments, and assigned narrow ranges of responsibility

(Dressel, Waters, Sweat, Clayton, & Chandler-Clayton, 1988). The private practitioner, on the other hand, has more opportunity to exercise professional judgment and to use the skills and knowledge acquired in professional education (Jayaratne, Siefert, & Chess, 1988).

Flexible Working Conditions

Unlike agency-based social workers, private practitioners are usually able to maintain their own work schedules based on their interests, needs, and life-style. The practitioner sets a personal pace, defines what hours to work, and decides independently when to take time away from the office. The practitioner can decide what professional meetings to attend. The agency worker, however, must conform to a predetermined work schedule and timetable.

One group of social workers for whom this scheduling flexibility is especially important and attractive is parents of school-age children. They find it difficult to blend the demands of their professional careers with the ways they want to care for their children. Part-time private practice gives them more flexibility than they would probably have in part- or full-time agency employment. Some of them maintain offices in their homes or in other settings where they are easily accessible to their children. Others are able to maintain private practice office hours while their children are in school or when their spouses are home. When their children become more independent, many mothers remain in private practice because they have become so well established.

For many private practitioners, however, especially full-timers, the idea of greater flexibility and freedom is more theoretical than practical. Many well-established private practitioners find themselves tied to their offices with little flexibility in their hours. They must be there when clients are scheduled for their appointments. And they usually are not inclined to turn clients away. In effect, they tend to demand much more of themselves than they would tolerate from agency supervisors. However, inasmuch as they do it of their own volition, they still feel a sense of freedom and flexibility.

Remaining in Direct Practice

After a social worker has worked for an agency for a number of years, the norm is "promotion." The worker becomes a supervisor or administrator and has much less direct contact with clients. These workers generally did not enter social work to become supervisors or administrators; if such had been their aspirations, they probably would have gone into different fields. If they do not accept their "promotions," they eventually find themselves coming under the authority of their former supervisees, and their relative income and credibility among peers remain static. Thus private practice becomes an appealing alternative.

It also has appeal for social workers who are not employed in direct practice jobs but who need to maintain and enhance clinical skills. For example, social work educators, especially those who teach clinical courses, find private practice a convenient way to work with clients and discuss their experiences with students. Many social work administrators, planners, and researchers are more productive in their jobs because, through private practice, they are keeping in direct client contact.

Financial Rewards

Money is not the most important reason why workers choose private practice over agency practice (Hass-Wilson, 1989). Nevertheless, it is one important consideration and remains a primary factor for some. The income that one receives from private practice is often not as great as expected, especially after overhead is taken out, but it is still significantly greater than the woeful earnings of many agency-based workers. In a 1987 study of its members, NASW reported that the mean income of self-employed private social work practitioners was $31,100 per year, higher than social workers in any other setting except a university (NASW, 1987).

Private practitioners have more control over the degree to which they are financially rewarded than any of their colleagues. Even when a social work administrator or university professor is relatively highly paid, the salary is limited. Organizations operate within their budgets, and no matter how motivated, skillful, and hardworking their employees are, they have limits on how much they can pay. However, if a competent private practitioner is willing to work long hours, the pay can increase commensurately.

The "Challenge" Motivation

Another motivation for many social workers is the challenge of private practice. Many workers want to test their professional capabilities without organizational constraints. They want to serve clients based on their knowledge rather than on the requirements of an employer. They also want to see if they can manage a business as well as perform a professional role competently. They know the risks, and they want to see if they can overcome them.

They see colleagues succeed in private practice and decide that they can do it, too. Conversely, they see agency-based colleagues who are locked into unsatisfactory or administrative jobs, too fearful about the loss of economic security to venture into new realms. Rather than encounter a similar fate, they want to move while they still have the motivation, capacity, and opportunity.

Working with Motivated Clients

Agency workers in direct practice often say they are frustrated in their attempts to provide services for clients who are undoubtedly in need but who lack some of the incentives, resources, or supports to care much about their difficulties. Agencies such as prisons, hospitals, public assistance offices, and juvenile courts often deal with clients who are forced to accept the worker's help whether they want it or not. In such cases, both the client and the worker sometimes merely go through the motions of the contact to satisfy the agency. The worker must spend a disproportionate amount of time filling out forms and acting as an agent of social control. Trying to provide effective services for clients who essentially do not want help often motivates workers to look for a different job.

Many social workers go into private practice because it seems like the antithesis of such experiences. Private practice clients tend to be motivated, cooperative, and appreciative of the worker's efforts in their behalf. They are more inclined to keep their scheduled appointments and to do any homework assigned as part of the intervention strategy. As a result, they are more likely to make progress in treatment than are clients in other settings (Luborsky et al., 1986). Social workers who deal with motivated clients tend to feel much more personal and professional satisfaction than do workers who work with less-motivated clients (Jayaratne et al., 1988).

Even though it may not be as rewarding for the worker to serve nonmotivated clients, these are usually the people who most need help. They are typically the most disadvantaged and have the least access to services. The heritage and tradition of social work demand that its members devote considerable attention to these people. Yet social workers began a gradual "disengagement" from needy clients more than three decades ago (Cloward & Epstein, 1965). This was long before private practice was much of a factor in the profession, so the trend can hardly be attributed solely to private practice. Nevertheless, the blame has been laid primarily on its doorstep. Some of this blame is rightly placed. Most private practitioners see relatively few of these clients. Unfortunately, what is a shame for the profession is, for some workers, an incentive to enter private practice.

Control over the Work Environment

The final motivation for entering private practice is the opportunity workers have to create their own pleasant and productive work environments. They can work in offices that they design and furnish to reflect their own tastes, styles, and practice specialties without being required to accommodate to colleagues. Private practitioners can locate their offices in neighborhoods that are convenient for themselves and the clients they wish to serve. They can decide on their own if they want to collaborate with others, and they do not have to work with any professionals with whom they feel no compatibility (Meloche, 1988).

Lamentably, this situation contrasts greatly with the conditions to which many agency-based workers are subjected. Typically, agency-based workers are assigned to whatever offices are available, if they have private offices at all. The offices can be furnished in spartan, institutional fashion, often with equipment that is inappropriate for the type of work that is expected of the professional. Agency workers are often assigned to work with colleagues with whom they have little affinity or few common professional objectives.

Although it seems unlikely that many social workers would leave agency employment for private practice simply because of the office furniture or other environmental factors, the importance of these conditions should not be underestimated (Mackey et al., 1987). Every business organization recognizes the relationship between worker morale and productivity and the ambience of the work setting. If this relationship exists in industry, it probably exists for social services organizations, too. Yet with their limited resources, the social services organizations have less opportunity to do anything about it. Workers who already have some morale problems might find that the harsh working environment is the final nudge that pushes them toward private practice.

EVERYDAY BURDENS IN PRIVATE PRACTICE

Looking only at the rewards of private practice can give one a false impression that it is unequivocally better than agency-based practice. However, many difficulties, some ordinary and some horrendous, confront private practitioners and balance the scale.

High on the list of ordinary or everyday burdens is the amount of time that must be devoted to the practice to achieve any of the aforementioned rewards. No one succeeds in private social work practice without working long hours, including evenings and weekends (A. M. Levin, 1988).

Much time has to be spent not in the rewarding experience of direct client contact, but in a myriad of dull, repetitious, and confining activities that are necessary in successful business management (Browning, 1989). Such tasks can include typing letters, sending out bills, bookkeeping, confronting former clients about failure of payment, shopping for supplies, and cleaning and maintaining the office (Seligman & Dougherty, 1987). These activities are rarely required of agency workers.

The private social worker has little respite from clients, is virtually on call 24 hours a day, and must find some other professional person to cover the office every time a vacation or a day off to attend a professional meeting is taken. Because of their professional isolation and the public demand for accountability, private practitioners find it more important than ever to attend professional meetings and to take continuing education courses (Hellman & Morrison, 1987).

The time taken from the practice for training reduces income. Yet the practitioner usually finds it necessary to devote many hours and considerable energy to activities for which no income is received. For instance, private practitioners often do community volunteer work, offer free consultation services to social services agencies, and give speeches to civic associations. Such activities are important for gaining the necessary public exposure that can lead to more referrals and keep a practice viable.

Those who enter part-time private practice while maintaining an agency job have even less time for developing referral resources, let alone for meeting personal or family needs. Moreover, their overhead costs can be as high as those of full-time private practitioners while their income from their private work is much smaller.

On the other hand, the full-time private practitioner usually gives up a secure job in a social services agency and a predictable if not munificent income. In private practice, it is difficult to plan finances because income can fluctuate dramatically from month to month, and the expenses of maintaining an office are great, continuous, and seemingly always increasing.

To enter private work, the practitioner gives up daily working relationships with agency colleagues, people with whom the burdens of caring for troubled clients could be shared. Such relationships provide an important buffer against professional burnout (Himle, Jayaratne, & Thyness, 1991). Private practice takes place in relative isolation, and the practitioner might go for hours or days seeing no one in the office but clients. Partly as a result, burnout is common among private practitioners (Gillespie, 1986).

Private social work practitioners are still at a disadvantage in competing with members of the other helping professions for the finite population of potential clients (F. Lieberman, 1987). The public seems to know what services the other professions render and what their qualifications are. But most people still have much less understanding of what social workers do and what their particular expertise is. Overcoming this disadvantage usually requires effective image building (Andrews, 1987) and careful marketing (Bailis et al., 1990).

In general, the spendable income of social workers in private practice, compared to that of agency social workers, is not as high as is commonly perceived (Hass-Wilson, 1989). Some clients are hesitant about reimbursing the private social work practitioner, somehow reasoning that members of this profession are volunteers or affiliated with charity organizations. Clients who are willing to pay often expect the fee to be less than that for the services of other professionals (Whittington, 1988).

This impression is often shared by insurance companies and other third-party financing institutions. Many of them will not help clients pay for social work services at all (Belser, 1989; Jewitt & Thompson, 1989). Many companies that do help pay require the social worker to be supervised by a physician. But many physicians are becoming increasingly reluctant to work with other professionals whom they see as competitors (Lesse, 1990). When social workers are paid by third parties, they often are reimbursed at a much lower rate than are other helping professionals. Furthermore, third-party institutions often change requirements for payment and use what seem to be capricious criteria to determine whether and how much to pay social workers.

CAREER PROBLEMS IN PRIVATE PRACTICE

Generally, most people can put up with, if not overcome, the difficulties posed by the ordinary negative aspects of private practice. However, some of these difficulties continually burden private practitioners to the point that their careers are jeopardized. These include such practical difficulties as professional isolation, loneliness, burnout, lack of opportunity for promotion or other advancement, and the pressures of helping people while conducting a business. Most workers who consider private practice believe they will have no problem overcoming these factors, yet more private practitioners return to agency work for these than any other reasons (Brown, 1990b).

It is not uncommon for social workers to enter private practice, work long and hard, become firmly established and financially stabilized, and then give it all up to return to agency employment. They succeed in a business sense but still find that private work is not what they wanted or expected. What is missing for them? It is not that they are overwhelmed by obstacles or that they lack the resources to maintain private offices; instead they often make conscious choices about the kind of work experience they want and come to believe that private practice does not offer it to them.

Professional Isolation

The difficulty most often mentioned to the author by private practitioners is professional isolation. Being away from colleagues is tough. Agency workers typically have frequent opportunities to talk with their colleagues, but private practitioners do not. Even when the private workers share an office, there is little opportunity for such exchanges because they are kept busy seeing clients, contacting referral sources, and managing the business aspects of their practices. As a consequence, the worker often feels alone and detached. As one social worker who left private practice to return to an agency wrote, "I enjoy working with a professional team. It is good to know that you can call on other people to fill in the gaps and share the responsibilities. As part of a team, I feel a broader effectiveness than I did as a private practitioner" (Rainier, 1990, p. 188).

Every worker needs to share worries, ventilate frustrations about jobs and clients, and get away from constantly performing a professional role. Feedback from one's peers, supportive relationships with colleagues, time away from the workday, and work sharing have been shown to be more important to social work job satisfaction than higher pay or variety (Pines & Kafry, 1978). The private worker can easily become emotionally depleted if there is only a one-way flow of emotion from worker to client; there is a clear need for a two-way flow of feelings, and this can best come from closer collegial and peer relationships (Koeske & Koeske, 1989).

A sense of isolation is a particularly serious problem for the worker who hangs out a shingle at a relatively early age and continues in private work for many years. Agency workers often change jobs or move within an agency to different roles during the course of their careers. Private workers, however, do essentially the same job throughout their careers. The only chance for variety is to return to agency practice or to change professions.

Burnout

For some private practitioners, professional isolation leads to burnout. This is a form of depression whose symptoms include apathy, boredom, intellectual stagnation, and lack of motivation to serve clients effectively (LeCroy & Rank, 1986). Agency-based social workers are also afflicted with this condition in great numbers because of their difficult working conditions and frustrations (Jayaratne & Chess, 1984).

It may be harder for the private practice social worker to prevent and recuperate from burnout. The private worker may not even be aware of burnout symptoms unless in contact with peers. No one is there to point out that it is happening or to encourage the worker to take corrective measures before its gets worse.

Problems of this type can best be prevented when the social worker maintains close contacts with other social workers, keeps intellectually stimulated, and grows in knowledge and skill. The danger for the private practitioner is that it is easy to put off taking the necessary steps and easy to let burnout creep in without suspecting its presence (Farber, 1990). The safeguard is to assume its inevitability unless opportunities for collegial relationships are sought (Arches, 1991).

Stress

Recent studies suggest that private practice may be less stressful than any agency-based alternative (Jayaratne et al., 1991). Nevertheless, no one suggests that the setting is stress-free or that all people feel stress about the same kinds of stimuli. Some workers in private practice are constantly worried about not getting enough referrals. Others worry about finances or malpractice and imagine that they would not have such concerns in an agency.

Employees in agencies work 40 hours or less each week and are able to leave many of their concerns at the office at the end of the day. Other workers cover for them in their absence, and they can give undivided attention to serving clients rather than to marketing and office management. Private practitioners, however, usually work many more than 40 hours per week and often work on weekends and evenings; clients frequently have access to them at all hours. Private practitioners are subjected to the pressures of single-handedly meeting office expenses and dealing with the myriad of details inherent in running a business. If the practitioner works elsewhere part-time, the stress can be even greater; spending 40 hours in an agency and then several hours each evening and all day on Saturday in private practice is a common and dangerous burden.

Full-time and part-time private practitioners who remain healthy mitigate such problems by pacing themselves so they can have respites and by maintaining good professional and personal relationships. It helps to take long lunch hours or have physical activities in the middle of the workday. Meeting with colleagues in agencies for intellectual stimulation is important, as are regular vacations and frequent variations in the working routine.

Blows to Professional Esteem

Private practice is sometimes seen by other social workers as among the most prestigious of the direct practice activities. Why, then, do private practitioners sometimes feel a lack of recognition as professionals? It is because status and prestige are relative. Agency workers work primarily among clients and other social workers. They meet with other professionals as representatives of the agency rather than as representatives of the profession. Private workers, however, deal with members of professions outside social work—physicians, lawyers, judges, and other officials. Among the mental health professions, social workers are ranked at or near the bottom by clients, colleagues, and other professionals (Borys & Pope, 1989).

A private practitioner must often spend inordinate amounts of time explaining the nature of the profession and its particular expertise. Skeptical insurance companies, potential clients, and referral sources must all be educated about the private worker's knowledge, abilities, and professional credibility. As a result, social workers in private practice are not regularly given the feeling that they are held in high regard by others.

Client Problems

Most private practitioners are not as selective of their clients as they should be; too often they take whatever clients come their way. Thus, if they are less equipped to work with certain kinds of clients or client problems, they will have less than optimal outcomes. In agencies where clients are screened and sent to workers on the basis of their special skills, this problem is usually less pronounced.

Private practitioners can minimize this risk for themselves as well as their clients by being objective about their own skills and interests, by being selective about clients, and by referring unsuitable clients to professionals who are more qualified.

THREE POTENTIAL DISASTERS IN PRIVATE PRACTICE

In addition to the problems listed above, social workers in private practice face three even greater hazards, the consequences of which can lead to bankruptcy, courtrooms, and professional banishment. These hazards are not unique to private practitioners but are far more likely to occur with them than with agency workers. Even so, the odds that any one of them will occur with a given private practitioner are not great. Nevertheless, when they do occur, the result can be personally and professionally devastating. Thus, the prudent private practitioner will want to know as much as possible about these hazards so as to be able to avoid them.

The first of these hazards is the financial difficulties facing most private practitioners. It is easy for inexperienced private practitioners to get into financial difficulty. Overhead costs, unless carefully managed, can get out of control. Savings for taxes, insurance, and retirement are often postponed until too late. An uncertain and highly variable income compounds the risk. Avoiding it requires careful planning and budgeting. Practitioners can reduce the risk only by knowing how to deal with the complex financial aspects of their businesses. (Money management is the subject of chapter 7.)

Malpractice and other legal difficulties constitute the next potential disaster area. Some social workers prefer to not think about this hazard, assuming that it will not be a problem for anyone who is always competent, ethical, and practicing within the norms of the profession. However, such avoidance of reality is dangerous. Many helping professionals have lost malpractice suits even though their competence and practice were considered appropriate (Besharov, 1985). In this current era of litigiousness, the practical social worker who enters private practice will learn as much as possible about how malpractice and other legal difficulties sometimes befall their colleagues. Knowledge is the best defense against these risks. (Malpractice and other legal difficulties are the subject of chapter 8.)

The final hazard centers on professional and public accountability, licensing, and qualifications for practice. Social work has lagged behind some of the other helping professions in the degree to which its private practitioners are regulated by and responsible to the public and to the consumers of their services. This is a serious problem for private practitioners because they must rely on their professional credentials rather than on agency or institutional employers to guarantee competence to the public. Yet it is not easy for the private practitioner to maintain the necessary credentials. (This issue is the subject of chapter 4.)

CHOOSING BETWEEN AGENCY AND PRIVATE PRACTICE

Having considered all the potential rewards and risks of private practice, one is still left with the crucial question: Which is better—private or agency practice? Obviously, there is no single best career decision for everyone. Some workers will always be happier and more productive in agency settings; others will be better suited to private practice no matter how many problems they must face (Demeo, 1990). Members of both groups can make a correct choice for themselves only if they consider their options objectively and realistically, anticipate likely problems, and learn how to minimize the difficulties before they actually enter private practice (A. M. Levin, 1988).

Careful study of the sizable literature on increasing the chances of private practice success is essential. Especially worthwhile and recom-mended are books by Biegel and Earle (1990), A. M. Levin (1983), Robertson and Jackson (1991), and Woody (1989). With careful study, the hazards of private practice are minimized and the potential for considerable reward is enhanced.

4 GETTING AND STAYING QUALIFIED

Once the decision is made to enter private practice, the next step is to make sure one possesses the necessary qualifications. These include complying with the relevant laws and licensing statutes and obtaining the appropriate credentials from the professional association. One should also consider certain personal characteristics to be qualifications for successful private practice, even though no institutional authority requires them (A. M. Levin, 1988).

QUESTIONS TO ANSWER

The necessary qualifications, credentials, and personal characteristics tend to vary from one jurisdiction to another; they may also vary depending on the type of specialty one seeks to enter and the type of practice setting to be established. And the qualifications change over time. Thus, it is important to review all the existing requirements for private practice and periodically reexamine them to be sure of continued eligibility to practice. Knowing, understanding, and complying with all the qualifications and rules are more difficult than one would think. The following true case illustrates these difficulties:

An agency-based social worker decided to go into private practice. She gave careful thought to its potential hazards and rewards and decided the risk was worth taking. She was very well qualified. She had several advanced degrees from accredited schools of social work and years of agency experience under good supervision. She had always been held in high regard by her colleagues, clients, and agency employers. She was professionally certified, and she had kept her knowledge up-to-date through many continuing education courses and professional seminars.

She was confident about her personal attributes for succeeding in the venture. She was a hard worker and able to work independently. She had the financial resources to support a practice until it became self-sustaining. Even the setting for her practice seemed ideal. She planned to establish it in her home, where there was an office directly accessible to the street. Her home was in a comfortable, upper-middle-class neighborhood, and a physician and a dentist had their practices in similar houses nearby. And so she placed a tiny sign showing her name, degree, and profession in the office window. She was now in private practice. How could anyone in this position go wrong?

She soon found out. After putting up her sign, the new private practitioner was taken to court for violating a county zoning ordinance that says that only members of "recognized professions" can operate practices in home offices. "Only recognized professionals?" she thought when the authorities notified her. "Then what does the county consider me to be—a fortune teller?"

In fact, the zoning statute had been instituted to protect residents from fortune tellers and others whose work was perceived as disruptive to the character of the neighborhood. However, because the ruling said no one except members of "recognized professions" could practice, the issue quickly became a question of whether or not social work was legally considered a recognized profession. If the worker could prove that it was, she could continue her private practice. If she could not, she would have to close her new office.

Her professional association, NASW, assisted in her defense because it appeared that the whole profession was on trial ("Association Assists Members," 1981). Witnesses were called on both sides to show why social work was or was not a recognized profession. The issue took many weeks to resolve and the outcome was equivocal. The county ultimately avoided saying that social work was not a recognized profession. Instead, it reworded its zoning ordinances. Thereafter, no one, regardless of affiliation or qualification, could operate a home office without prior county approval. The worker was permitted to keep her private practice, but the costly legal defense meant her office was already thousands of dollars in the red.

WHAT CREDENTIALS ARE NEEDED?

The above example is not uncommon. Unfortunately, many social workers going into private practice have had to learn their lessons the hard way, the expensive and ego-deflating way. They must look carefully at all the laws and credentialing authorities to determine exactly what is required. If they ignore any of these before they start their practices, even those that seem only peripheral to their work, they almost always end up paying a painful price.

Even when private social work practitioners have all the necessary credentials, they still may encounter difficulties because others do not accept those credentials. This is illustrated often in the *NASW News,* which describes how social workers are challenged about their qualifications for private practice. In one story, a social worker in Ohio had a successful private practice, served clients effectively, and was credited with providing a valued community service. One day, however, the state authorities said he had to suspend operations immediately. They claimed he was violating the state's psychological-licensing laws. He was alleged to be providing a "psychological service" without a license as a psychologist. In another story, a social worker in a New Jersey private practice was told by the state that he was unqualified to practice marital and family therapy because he was a social worker ("Association Assists Members," 1981).

Such incidents lead to the important questions that must be faced by every social worker who contemplates private practice: What qualifications and credentials are necessary before one can have credibility as a private practitioner? What is the necessary training and experience? Is a license needed, and, if so, how can one be obtained? What tests have to be taken, and what preparations for them are advisable? Once in private practice, how does one prove that one's qualifications are current? Are continuing education credits required, and if so, where are the continuing education records kept? What do insurance companies require before they will help pay for the services? Where is it permissible to practice, and where is it not? Are private practitioners required to join any organizations? If not, is it advisable to join one for acceptance and protection in the practice? To answer such questions properly, the practitioner should first consider what it is that constitutes a qualification or credential.

THE NATURE OF CREDENTIALS

Professional credentials are a social institution's implicit or explicit standards to which an individual (or group) must conform to have the endorsement of that institution. If, for example, the institution is a profession or a professional association, endorsement will be given only to those individuals who complete its educational and experiential requirements and who meet its assurances of quality. If the institution is the legal system of the relevant jurisdiction, approval comes by obeying the laws (Thyer & Biggerstaff, 1989). The institution usually, but not always, explicates its criteria for those who seek its endorsement. The endorsement is then granted to those who offer proof that they have conformed to the criteria. The proof may be offered in the form of certifying exams that must be passed, academic degrees, types of experiences, documented professional activities, or demonstrable skills.

What is offered as proof is supposedly, but not necessarily, relevant to the activity that is to be endorsed. What counts is whether the endorsing institution considers the proof to be relevant. For example, in some states, pharmacists are still required to demonstrate that they can competently mix medical compounds to get their licenses. In recent years, however, the nation has established such rigorous food and drug laws that virtually all prescriptions have to be made under highly controlled laboratory conditions. In effect, the ability to mix compounds in a pharmacy is virtually irrelevant, even though the pharmacist will not be endorsed without proving his or her ability to do it.

In another example, professional social work associations will not endorse an individual who does not hold certain academic degrees. The degree itself does not prove that the individual is competent to practice social work, but it does show that the person has followed a course of training that has provided information pertinent to the practice of the profession.

ORGANIZATIONS PROVIDING CREDENTIALS

Formal credentials are issued to private social work practitioners by many different institutions and associations. In 49 states and the District of Columbia, legal regulation is available to the private practitioner. Private practitioners can also belong to one or more additional credentialing authorities (Flynn, 1987).

Many professional organizations also offer credentials (Brooks & Gerstein, 1990). The largest of these groups, by far, is NASW, which has over 135,000 members. In addition to being NASW members, many private practitioners are also members of two NASW-sponsored authorities, the Academy of Certified Social Workers and the NASW *Register of Clinical Social Workers,* which offers the Qualified Clinical Social Worker credential. Many private social work practitioners belong to the National Federation of Societies for Clinical Social Work. Although this organization of about 6,500 members is much smaller than NASW, it is especially popular with private practitioners. Another organization is the independent American Board of Examiners in Clinical Social Work, which offers the Board Certified Diplomate credential.

Many social workers in private practice also belong to one of the associations that provide related psychosocial services, many of which have their own certification authorities. The most popular of these for private social work practitioners are the American Association for Marriage and Family Therapy; the American Group Psychotherapy Association; the American Association for Sex Education, Counseling and Therapy; the American Association of Orthopsychiatry; the American Psychotherapy Association; the American Society of Clinical Hypnosis; and the American Association of Industrial Social Workers.

Although it is the institution's right to determine whom it will endorse, it is the individual's right to determine which endorsements to seek. The worker may legally engage in private social work practice without belonging to any professional association or certification authority or body. However, the worker must gain the endorsement of the licensing board in those jurisdictions where licensing is a condition of practice.

The practitioner's ultimate choice about which endorsement to seek rests basically on an estimate of how much good the endorsement will do compared to how much resource expenditure it will take to meet the standards of the endorsing body (Barker, 1987a). In effect, the practitioner makes a cost-benefit analysis.

SEVEN QUALIFICATIONS FOR PRIVATE PRACTICE

Regardless of which endorsements the private practitioner chooses to seek, it is important to fulfill seven requirements. They are (1) licensing requirements, (2) local business and zoning laws, (3) professional credentials, (4) continuing education requirements, (5) third-party conditions for reimbursement, (6) consumer expectations, and (7) personal attributes. Although only the first two of these are usually required and enforced by law, conforming to the other five is just as vital to the health of a private practice.

Licensing Requirements

It is necessary to get a professional license for social work practice in virtually every jurisdiction of the nation (Hardcastle, 1990). At present, all but one state have legal regulation. The requirements for obtaining the relevant license vary to some extent in each of the licensing jurisdictions. All of them require the practitioner to have a professional degree from an accredited school of social work. Some add the requirement of a certain amount of supervised practice experience. Fewer states require that the applicant pass written, and sometimes oral, examinations. And some jurisdictions require that the license holder maintain knowledge currency by fulfilling certain continuing education requirements.

The wide variation among states as to requirements makes it impossible to spell them all out here. The aspiring private practitioner should check with the jurisdiction's licensing authority. The names, addresses, and telephone numbers of these authorities appear in appendix B.

Local Business and Zoning Laws

Because private practice is a business as well as a profession, the practitioner must usually conform to local laws pertaining to the operation of a business. In many jurisdictions, the practitioner must obtain a business operating license as well as a professional practice license. Business licenses, especially for professional service providers, are usually rather simple to acquire. They often can be obtained by simply filing an application and paying a modest fee.

In some jurisdictions, it is also necessary to notify the local tax and revenue board. The board may want to assess the equipment and physical aspects of the business and to require that annual taxes on them be paid. It is necessary to determine if such requirements exist in the jurisdiction. Usually this can be determined by asking the authorities at the business licensing bureau or by calling the board of assessments and taxation (Baumback & Lawyer, 1989).

The practitioner must also make sure the location of the practice does not violate zoning ordinances. This is especially crucial for home offices and other settings outside traditional office buildings. The worker can determine these requirements in advance by contacting the county or city licensing and zoning offices. The names of the offices vary by jurisdiction, but they are easily located in the county directory.

Professional Credentials

To have credibility as a professional, the social worker should also have some professional endorsement through membership in one of the professional associations. Theoretically, one could maintain a legally valid private social work practice without any professional affiliations; however, this would be most unwise. Without affiliation it is difficult to stay informed, maintain needed contacts with colleagues, and demonstrate to consumers and third parties that one adheres to a specific ethical code.

Most private practitioners choose to be affiliated with and credentialed by both of NASW's certification programs (ACSW and QCSW) or by ABE's BCD credential. To be a member of ACSW, the applicant must have NASW membership; a master's or doctoral degree from a graduate school accredited by the Council on Social Work Education (CSWE); two years of full-time supervised practice experience after receiving the degree (or 3,000 hours of paid, part-time work); three acceptable professional references, including one from the applicant's supervisor; and a passing mark in the ACSW examination. This multiple-choice exam is offered twice a year at centers throughout the nation. Information about it can be obtained by contacting NASW headquarters or one of the local chapter offices listed in appendix C.

The other credential offered by NASW, the QCSW designation, enables the worker to be listed in the NASW *Register of Clinical Social Workers*. Requirements for this credential are a master's or doctoral degree from an accredited school of social work, membership in ACSW or a state license that requires an examination, and two years of post-master's clinical social work practice under the supervision of a master's-level social worker or the part-time equivalent of 1,500 direct client contact hours within a period of not less than two years (NASW, 1991a). Information about QCSW can also be obtained from NASW headquarters or one of the chapter offices.

ABE's credential, the BCD, has the following requirements: a graduate degree from a CSWE-accredited school of social work in which courses and field placements include specified clinical content, a total of five years or 7,500 hours of direct client contact, and 3,000 hours of supervised clinical practice (1,500 of which may be under the supervision of a qualified professional from a specified discipline other than social work). The BCD member must also pass the qualifying exam, be licensed at the highest level possible, and be recertified annually through documenting a current license and continuing education requirements (ABE, 1989). More specific information about this credential may be obtained by writing ABE (8484 Georgia Avenue, Suite 700, Silver Spring, MD 20910).

Continuing Education Requirements

To ensure that the worker has kept current, some state licensing boards and professional associations have established continuing education requirements. Each licensing board and credentialing authority has established its own requirements. The continuing education requirements of associations are not necessarily the same as the requirements of the state licensing board (Sancier, 1987). Legal enforcement of continuing education requirements has not been achieved, but the practitioner who gets sued or reviewed by peers is certain to be questioned about adherence to these requirements (Seelig, 1990).

Many state licensing authorities have followed the standards recommended by NASW or ABE. NASW's current recommendations for continuing education of social workers in private practice include 90 hours of continuing professional education every three years: 40 hours of formally organized learning events in classrooms, practice-oriented seminars, or accredited training activities; 30 hours of professional meetings or symposia sponsored by social work or allied organizations; and 20 hours of individual professional activities such as research, teaching, writing, and independent study (NASW, 1982). So far, NASW does not enforce these continuing education standards or keep records of the continuing education of its members, but it is likely to do so in the future (Barker, 1990b).

The requirements and documentation of continuing education have been changing fairly rapidly in some jurisdictions and with some associations. Thus, it is necessary to check regularly with the credentialing organization to see what the existing standards for continuing education are.

Third-Party Conditions for Reimbursement

Even though social workers are not legally or professionally required to meet the standards of the third parties who help clients pay their bills, it is almost impossible to maintain a viable private practice without doing so. The vast majority of the clients who use the services of private social work practitioners are covered by health insurance programs and expect to be reimbursed by those companies for most of the treatment costs (A. A. Lieberman & Turner, 1991).

Social work has made significant strides in the past decade in getting insurance companies to reimburse for its services (Saxton, 1988). Most health insurance companies reimburse social workers who meet their qualification standards (Shatkin, Frisman, & McGuire, 1986). Some of the larger ones, such as the Civilian Health and Medical Program of the Uniformed Services (CHAMPUS), cover clinical social work services without requiring physicians to supervise the intervention. However, they do require peer review mechanisms within the provider's profession (Jackson, 1987). Most states now have laws that require insurance companies that have mental health care benefits to cover Qualified Clinical Social Workers without their having to have been referred by other health care professionals (NASW, 1991b). Members of some professional groups, such as some marital and family counselors, are still required to be supervised by physicians (AAMFT, 1991).

Even so, the health and mental health care coverage situation is in a state of rapid fluctuation, with insurance companies and state legislators changing their rules considerably. The movement toward national health care, the increasing influence of managed health care programs, and the competition and cost problems facing insurance companies have all influenced these changes. One rule that has remained consistent among all third parties, however, is this: No reimbursement can knowingly be made for professional services if the practitioner is not licensed in those states where licensing exists. And few vendors will reimburse professionals who lack professional certification. They require that the worker belong to a professional organization, such as NASW, that has a peer review mechanism or a quality assurance program (Shatkin et al., 1986).

A social worker should ascertain the specific reimbursement requirements of a new client's coverage before getting very far into treatment. Clients often expect their health insurance to cover the services of the social worker as it does those of other health care professionals. A financial problem for both worker and client could occur unless this information is known in advance. The worker should call the nearest office of the relevant company for their criteria for provider reimbursement. It is important to get this information in writing, however, to protect against future problems. NASW publishes a helpful guide to the federal and commercial insurance programs and managed health care programs, which delineates their policies for covering social workers. Entitled *Professional Social Work Recognition* (NASW, 1991b), the publication is available from NASW headquarters for a nominal fee.

Consumer Expectations

In previous years, clients had to take an approach of caveat emptor with professionals. They have few protections against incompetent or unscrupulous practitioners. However, in recent years, consumer protection laws have rightly been applied to professionals as well as to merchants. With these laws, government agencies play the role of watchdog with professionals.

Professionals who wish to avoid confrontations with consumers need to belong to organizations that have peer review or quality control mechanisms. Without such affiliations, the worker is vulnerable to malpractice suits and other legal problems if a client ever experiences difficulties as a result of the contact with the worker (Coulton, 1987).

This criterion is met if the private social work practitioner is a member of NASW, NFSCSW, or AAMFT. These organizations have strong codes of ethics and require their members' adherence to the codes. They also have ethics and grievance committees to which clients can go if they have any problems with the worker (NASW, 1980). The criterion is usually also met if the worker is affiliated with a managed health care organization such as a health maintenance organization or a preferred provider organization.

Personal Attributes

Social workers should also possess certain personal attributes if they hope to be successful in their private practices (Matorin, Rosenberg, Levitt, & Rosenblum, 1987). Of course, the most important characteristics necessary for a successful private practice are knowledge and competence. Other qualities that various writers have indicated are important for private practice include higher than average degrees of (1) motivation, (2) adaptability, (3) perseverance, (4) assertiveness, (5) energy, (6) independence, and (7) initial financial resources.

Motivation to be a private practitioner is crucial. To be able to face and overcome all the obstacles one is likely to encounter, these workers must sincerely want to be private practitioners. Workers who are in private practice because they cannot find agency jobs do not tend to stay with it for long (A. M. Levin, 1988). Adaptability is important because the work of the private practitioner is varied and requires a variety of skills and the ability to change plans easily (Tamkin, 1976). Perseverance is necessary because the novice private worker is likely to encounter so many unexpected disappointments and economic shifts that it becomes tempting to give up (Barker, 1983).

Assertiveness, energy, and a sense of independence are also traits usually found in successful private practitioners. Many social workers seem to do better when they are encouraged or pushed to get their jobs done. Workers who put things off or need to be pushed by others to do their jobs do not do well in private practice. Instead, the worker must be a self-starter who can maintain a self-imposed schedule.

Finally, the worker who succeeds in private practice needs to have other financial resources, at least at first, as well as a certain amount of business sense and management skills (R. Levin & Leginsky, 1990). For example, the worker has to be able to ask clients for money and to apply pressure to those who do not pay their bills. Other financial resources are essential because workers have to spend substantial sums before they start seeing clients and drawing revenue.

These personal characteristics are as important as licensing, professional certification, or any other requirement. Without them, the practitioner would have few clients, no referrals, financial problems, and disorganized records.

PRACTICING WITHOUT MINIMUM QUALIFICATIONS?

Private practitioners have been known to operate without possessing even the minimum standards delineated above. Some do not have appropriate licenses, certificates, education, or experience and seem to hope that no one will notice. Indeed, it is not uncommon for members of some specialties to call themselves "social workers" even though they were educated in different fields. Often, they belong to counseling specialties that have little public or institutional recognition. Sometimes social services agencies or institutions employ such people and eventually call them "social workers" because that is the existing job title. When these people enter private practice, they retain the title, claiming they are experienced social workers.

Trying to operate a practice with less than the minimum requirements is tempting to some because it seems so easy. Enforcement is still lax, and punishments are usually not severe. In those states where the social work licensing laws are weak, the legal authorities may be unable to do anything at all about practitioners who lack credentials, as long as the practitioners keep a low legal profile.

When licensing laws are weak, there is little protection against this practice (Hardcastle, 1990). Even the professional association can do little, except generate negative publicity for the practitioner. NASW would have a strong case only if the unqualified practitioner tried to use the designation ACSW or QCSW.

Nevertheless, practitioners who count on inadequate laws, little enforcement, or minimal requirements to maintain their offices are being shortsighted. The national trend is rapidly moving toward stronger regulations, higher standards, and more stringent means of enforcing them. Tremendous efforts are now being made by the various professional groups to show the public and those who pay for services that high standards exist. Consumer groups and third-party organizations will require high standards even if state laws do not. Consumers will not go to practitioners who do not demonstrate competence or to agencies that lack quality assurance programs.

Anyone who hopes to remain in private practice will find it imperative to upgrade skills and qualifications regularly. When professions and state licensing boards impose higher standards, it may seem threatening and needlessly intrusive, but it is in the social worker's interest as well as the client's. In the near future, the only way a profession will be able to compete with other professions is through possessing and enforcing high standards. The existence of these standards will be one of the private practitioner's greatest assets in maintaining a viable practice. The qualifications of the social worker and the profession require taking quality assurance measures seriously and living up to them consistently.

QUALITY ASSURANCE CONTROVERSIES

Quality assurance refers to the procedures used by professional organizations to demonstrate that their services are worthy and not harmful to the consumer. In this general sense, quality assurance includes the profession's ethical code, licensing and certification requirements, competency and currency testing, peer review procedures, and any other devices used to encourage and force practitioners to live up to specified standards (Coulton, 1987).

Social work was once at the forefront of the helping professions in its quality assurance procedures, providing protection against incompetence or malevolence by its members. Long before many other professions displayed concern about protecting consumers from their own incompetent or unscrupulous members, social work had comparatively rigorous measures—a strong code of ethics and institutionalized use of supervision to maintain standards. After receiving their MSW degrees, workers were generally employed in social services agencies where their practice was supervised for several years by experienced professionals. After the supervised apprenticeship was completed, the worker maintained a close association with peers in a consultative relationship. If the worker displayed deficiencies in knowledge or performance, the supervisor or agency provided extra guidance or applied pressure to upgrade skills. Often agencies encouraged and paid their employees to take courses and attend professional meetings.

Naturally, not all social workers enjoyed this procedure. Some studies have indicated that workers see supervisors not only as teachers and role models who socialize the new person into the established way of doing things but also as agents controlled by the social services agencies (Miller, 1987). The respondents said supervision taught them to conform rather than to innovate. Other studies suggested that tensions exist between supervisors and practitioners and that workers perceive supervision as an encroachment on professional judgment, responsibility, and competence. Supervision may have existed more to exert the agency's bureaucratic control on its employees than to protect the consumer from incompetence, but the effect was the same—the client had some protection.

In the private practice model of delivering social services, supervision cannot be used to show the public that practitioners measure up to the standards. The appropriate alternatives are the same quality assurance devices that other professions use: rigorous competency testing, enforced demonstration of practice skill, proof of currency, strong and consistent licensing and certification requirements, and formal grievance and peer review procedures. If these programs exist within the profession, they are less likely to be externally imposed.

Unfortunately for private social work practitioners, the profession is in serious conflict about its quality assurance devices, just as it has been about licensing. The problems stem partly from the ambivalence of social workers themselves about standards. Some social workers fear, perhaps with justification, that they will become victims of discrimination or that they will not be able or willing to meet the standards. Many social workers want to raise educational standards for entry into the profession, whereas many others advocate a greater role for the bachelor of social work (BSW) social worker, even in private practice. Many competent social workers resist the idea of competency testing because they fear it would be too clinically oriented (Barker, 1988a). They believe the profession should assume more of a macro than a micro perspective and think standards enforcement measures take the profession in the wrong direction.

NASW and NFSCSW cannot force their members to accept higher or different quality assurance standards; they do not make autocratic decisions that their members must accept. These associations reflect the mood of their members, and if the members are in conflict with one another, the association can only mirror the internal turmoil. Nevertheless, the profession and its private practice sector will have difficulty gaining public acceptance without unity (Hartman, 1990).

COMPETENCY TESTING CONTROVERSIES

Another controversy in social work that has a particular impact on private practitioners is the issue of competency testing. Social workers have long argued about whether such tests are necessary, useful, relevant, and fair (Borenzweig, 1977; Johnson & Huff, 1987; Thyer, 1990). Proponents of these tests say they are needed as tangible evidence that the worker possesses the knowledge required for competent professional practice. They also argue that such tests help keep out incompetent and unknowledgeable practitioners who would harm clients and the professional image. And, they argue, all the other professions have such tests in place, and any profession that does not would be at a competitive disadvantage. Opponents argue that pencil-and-paper tests for social workers do not really measure social work's knowledge and skills. Moreover, say the opponents, the tests discriminate against some minorities and have been administered so poorly that they are worthless.

Gradually, the proponents are having their way, and written tests of competency are becoming the norm in clinical social work practice. Most of the state licensing boards have become affiliated with the American Association of State Social Work Boards (AASSWB). AASSWB has sponsored the development of a standardized test of social work knowledge and help design questions, administer the test, and interpret the results. AASSWB also helps state boards modify the test for local use and update it to include current social work knowledge. The prototype exam is a pencil-and-paper multiple-choice test whose questions, answers, and "distractors" are written by licensed practicing social workers. In two states—Virginia and California—the applicant must pass the test as well as an oral exam. Information about the test can be obtained from AASSWB headquarters in Culpeper, Virginia, or the relevant state board of examiners listed in appendix B.

Another exam for the ACSW professional certification is administered twice yearly in a number of test centers nationwide (Middleman, 1989). It consists of 175 multiple-choice, continually updated questions developed with the help of the American College Testing Service, and it is administered under NASW auspices. The exam is given not only to clinical specialists but also to all those who seek the title "certified social worker." It attempts to be comprehensive, covering the range of knowledge and skill that is supposed to be within the social worker's grasp: general social work knowledge with a heavy emphasis on social work values, principles, and methods, from community to individual interventions.

Passing the exam and becoming certified are not essential for private social work practice and seem to be of declining value as other credentials become more meaningful. The public seems to have little awareness of the meaning of the credential, and third-party organizations and overseeing bodies still do not see it as a way of ensuring conformity to high standards. The new NASW credential for clinical social workers, the QCSW, or the ABE credential, the BCD, may supplant ACSW as the professional certification most important to private social work practitioners.

CONTINUING EDUCATION CONTROVERSIES

The knowledge base for social workers in private practice keeps growing. A practitioner who does not keep up with the advances in the field is not conforming to professional social work standards. Of course, the same is true for other professions. Studies have long confirmed that every five years medical doctors have to acquire half again as much knowledge as they obtained in medical school just to keep up with advances in their profession (Robinowitz & Greenblatt, 1980). Psychologists have a knowledge half-life of 10 to 12 years (Dubin, 1981). Professionals who do not maintain knowledge of their field do a disservice to themselves and their clients; some call it negligence.

What can the profession do to assure the public and the overseers that the practitioner has kept up? What can be done to encourage or force unmotivated practitioners to stay current? Most professions rely on two possibilities: recertification of members through periodic testing and enforced continuing education requirements. Social work is behind most of the other professions in pursuing both possibilities.

Continuing education standards for social workers are rarely imposed or enforced. Most of the state licensing boards, while saying that continuing education is necessary, do little to ensure that the worker has fulfilled the explicit requirements.

As is mentioned above, NASW's requirement of 90 hours of continuing education every three years is not rigorously enforced. The association does not keep records of how many units each member has acquired, as do some professional associations. It does not monitor the quality of the educational experience that the member receives. The member is on the honor system in keeping track of relevant units.

Some social workers justify the lack of enforced continuing education. They point out that there has been a lack of evidence to show a relationship between continuing education and continuing competence (Edwards & Green, 1983). The suggestion is that if a person demonstrates no more competence with continuing education than without it, what is the purpose of requiring it? Obviously, the same argument could be applied to requiring attendance at schools of social work in the absence of adequate competency testing, but that is another issue. In any event, testing, not training, is seen as the more appropriate way of proving that the person has kept current.

However, there is also a paucity of periodic examinations for social workers. Nurses, lawyers, physicians, and psychologists take tests every few years to assure the public they are maintaining skills and knowledge. Psychiatrists must be recertified every six years by passing a multiple-choice exam of 400 items and an oral test. They are eligible to take the exam only after demonstrating that they have successfully completed a specified number of qualified continuing education units. Some might argue that the exam and the education do not prove psychiatric competence, but, at the very least, it has some public relations value. The requirement tells the public, third-party underwriters, and government overseers that efforts to encourage currency standards are in effect.

Social workers have little that is comparable, either in state licensing laws or in professional credentialing. The profession has not pushed the boards or the associations to institute these requirements. As a result, there are few ways that a private practitioner can prove up-to-date knowledge.

Many social workers not only resist currency examinations but defend a norm, the grandparent clause, that undercuts and precludes them. *Grandparenting* is the practice of automatically granting an experienced social worker the same credentials, licenses, and professional certifications granted to younger workers merely because the experienced workers obtained the necessary qualifications before a certain date. This practice improperly assumes that social work knowledge and skills, once acquired, are mastered for life or that the profession is not generating new knowledge and skills. Only if knowledge and skills were static would there be justification for grandparenting. Nevertheless, social workers who received their state licenses before a certain date, or their ACSW certificates before the exam was instituted in 1971, have not been required to take the exam or show proof of continuing competence. Instead, these workers merely have to pay renewal fees to renew their licenses. As Barker (1988a) once editorialized, "It's time to retire grandfather."

ADJUDICATING GRIEVANCES

Peer review is considered essential by many government and third-party financing organizations. To them, it is a way of assuring the public that a profession or any one of its members is being internally monitored so as to minimize the risk of ethics violations or incompetence. Peer review is also important for private practice for another reason: It provides some of the supervisory controls that these workers would otherwise not receive. Peer review mechanisms are also demanded by consumers and consumer groups. Clients are entitled to the opportunity to express any grievances or alleged wrongdoing by the professional to the practitioner's peers. The reputation of the profession itself could be harmed if a member continued working at lower than professional standards with no accountability.

All the traditional helping professions have peer review systems, even though each has somewhat different objectives and procedures for implementing them. Some use the system only to adjudicate grievances lodged with the profession by unhappy clients. Others use peer review as a way to encourage members to improve certain practices even though no complaint has been made. Some procedures are informal, consisting merely of regular meetings of professionals who teach each other; others are formal, with prescribed procedures, elected officers, and appeal procedures.

Social work already compares favorably with other professions in its peer review procedures. NASW's system is built around its National Committee on Inquiry (NCOI) and local committees on inquiry (COIs) at each chapter office. The NASW chapters maintain standing or ad hoc committees composed of designated chapter members.

The adjudication guidelines specify that a case will not be considered for review unless the complaint is made within 60 days after the client or worker comes to believe that a wrong has been committed. However, because complainants often need more time to recover or summon the nerve to formally make the allegation, this time limit is often waived (Berliner, 1989).

When a complaint is filed, the committee has to act rapidly. Within 10 days the chapter must inform the complainant that action is being taken. Hearings begin within 45 days if the complaint meets the necessary criteria, and a written report with recommendations must appear in another 45 days. Either party in the adjudication procedure may appeal the decision and recommendations with the NCOI. If there is no appeal, or if the decision is sustained, the recommendations are implemented within four months. When the committee rules against a member, membership in NASW may be temporarily suspended, or the member may be given a written reprimand and have his or her practice monitored for a specified time. Private practitioners could be required to receive approved supervision, and the fees they ordinarily receive from their clients could be waived for a specified time (NASW, 1980).

Even though the number of complaints has been relatively low, the COIs have determined in 41 percent of the adjudicated cases that some violation of ethical standards did take place (Barker & Branson, in press). The most common grievances are sexual misconduct; breach of confidentiality; fee splitting; soliciting the clients of other workers; overall professional misconduct; failing to adhere to ethical responsibilities to colleagues; and failing to adhere to ethical responsibilities to organizations, the social work profession, and society.

The adjudication procedure has been criticized, especially for not permitting the opposing parties to be represented by legal counsel and for not requiring that written transcripts of the hearing be taken (Zastrow, 1991). Nevertheless, most professionals are satisfied that it meets its objectives well. The procedure has even been used as a model for similar procedures by other professional associations within and outside social work. It is also used as a guide for the licensing regulations of some states.

5 PLANNING AND ORGANIZING THE PRACTICE

Once the social worker has the qualifications for private practice and is willing to take the necessary risks, it is time to begin to organize the practice. To have a viable practice requires serious advance planning; otherwise, the social worker is likely to encounter many problems that could have been avoided.

Before looking for an office and certainly before seeing the first fee-for-service private clients, the practitioner has many important decisions to make, such as whether the practice will be a solo or a group venture and how the office will be staffed. The practitioner should know the jurisdiction's legal regulations for small businesses and professional practices and must look into malpractice and business liability insurance. Plans for retirement and for insurance against illness or incapacitation need to be established. The practitioner must determine how to satisfy the income, property, and professional tax requirements of both federal and local laws. If helpers are employed, either part- or full-time, the employer must consider how to fulfill the legal requirements for their Social Security, retirement, and unemployment compensation programs.

Decisions concerning other aspects of the practice—office location and equipment, kind of clientele, fees and billing, and so on—also need to be made in the early stages of planning. These other topics are covered in later chapters.

Once all of these decisions are made and their implementation worked out, the practitioner will be able to turn full attention to the task of effectively providing quality service for clients.

SOLO OR GROUP PRACTICE?

Perhaps the most important preliminary decision is whether to establish a solo practice, a partnership, or a group practice. This choice influences almost every other decision that will have to be made about the way the practice is managed.

In a solo practice, of course, the worker is entirely responsible for the operation of the management and professional aspects of the practice; there is no sharing of office equipment, clients, problems, or decisions. Solo practice has been the most popular model for newly establishing part-time practitioners, at least until recent years. It has been popular because of its flexibility; workers do not have to worry about how colleagues want the office decorated or what hours to keep. It has also remained common simply because it is so difficult to find compatible partners.

The disadvantages of solo practice, however, are numerous. The expenses are always higher, and income is usually lower. It is more difficult to get referrals in solo practice. Most solo practitioners feel more isolated, and they have the unrelenting burden of caring for their clients without respite; there are no convenient colleagues with whom to share information, ideas, resources, and coverage during illnesses and vacations. Without collegial stimulation, there is often less inclination to keep professionally current. For these reasons, group practices have become the most common model of private social work practice in recent years.

Whatever choice is made is not irrevocable, however. In fact, a high proportion of social workers who enter private practice change from one type of practice to another as their circumstances, interests, skills, contacts, and social conditions change over the course of their careers. Most part-time practitioners originally opt for solo practices, and most full-timers develop partnerships or group practices. Overall, the trend for all private practitioners is away from solo practice and into the various forms of shared practices.

TYPES OF GROUP PRACTICES

There are many models of group practice. The simplest one is the informal partnership, wherein two social workers agree to share some office space and the expenses pertaining to their mutual needs. Everything else—individual office expenses, client records, billing, and income—is separate. At the other extreme of complexity is the professional corporation partnership, in which two or more social workers (or members of different disciplines) agree to share the entire operation, including its responsibilities, expenses, income, workload, physical setting, and employees.

There are advantages and disadvantages to both types of arrangement. When the social worker's partner is another social worker, their methods are more understandable to one another. They can usually cover each other's clients during absences because their intervention strategies are likely to be similar. Newcomers to social work can enter private practice sooner and obtain supervision from a qualified, experienced social work partner. Including members of other professions in the practice, on the other hand, can broaden the range of services the office provides and offer different viewpoints. If the partner is a physician, there are fewer problems about medical backup. Psychologists, marital therapists, and other specialists also bring unique areas of expertise to a partnership.

PROFESSIONAL EMPLOYEES IN GROUP PRACTICES

Another form of group practice consists of an experienced private practitioner or partnership employing another professional. The newcomer is not a partner—does not share in decisions, expenses, or profit—but does see clients. Employees who are professionals are not, strictly speaking, private practitioners. Because they do not make the ultimate decisions about who their clients will be or take ultimate responsibility for their care, they are more like agency employees.

Such an arrangement typically comes about when an experienced practitioner, sometimes from a different profession, has an overload of referrals and uses the new worker to see them. The new worker is paid a straight salary, or, less desirably, a percentage of the fee collected from the client.

To a social worker with relatively little experience or few financial resources, even an arrangement whereby only part of the fee is received might be tempting. However, workers can get trapped in these arrangements by entering a contract with the experienced professional that precludes their establishing their own independent practices in the community. Becoming involved in such an arrangement is most unwise for a new worker and may be illegal and unethical for the experienced professional. This practice, called "fee-splitting," is discussed further in chapter 8.

ADVANTAGES AND DISADVANTAGES OF PARTNERSHIPS

When shared partnerships are legitimate, they have many advantages. Not only are there substantial cost savings in office space, but problems of isolation, coverage, and consultation are minimized. Partners can provide more specialized services and team approaches. Income- and clientele-building opportunities are increased because shared practices provide better opportunities to participate in managed health care programs, preferred provider organizations, and employee assistance programs. In addition, credibility with other professional groups in enhanced.

Some workers find disadvantages in shared practices. The partners may not be compatible because of different tastes or work habits or noncomplementary types of clients. Problems can also occur over sharing equipment and keeping track of expenditures. In addition, if allocating responsibilities and dividing the workload become too time consuming, the workers are soon facing some of the very problems they had hoped to leave at the agency.

The biggest problem for many is finding compatible partners. Most partnerships derive from personal friendships established in agencies or in school. Some workers find compatible partners through advertisements in professional journals and professional association newspapers and newsletters or through brief meetings at conferences. Partnerships from such encounters are risky because the new partners do not know each other well enough. A better way is to develop working relationships with fellow professionals, say, by working together in a professional organization on a committee project, or, if the worker wants a partner from another profession, by volunteering on civic projects or working for political causes, hospitals, or institutions. This method will take much longer, but the decision about a partner is important enough to deserve this kind of patience.

PARTNERSHIP AGREEMENTS

Whatever kind of group practice is established, the participants should put their agreed arrangement in writing. Even if the partners are good friends, a written agreement can keep issues clear and mutually beneficial. The partners should make a formal contract through a lawyer after discussing issues with a financial consultant (Seelig, 1988b).

The agreement should specify the nature of the partnership, the mutual responsibilities of the partners to the organization, and the way proceeds from the organization are to be disbursed to the partners. The agreement should also specify which costs are to be borne by the group and which by the individuals. In addition, the responsibilities of each participant in covering for the others and providing consultation or supervision should be outlined, and the use of office space and the procedures for deciding on what equipment, furniture, and supplies to acquire should be defined.

Other important matters to be covered include the procedures for billing clients, collecting and bookkeeping, record keeping, and hiring and supervising employees. It is especially important that the agreement also specify that all partners get adequate malpractice insurance coverage; to the extent possible, it should include a "hold-harmless" clause in which the partners are not liable for malpractice actions brought by a client against another partner. The contract should also spell out the conditions for dissolving the partnership and dividing its assets and obligations in the event of death, retirement, disability, personal conflict, or other circumstance (Seelig, 1988a).

MANAGED HEALTH CARE SYSTEMS

Whether private practitioners opt for solo or group practice, they also must decide whether to participate with colleagues in some form of health care provider network. These networks have different names and models of organization, including preferred provider organizations, health maintenance organizations, and managed health (or mental health) care programs. The term now preferred by those in the system is "coordinated health care system." Whatever they are called, they are health insurance–health benefit plans originated by government and third-party financing organizations to help contain the costs of service while maintaining quality of care. They administer the provision of health care to people who belong to a group coverage system; they collect funds from these members or their employers and then pay the health care professionals registered in the system for their services.

Given current economic and political trends, it is probable that nearly all private practitioners will eventually become members of these networks. The reason for this is clear: Virtually all potential clients will eventually be participants in such programs, and having prepaid for the services, they will go only to participating health care providers. Insurance companies increasingly use such systems, and the long-discussed national health care system would do likewise. Some professionals may remain outside these networks, but these professionals are likely to be few in number and to provide highly specialized services only for very affluent clients (Moldowsky, 1989).

Participation in most of these networks would not necessarily require providers to give up their independent offices or helping methods, but only to work within specified guidelines in exchange for being eligible to receive client referrals from the network. Clients would still choose which provider to consult, so the practitioner's need for marketing would remain. The practitioner's need to be fully qualified, current, and connected with professional organizations would also remain because the network would scrutinize the provider's activity carefully.

Every community now has one or more managed health care systems, and most of these include social workers. Because these systems are comprehensive and include inpatient, outpatient, and in-between health and mental health care, prevention, and social services, social workers have proved to be important contributors (Dumont, 1990). Every social worker who establishes a private practice should contact these organizations to discuss participation. However, before signing any agreement to be a part of a system, the worker should review the contract with a lawyer, compare alternatives, and discuss the arrangements with other professionals who do and do not participate (NASW, 1990a).

TO INCORPORATE OR NOT?

If the practitioner establishes or enters a shared practice, a decision about whether to incorporate must also be made. It would be somewhat less complicated to incorporate before the practice is actually established, but many practitioners start the practice and incorporate later. It has become quite common to see such designations as "Joan Smith, MSW, PA" (for professional association) on office stationery and shingles.

In the past decade, there have been changes in federal tax laws and new court rulings about financial obligations and malpractice liability that considerably reduce the advantages of professional incorporation. Many believe that incorporating allows the purchase of yachts, large cars, cottages in the Caribbean, and unlimited luxuries without many tax consequences. In fact, business corporations can write off these expenses only when the company owns such luxuries to enhance its profitability, and unincorporated practitioners can also write off any purchase justifiably needed to operate or improve the business or practice anyway.

Another misconception about incorporating is the belief that a practitioner's personal assets are separate from business assets. The premise is that in case of litigation, only the practice assets are vulnerable. Again, although this may be true of some other businesses, it is not so with professional corporations. Malpractice suits are still filed against the practitioner and the practitioner's personal assets as well as against the corporation.

Incorporating does offer some benefits, however, and should be considered, particularly if a group practice is contemplated. The major advantage is in insurance payments. Life and disability insurance premiums may be paid with pretax dollars by the corporation in the practitioner's behalf. The unincorporated practitioner pays these premiums after paying income taxes. Furthermore, much of the practitioner's total medical and dental expenses may be deducted from the corporation's taxes, but the unincorporated practitioner can deduct only the standard 3 percent of adjusted gross income for health care costs.

The 1982 tax law changes eliminated what had been the best reason to incorporate. At that time, the unincorporated practitioner could set aside only 15 percent or up to $15,000 of net income for tax-deferred retirement. Practitioners in the higher income brackets found this quite limiting. Through incorporating, they could set aside substantially more. Since 1984, the amount that can be set aside for tax-deferred retirement has been increased to up to $30,000. This increase negates the tax advantage of incorporating for all practitioners who net less than $100,000 annually.

Incorporation can cost the practitioner over $1,000 to establish and several hundred dollars annually to maintain. It requires formal record keeping, appointment of officers, and regular meetings of those officers. These costs are no longer offset by tax savings, except for practitioners in very high income brackets. Any worker who reaches such income levels should retain a management or investment consultant and discuss any further advantages of incorporating.

MANAGEMENT AND PROFESSIONAL CONSULTANTS

If the services of a management consultant are going to be used, the best time to hire one is before opening the practice. A management consultant can advise the beginning practitioner on bookkeeping procedures, tax records, tax savings, investment programs, retirement accounts, and many other essential aspects of the business. After the practice is well-established, the worker may want to forgo help from a management consultant and employ an accountant who specializes in income tax. The accountant may keep all the worker's books but is primarily needed for annual assistance with taxes. Management consultants and accountants, while rather expensive, usually pay for themselves by finding savings and ways to make the practice more efficient.

Many private social work practitioners also find it valuable to employ professional consultants. They may be colleagues who are more experienced and who assume some of the functions of the agency supervisor. The consultants may be social workers or members of other professions. Usually, they have private or agency practices of their own. Private practitioners would regularly go to their offices to discuss cases and sometimes even send their clients there for further evaluation.

Should the consultant be another social worker or a member of another profession? There are advantages and disadvantages in each choice. Many practitioners hire experienced, professionally certified social workers as professional consultants to act as supervisors in order to meet the credentialing requirements. Most credentials and certifications require workers to have a specified number of hours of client contact under the supervision of a qualified social worker. Using members of other disciplines does not meet this criterion. Even if the social worker no longer needs supervision for credentialing, consultation with professional colleagues is still beneficial. An objective social work view of the case helps refine one's professional skills and knowledge. If the consultant is a colleague, it is often more convenient to reciprocate consultation services; coverage of clients during absences is also more feasible than with professionals from other disciplines.

Many social workers employ the services of a physician in addition to, or instead of, their professional colleagues for regular professional consultations. There are several reasons for this. With medical backup, the worker can more easily know if the problems have physical origins. Medication can be prescribed and monitored, and, when necessary, hospitalizations can be facilitated. Finally, some social workers use physicians to meet the reimbursement criteria of some insurance companies. Most third parties no longer require physicians to oversee the worker's intervention with the client, but the value of medical review remains.

All private practitioners, especially those in solo practice, should employ professional consultants. Even practitioners with ample experience and excellent training benefit from reviewing their cases through the eyes of others. It is easy to develop "blind spots" or bad practice habits that go undetected and that can be harmful to clients. If a client is harmed through the worker's negligence, an issue that is sure to be raised in the malpractice trial is whether the worker used any consultation. Ironically, it has become more difficult for professionals to employ and retain good consultants because of legal liabilities; consultants and supervisors can be included in malpractice suits (Reamer, 1989).

CLERICAL EMPLOYEES

Most private social work practitioners in established practices have some secretarial or office assistance. The activities of a solo private practitioner rarely require the services of a full-time secretary, especially now that computer systems fulfill so many secretarial functions efficiently. Group practices, where one secretary can meet the office management needs of several professionals, still employ clerical staff even when they use computer systems. The essential jobs performed by clerical staff include preparation of monthly bills, filling out and filing insurance claims, typing letters, keeping files orderly, receiving clients in person or on the telephone, scheduling appointments, procuring supplies, and maintaining the office. Computer programs are effective in calculating and preparing monthly bills and preparing insurance claims, but typing personal letters and providing the "human touch" for clients is another matter.

Many workers try to economize by doing the secretarial tasks themselves, but it is an inefficient frugality. Hiring a part-time secretary for a few hours weekly is not very expensive, and the social worker is freed to carry out those tasks that enhance practice skills and build clientele.

EMPLOYEE BENEFITS

When employees are hired, whether they are part-time or full-time secretaries, janitors, or professionals, the law says they are entitled to certain benefits. They are entitled to just compensation that, at the least, meets federal minimum wage laws. A portion of their pay must be withheld and paid to the Internal Revenue Service (IRS) and usually to the relevant state tax authorities. Social Security funds must also be withheld and sent to the IRS along with matching employer contributions. Employers are required by federal law to pay half of the employee's Social Security (FICA) tax. In other words, 7.65 percent of the employee's taxable income must be withheld, and another 7.65 percent must be contributed by the employer (Webster & Perry, 1990).

If the practitioner has a federally regulated retirement plan, employees must be included in the plan to provide for their retirement. One employee retirement system is the Private Retirement Incentives Matched by Employers (PRIME) account, in which the employee makes pretax contributions of up to $3,000, which the employer matches, dollar for dollar, up to 3 percent of the employee's salary. Employees must also be covered for worker's benefits such as unemployment and on-the-job injury compensation. Before employing anyone, practitioners must contact the relevant state department of labor for all the necessary forms and regulations. Other employee benefits are optional and should be negotiated before hiring takes place. Benefits other than direct fees for service are not required for independent consultants.

RETIREMENT PROGRAMS

Practitioners may also want to establish their retirement plans before they establish their practices. The plans, except for Social Security, are optional but may be opened with minimal initial investment and maintained with minimum or no regular contributions. If the accounts are established in advance, the contributions made to them can follow the fortunes of the practice and provide considerable income tax savings.

Prior to 1984, the foundation of the private practitioner's retirement planning was the federally regulated Keogh Plan for self-employed taxpayers. The Keogh Plan permitted the social worker, whether in part- or full-time practice, to set aside 15 percent of net practice receipts (or up to $15,000) per year and pay no income tax on this money until retirement.

The Tax Equity and Fiscal Responsibility Act (TEFRA) was designed to replace the Keogh Plan and provide more retirement protections for employees. TEFRA permits the private practitioner to set aside up to 25 percent of net earnings (or up to $30,000) per year in certain defined circumstances.

The TEFRA rules are more rigorous in providing eligibility and vesting requirements for the practitioner's employees, but otherwise they differ little from the Keogh Plan. In both cases the worker cannot begin to withdraw the money until age 59 1/2 and must begin to withdraw it by age 70; if the money is withdrawn before this time, tax on it will be paid at the current income rate, and a 10 percent penalty is levied by the IRS. If the practitioner or employee becomes permanently disabled before this time, withdrawals may be made without penalty. The money is held in a government-designated and government-regulated financial institution that is set up for TEFRA and Keogh programs.

The practitioner may choose from a variety of investment possibilities for the program by informing the qualified institution where to invest these funds. Most private social work practitioners have their retirement accounts held in banks, where the money is invested in one of the bank's own programs or in mutual funds, stocks, or insurance annuity programs. It is easy to establish a retirement account of this type by contacting almost any bank, securities brokerage firm, or insurance company.

SOCIAL SECURITY AND SELF-EMPLOYMENT TAXES

Although the TEFRA and Keogh programs are optional, Social Security— Old Age, Survivors, Disability, and Health Insurance (OASDHI)—is not. Social Security benefits are important, especially for self-employed people, and may include significant retirement income, income for one's surviving dependents, payments for individuals who become disabled, and medical care payments for covered individuals who reach the age of 65. These benefits are paid for not out of government general revenues, but by the workers themselves and by their employers. Social Security collects 15.3 percent of the individual's taxable income; this amount is disbursed to the Social Security fund (12.4 percent) and to the Medicare fund (2.9 percent).

Unlike employees, private practitioners must pay all of the 15.3 percent and withhold their own funds from their taxable incomes. They do so through the Social Security self-employment tax. This tax is calculated on IRS form 1040 SE and paid through the IRS at the same time the private practitioner pays income tax, in the quarterly estimated payments and at the end of the tax year.

INCOME AND OTHER TAXES

Private practitioners, like all self-employed persons, are required by the IRS to estimate their annual taxable income at the beginning of the year or when they first open their practices. Income taxes are the same as for employed workers, except that the self-employed person may take a deduction for the 7.5 percent of the Social Security self-employment tax that is not paid for by employers.

The IRS requires the self-employed person to pay income taxes quarterly. At the beginning of each taxable year, or at least by April 15, the practitioner must estimate approximately how much taxable income is going to be received during the year. This estimate is sent to the Internal Revenue Service on IRS form 1040 ES (OCR). (This form is available at IRS offices and at tax time at most post offices and public libraries, or it may be obtained by calling the IRS at 1-800-829-3676.)

Based on the estimate made, the practitioner must send a check to the IRS every quarter of the year (by the 15th day of April, June, September, and January). The amount is one-fourth of the annual total estimated tax due. If the practitioner's estimate turns out to be too low (less than 90 percent of the annual income) when the year-end tax is figured, the additional tax and a penalty must be paid. This need not happen, however, because the practitioner can easily raise the estimate each quarter if earnings exceed the estimate. If taxes are overestimated, the practitioner gets the refund but no interest.

If net income rises rapidly after entering private practice, the practitioner's taxes will greatly increase. Because the private practitioner pays taxes directly instead of through payroll withholding, there can be a difficult adjustment process. It is tempting to delay making the tax payments until the end of the year, but then one can be hit with a tax obligation that is hard to meet. One way to lessen the crunch is to be sure to set aside approximately 25 percent of practice receipts for taxes. Another way is through "income averaging." In effect, the practitioner can, for tax purposes, spread the increased earnings over several past years when earnings were lower. It is advisable to employ a certified public accountant to help with the first year's taxes if income averaging seems a possibility.

State and local income taxation, if applicable, is usually based on a proportion of one's federal taxes. State income tax laws usually require estimated quarterly payments just as for federal taxes. However, some localities tax the incomes of professional practices even if the jurisdiction has no personal income tax, through a sales tax on services rendered. Some jurisdictions also have property taxes on the contents of the practitioner's office. And some jurisdictions extract taxes from private practitioners through business licenses. The beginning practitioner would do well to check with the relevant locality's revenue departments before seeing clients. It might be tempting to ignore these local taxes in the hope that no one will notice, but eventually the taxes will have to be paid, and possibly with penalties.

Those in private practice and other small businesses tend to be scrutinized by the Internal Revenue Service more carefully than paid employees. This is because the IRS recognizes that it is more difficult to track receipts that come from individual customers and clients; many business people take advantage of this difficulty and do not provide a full accounting of their income. The extra scrutiny makes it essential to maintain well-documented financial records.

MALPRACTICE AND OFFICE LIABILITY INSURANCE

Before the first client is seen or even spoken with on the telephone, the private practitioner must become insured against the risks of malpractice and office liabilities. As is discussed in detail in chapter 8, the current social trend of litigiousness necessitates the need for this protection.

Many commercial insurance companies underwrite social work malpractice risks, and their premiums are far lower than the rates charged to other mental health care providers. However, the rates for social workers' coverage are going up as, increasingly, social workers are being sued. Currently, the NASW-sponsored plan underwritten by the American Professional Agency has the most competitive rates and coverage generally available. The agency-employed social worker can easily transfer or add malpractice coverage obtained for an agency practice to a private practice setting with minimal rate changes. One must be a member of NASW and hold a master's degree in social work to apply for NASW-sponsored liability insurance coverage as a private practitioner. In most cases one also must not be under review for possible sanctions due to ethical violations.

The practitioner will also need office liability insurance. This coverage is to take care of anyone who is accidentally injured on the practitioner's premises. These policies are analogous to homeowner's insurance and may also cover against vandalism, theft, and weather damage to the office facilities. They may cover people who are injured as a result of another client's actions, too. The rates are relatively low, and these policies are available through most commercial homeowner insurance companies that offer "umbrella coverage." This coverage is important even if the practitioner is in part-time private practice and using another professional's office. Again, coverage should be obtained when the office is in the planning stages so that it is in place when the practitioner is ready to see clients.

The private practitioner, especially one no longer affiliated with an agency, may also want insurance against sickness and resulting loss of income and permanent disability. Social Security does not cover for loss of income or sickness (unless one is below the poverty line and thus eligible for Medicaid), and its disability coverage is minimal. Thus, some form of supplemental insurance protection is essential. Many companies offer such coverage, but nongroup rates can be very high. The NASW-sponsored plan for health, income loss, and disability has rates and coverage that are competitive with those of other group policies.

6 CHOOSING THE PRACTICE SETTING

Making one's own decisions about the location, style, and contents of the office or setting for the practice is one of the most satisfying aspects of being in private social work practice. If the right decisions are made, practitioners can create work environments that complement their unique styles and the needs of their particular clientele. Even though this process can be somewhat tedious—involving the research for the right location and furniture, as well as negotiations with realtors, landlords, furniture salespeople, contractors, and bank loan officers—the end result can make it worthwhile.

However, all too often, private practitioners do not plan their setting very carefully. They merely fall into a location because someone they knew was there. They furnish it with the most easily available and least expensive equipment, making these decisions through trial and error.

A better approach is for the practitioner to consider what the typical workday will be like in this office; it is helpful as well for the practitioner to try to imagine the office as the client will see it. Will it give the client the impression that the worker is a well-organized, thoughtful professional, or one who is slapdash about everything? The practitioner also needs to make certain that the office and equipment are suitable for the type of practice specialty that is to be established.

THE RIGHT LOCATION

Careful planning about where to locate is a prerequisite of establishing a successful practice. Thoreau was wrong in claiming that people would travel through the deepest woods to reach the person with a better mousetrap. Thoreau failed in three major business ventures in his lifetime and had to live off his friends. No business, including that of private psychotherapy practice, is likely to succeed if it is badly located.

The right location for a social work practice does not depend on heavy traffic patterns, but it should be accessible to the type of clientele one hopes to reach. The location should be one in which the clientele will feel comfortable. In addition, clients should feel comfortable in the office, and the neighbors should feel comfortable with the practice in the neighborhood. For example, downtown office buildings are ideal settings if the desired clients are mostly professional people, but less satisfactory for a clientele composed of children or families who rarely venture from the suburbs. On the other hand, if the clients are economically disadvantaged or mentally ill, or if they are members of the gay community, offices in suburban homes might not always be welcomed by the neighbors.

If the office has an opulent or formal atmosphere, it might be ideal for older, more affluent couples, but it might make children, adolescents, or economically disadvantaged people feel ill at ease. If the office has been decorated and equipped in a spartan fashion, it might suggest to some potential clients that the worker is not very successful and perhaps incapable of providing the needed service. Clients develop impressions about the worker based on the look of the office as well as on the number of diplomas on the walls; clients will be less likely to pay their bills, return for subsequent visits, or refer others if the office makes them uncomfortable (Mackey et al., 1987).

Therefore, the worker should determine in advance the clientele to serve and then locate and decorate accordingly. Even a practitioner with limited financial resources can lease appropriate office furniture at affordable rates. If limited finances preclude getting the type of office desired, a short lease, followed by a move, might be workable. But the best investment the new private practitioner can make is the most accessible and comfortable office possible.

SIX POSSIBLE SETTINGS

Private social work practitioners have six possibilities when it comes to choosing their office settings. They are (1) professional office buildings, (2) office suites in residential apartment complexes, (3) offices in small detached buildings or converted homes, (4) rented space in the office of another professional, (5) the social worker's home office, and (6) after-hours use of an office in the agency where the part-time private practitioner is employed.

Each of these settings has advantages and disadvantages. Because each practitioner's needs, clientele, specialty, style of practice, and financial circumstances are unique, it is up to the practitioner to decide which setting is best for his or her own practice. In weighing all the variables, one must also take into account that one's immediate practice needs and circumstances will not be the same in a few years; thus, the flexibility of various features being considered is also an important factor.

Professional Office Buildings

Office buildings for professionals are appealing to full-time private practitioners, especially those in group practice. The building itself sets the tone for the businesslike nature of the therapy relationship. Clients feel they are going there to work. This no-nonsense ambience might repel some potential clients, but the ones who are attracted to it are more likely to be serious about confronting their problems and more willing to pay for the service. Such buildings are generally easy for clients to get to, usually being located on major streets near public transportation or parking facilities.

A source of additional referrals is another advantage of such buildings. Other professionals in the building, especially if the social worker cultivates a relationship with them, may refer clients. Many people who seek professional services pass through these buildings. When they see the worker's name and specialty on the directory or the practitioner's office door, some inevitably inquire about an appointment.

Isolation, the problem facing many private practitioners, is minimized in this setting because of the possibility of cultivating friendships and consultation or collaboration contacts in the building. Furthermore, the maintenance of the office can be done by building personnel, freeing the worker from this task. Finally, the office building choice avoids some problems found in the alternatives. For example, there are no zoning problems in such a location, and there is no difficulty convincing the Internal Revenue Service that the office is used entirely for one's professional activity.

The financial expense of this setting is the greatest disadvantage, and rents go up every year. Also, such buildings may seem rather forbidding to some people, especially children. If such buildings have inadequate parking facilities, it is discouraging to those who prefer driving. Finally, some clients do not like office buildings because such buildings are often crowded and the clients are seeking confidentiality.

Office Suites in Apartment Complexes

Office suites in apartment complexes are among the least popular options for most private practitioners. This is surprising because this kind of location has many desirable features. Many of these apartment complexes have office suites on the ground floor, often with private entrances and thus more confidentiality for clients. There may be other professional offices in the complex, so the worker will not feel isolated. The buildings generate some "drop in" clientele from residents who see the worker's name and specialty listed.

These facilities offer a more "homey" atmosphere for warmer relationships with clients who are intimidated by office buildings. In addition, these buildings often feature such amenities as swimming pools and tennis courts, which can offer a short respite for the practitioner in the middle of the day. Many of these suites are similar to apartment units in that they have kitchens and bathrooms. And, during the weekdays at least, the parking problem is not as severe as it can be in an office building.

The best feature of all is the cost. Although such suites are usually more spacious than suites in office buildings, they typically cost one-third less for equivalent amounts of space.

The disadvantages are few but important. Sometimes residents in the complex are uncomfortable with the behavior or appearance of the clients and exert subtle pressure on the clients or worker that indicate their presence is unwelcome. There is typically less tolerance for anything that appears deviant wherever people live; such reactions may be inevitable.

Offices in Small Buildings or Office Condominiums

Detached buildings, converted houses, or office condominiums are a third possible choice of office location. Frequently, these office condos or small buildings are located in areas that are more commercial than residential, and they are usually owned by the professionals themselves as an asset of their shared practice. They feature fairly homey atmospheres and no parking problems, and they can be modified to meet the needs of the therapist and the clients much more easily than suites in office or apartment buildings.

The start-up costs for these arrangements are relatively high because of conversion expenses and utility costs. However, units owned by the practitioners become relatively cost-efficient in the long run. Fixed mortgages remain stable, whereas rents in office buildings and apartment complexes keep rising. Because the building is used exclusively for offices, income tax savings are considerable. It may be depreciated rapidly for tax purposes, even though it is in reality likely to appreciate in value.

The disadvantage of this setting is that the building usually requires more maintenance than the other choices, and the practitioner-tenants must either maintain it themselves or hire service people. Otherwise they pay a high condo or management fee. If the building is shared by several professionals, the sense of isolation is minimal, but it is crucial that the partners be compatible. If they turn out not to be, there may be no escape from the unpleasant conflicts short of the cumbersome process of extricating, selling, and relocating.

Space Rented from Other Professionals

Renting space in the office of an established private practitioner is another option that has attractive advantages, especially for the social worker who is just starting out in private practice. It enables the newcomer to become somewhat established without a major financial outlay. The newcomer can concentrate on building a clientele without having to worry, for the time being, about the physical setting. The start-up costs are low, and the new social worker can learn firsthand what will be needed to establish the setting for a separate and independent office later.

The basis of charging for sublet space from established practitioners varies tremendously. Some practitioners simply charge a flat rental fee each month, the amount of which is negotiated by the two parties. Others charge on the basis of hours of use or number of clients seen. An increasingly common system is for the established practitioner to receive a percentage of the amount that is collected by the new practitioner. Often in this system, the established worker provides clients for the newcomer, too, and perhaps some "consultation." This is a highly dubious system of which the new practitioner should be wary. A flat monthly charge is the fairest and most equitable system for all involved.

Even with a fair charge system, there are some disadvantages for the newcomer in subleasing space from an established practitioner. Newcomers can often feel very isolated in such systems. They might be using the office only in the evenings and weekends during the owner's absence. New workers will not be able to equip the facility with much that is their own, and their own files, materials, and references will usually have to be moved in and out of the office nearly every day. In addition, they may be concerned about the possibility that they or their clients might damage some of the property or otherwise disrupt the operations of the owners. The disadvantages of this method are so serious that it must be considered only a temporary solution and one that the newcomer should become free of as soon as possible.

The Home Office

The home office is, of course, less expensive and more convenient than the other choices, and it is immediately available. The initial investment is not as great, and the worker might be able to get double duty out of the office by using it for other purposes when no clients are there. The home office usually reflects the worker's specialty, values, and style better than any other possibility and therefore can be a very comfortable environment for practice. However, the disadvantages are considerable.

If the home is located in an area inconvenient for the target clientele, it will be more difficult to attract new referrals. When the home is geographically accessible, the worker may lose some sense of privacy. Clients can observe many personal aspects of the worker's life and make judgments based on factors other than practice skills. Finally, of course, the practitioner cannot avoid bringing work home.

One caution about home offices regards regulations of tax and zoning authorities, landlords, and neighborhood associations. For example, although it is possible to deduct some of the costs of maintaining a home office from federal and state income taxes, one cannot legally deduct the costs of the entire office if it is used for purposes other than the practice. In addition, even if the rooms do qualify exclusively as a home office, the worker still might not want to deduct it because those rooms are then no longer considered part of the residence for resale or capital gains purposes. The worker must keep careful records about household expenses to use in documenting tax claims. Zoning regulations can present another problem; as discussed in chapter 4, if the worker's home is in a residential area where businesses are not permitted, difficulties may be encountered.

After-Hours Use of the Agency's or Employer's Office

Many social services agencies are now permitting their social work employees the use of agency offices to see private clients after hours. This privilege often salves the wounds of meager pay and benefits and prevents loss of good employees. For the practitioner, this arrangement has the advantage of economy and convenience. In addition, the worker spends less time commuting if there is only one place of business, and opportunities exist for gaining referrals from those who use the agency.

There are two disadvantages. One is that the worker has little choice about decor and equipment and does not have much chance for variety in work experiences (unless the worker performs only administrative duties during agency work hours). The other disadvantage is that conflicts of interest can easily occur. Clients may be shifted from the care of the agency to the care of the private practitioner without even knowing it. And when a client runs out of money or insurance, he or she may be shifted back to the agency. With no clear demarcation between the practitioner's agency work and private work, such circumstances can occur. Clients, colleagues, tax collectors, third parties, and agency board members are likely to become confused and to require the practitioner to clarify things.

Even though such conflicts of interest may not occur frequently, given social workers' strong adherence to ethics, such problems have occurred often enough for agencies and professional associations to re-act. NASW has explicitly stated in its *Guidelines on the Private Practice of Clinical Social Work* (Robertson & Jackson, 1991) that the private practitioner should refrain from soliciting or accepting clients for private practice who have requested the services of the employer when the employer is able to provide those services.

AMBIENCE: THE "SOCIOPETAL" OFFICE

After deciding on the office location, the worker begins planning the physical layout, decor, and amenities of the office. This is one of the nicest aspects of private practice—the opportunity to decorate and equip the practice setting to suit one's own taste and pocketbook.

Thoughtful planners organize their new offices to create settings that have "sociopetal" rather than "sociofugal" characteristics. These terms were first applied to the design of psychiatric wards and later came into use by designers of restaurants, shopping malls, and offices where communication and optimal helping are important. The sociopetal setting is one that encourages interaction and promotes feelings of warmth and intimacy, whereas sociofugal arrangements inhibit interactions. For example, metal desks, tile floors, and furniture arrangements placed in severe right angles are sociofugal. Interview chairs placed farther than five feet apart and side by side or directly face to face are also sociofugal arrangements. So, too, is the arrangement in which the practitioner's desk is between the worker and the client.

The sociopetal private practice office is about twice as long as it is wide (approximately 16 feet by 9 feet, for practitioners who work mostly with individuals) and contains a couch, bookcase, desk, several soft chairs, small tables, and a large plant. Soft carpets, tasteful wall hangings, and diplomas make the room feel more like a den or living room than an office. In these settings, the chairs where interviewing takes place are seldom more than a few feet apart, and many are two or three feet apart. They are placed at 45-degree angles to one another for the most comfortable interviewing situation. The practitioner's desk is nearby but not within the interview area.

The sociopetal office makes the client comfortable in many little, less apparent, ways, too. Clients should know where the nearest available washroom is and should have easy access to it without having to ask. The practitioner's name should be displayed to avoid embarrassment should the new client forget. Facial tissues should be located near the client's chair in case of tears. A mirror could be located near the door so the client can get presentable before returning to the outside world. Clocks could also be placed where they can be seen by clients. As F. J. Turner (1978) wrote, "The increase in tension toward the end of an interview may be related to significant psychodynamic material but it may just as well be related to worry about missing a bus" (p. 74).

Obviously, the outcome of the social worker's intervention does not depend on the arrangement of the office or on the amenities it contains. However, there is strong evidence that the physical arrangement of the office influences the nature of the relationship. It helps increase the level of security, trust, and comfort experienced by the client and practitioner.

ESSENTIALS FOR THE WORKING OFFICE

For offices to be effective and efficient, some elements are mandatory. It is essential that the interview room be separate from the waiting room. The walls between them must be soundproof to preserve client confidentiality. If soundproofing is too expensive, a radio or sound device may be kept on in the waiting room to mute any sounds coming from the interview room. In addition, the waiting clients should have easy access to a lavatory.

No filing cabinets or information about clients should be in the waiting room or accessible to anyone but the worker and worker's staff. A lockable desk and a lockable file cabinet are also needed. These safeguard client files as well as cash payments that have not been deposited.

The practitioner's office needs little equipment unless the specialization requires toys for work with children. Otherwise, one needs only a telephone with a switch to turn off its ringing and a typewriter or word processor and printer. Some workers find it convenient to write out bills in longhand, but typed or computer-printed statements are more professional and businesslike. In any case, the typewriter or computer and printer are needed for the many letters that have to be written.

The telephone may be in the interview room, but it should be shut off during interviews. It is improper and inconsiderate to interrupt worker-client sessions to take calls. If the phone has an extension in the waiting room, it can be answered there by a secretary or by an answering machine or service.

Answering machines are irritatingly ubiquitous in all walks of life, including private practitioners' offices. However, unless the worker employs a full-time receptionist or uses an answering service, answering machines are necessary. Although annoying, they are inexpensive and convenient, and they protect the worker from interruptions when talking with a client. Their major drawback is that they can be intimidating for many clients, who simply hang up rather than talk to a machine.

A more expensive alternative is the answering service. The worker's phone rings in another office, sometimes across town, where full-time receptionists take all messages for the worker. This service is more personal than a machine, and the client can leave a more thorough message. The disadvantage of the service, in addition to higher costs, is that operators sometimes receive many calls at once and put the caller on hold for long periods; if the client gets tired and hangs up, the worker is often not informed. Operators can also write down incorrect messages and telephone numbers in their haste.

The acquisition of any other office equipment the worker may want can be delayed until the worker's financial position is solid. Such luxuries include photocopy machines, fax machines, audio and video recorders, postage meters, one-way mirrors, and computers and computer printers (to replace typewriters). Although these items are expensive and dispensable, most private practitioners eventually acquire some of them; the convenience they provide enables the worker to devote more time to marketing and professional activities (Kreuger, 1986). The costs of these items are tax deductible as office expenses if they are used for no other purpose.

LEASING OR BUYING OFFICE FURNITURE AND EQUIPMENT

To save on start-up costs, many new practitioners lease rather than buy furniture and equipment. The costs of establishing and equipping the private practice office, even a relatively spartan one, are considerable, usually much more than the beginning practitioner anticipates. If the practitioner purchases all the needed equipment and furnishings for the office at once, the cost could easily reach five figures. This is a considerable investment, especially when there is no proven formula for estimating the probable or even hoped-for return. Borrowing money to get started might be difficult for beginning social workers because of the uncertainty inherent in their venture. They often must pay a very high interest rate or points on their loan.

Leasing the needed equipment is an attractive alternative for many social workers until they are in a better financial position. Many practitioners think nothing of leasing their office space but do not even consider the same possibility for equipment and furniture. This oversight is unfortunate because there are major advantages to leasing. The most important is that the initial outlay is considerably reduced. The monthly fee for the rental of the furniture and equipment is totally tax deductible and is deductible from the overhead of the operation. Often the amount spent on the rent can be applied to a purchase at a later time if the social worker decides to retain the equipment. Another advantage is that leasing permits the worker to experiment with different types of equipment or different styles of furnishings and then to eventually buy whatever is most suitable and desirable.

Of course, in the long run the costs of leasing are far greater than those of outright purchases, and the selection is sometimes smaller than that available to buyers. After workers become well-established, they usually want to buy their own furniture and equipment. The purchase price of the items is tax deductible if records showing the date of purchase are retained. It is possible to depreciate these items each year as they wear out, a technique that adds considerably to one's tax savings.

STATIONERY AND OTHER SUPPLIES

Essential office supplies should be on hand before the first client is seen. Printed stationery items are the most important and should be ordered long before one sees clients to be sure that everything is correct when needed. Supplies needed include long and short envelopes (plain and with windows for inserting bills); matching letterhead paper, business cards, billing statements; and a book of receipts. All these items are printed with the worker's name; highest academic degree; appropriate designation if incorporated; professional affiliation; practice address; telephone number; and, where applicable, professional license numbers.

Most local print shops can provide such materials affordably and quickly, but many practitioners find it convenient to use the large mail-order printing firms that specialize in printing for physicians and other professionals. These firms provide catalogs and order forms. Orders are usually filled promptly and returned with guarantees, by direct mail or parcel delivery, within a few days if needed. (The largest of these companies include Histacount Corporation, Walt Whitman Drive, Melville, NY 11747; Professional Offices, Box 450, Waterloo, IA 50704; and Feld Printing Co., Box 44188, Cincinnati, OH 45244.)

Other important supplies include tissues for tearful clients, manila folders for filing client records, and perhaps coffee equipment. These last items are easily purchased after the office is opened.

THE ESSENTIAL REFERENCE LIBRARY

Professionals who maintain private practices do not usually have ready access to libraries, as do those who work in agencies, hospitals, or institutions, and so they must maintain their own mini-library of essential reference books. The most important of these, of course, are the definitive textbooks that are concerned with the social worker's specialty and primary clientele. Others that will be used frequently include the following:

• The American Psychiatric Association's (1987) *Diagnostic and Statistical Manual of Mental Disorders, Third Edition—Revised* (DSM-III-R): The DSM-III-R (the fourth edition is to be published after 1992) summarizes and categorizes each mental illness and related condition, including the symptoms, genesis, and prognosis of each. Each illness or "diagnostic category" is given a number, which is recognized and officially sanctioned in the psychiatric community of the United States and most of the Western world, and the numbers and categories are standardized internationally with the World Health Organization's (1990) *International Classification of Diseases*. It is important for the social worker to have ready access to this code system, because it is often necessary to write the number rather than a description of the diagnostic category to fill out insurance forms or to maintain confidentiality. This book is also useful to have when one is perusing information about the client from medical or other records in which diagnostic numbers rather than labels are given. The DSM-III-R also gives the worker a convenient, shorthand way of communicating with other professionals about the client. A useful alternative to the DSM-III-R for workers who have the right computer system is the DTREE (First, Williams, & Spitzer, 1988), an electronic version of the DSM-III-R.

• *The Merck Manual* (Merck & Co., 1991): Another book that is useful for social workers in private practice is *The Merck Manual*. This compact volume is written for physicians as an abbreviated summary of the various physical and mental diseases, their symptoms, symptom progression, and prognoses, and some treatment perspectives. *The Merck Manual* was first published in 1899 and is periodically revised. Social workers use the manual to help understand the physical diseases and treatments of their clients.

• The *Physician's Desk Reference* (PDR): The PDR is produced for physicians to provide extensive and inclusive information on every prescription drug in the world. The book is divided into four sections. One describes, in alphabetical order, all the drugs that are currently prescribed, how they are to be used, their chemical nature, the effects they have on the patients, the uses and contraindications, and the occasional side effects. Other sections list the same information by manufacturer, by generic name of the drug, and by illnesses for which the drug is generally prescribed. The book also contains pictures, in full color, of virtually all prescription drugs commercially available. Of course, social workers never prescribe medications and should not attempt to give information to clients about their prescriptions. However, when the worker's client is taking medication, the PDR is informative about the nature of the drug and its possible effects on the client's behavior. Many social workers prefer *The Psychotherapist's Guide to Psychopharmacology* (Gitlin, 1990) because it provides the PDR information in a way that is specific to the needs and interests of nonmedical helping professionals.

• *The Social Work Dictionary:* First published by NASW in 1984 and now in its second edition (Barker, 1991), this dictionary concisely defines 5,000 terms that are used by social workers and members of related disciplines. Written by the author of this book, the dictionary also includes a chronology of the milestones in social welfare history, the NASW *Code of Ethics,* and the names and addresses of each state's licensing boards and NASW chapter offices. The dictionary is now widely used by licensing boards and exam preparation services, social workers studying for their licensing examinations, and social workers in clinical practice.

• *The Encyclopedia of Social Work:* This NASW publication, now in its 18th edition (Minahan, 1987), provides the worker with an outline of the major issues, trends, treatment formats, client groups, social problems, and influential social workers of interest to the profession. Each article is written by one of the profession's most informed experts in that area of interest. For the private practitioner, the encyclopedia offers a chance to remain in touch with the current thinking and knowledge of the profession.

• Clinical reference books: Social workers in private practice often benefit from ready access to review articles about different kinds of clinical problems. Several current textbooks on clinical problems are presented from a social work perspective. One of the most useful of these is the *Handbook of Clinical Social Work,* edited by Rosenblatt and Waldfogel (1983). It offers an evaluative description of the range of social work treatment methods most commonly in use with clients. Another useful reference is the three-volume series on the various psychopathologies edited by Francis J. Turner. These books are entitled *Adult Psychopathology* (1984), *Child Psychopathology* (1989), and *Mental Health in Older People* (in press), all with the subtitle *A Social Work Perspective.* Most of the major mental illnesses and their biopsychosocial origins and consequences are discussed by various experts in the field.

• Legal references: It would also be useful for many practitioners to secure the law book pertaining to the relevant state's statutes regarding marriage, divorce, adoption, wills, custody, commitment, equal rights, and the myriad other legal issues that are often discussed in the practitioner's office. If such law books are unavailable or too expensive for their anticipated degree of usefulness, the practitioner can get copies of relevant laws through a good local library.

• Directories of agency and referral resources: Private social work practitioners will need to know where to send clients for additional needed services in the community. Every client is likely to need social services and other community services that are beyond the capacity of the practitioner to provide. Every social worker is also going to encounter clients who may also need the services of other professionals. Many communities produce these referral guidebooks or pamphlets. Some are sponsored by public human services departments, and others are done in conjunction with United Fund appeals. The best ones list all the agencies supported by public monies or the United Fund and describe their location, the services they provide, and their service eligibility requirements. An example of a community resource book is the *Sourcebook 1991–92: Social and Health Services in the Greater New York Area* (1991). The professional associations of various communities also produce registries of their members, indicating their specialties, educational backgrounds, and other useful information.

• Social work directories: Social workers have their own directories, including NASW's (1991a) *Register of Clinical Social Workers*. The American Board of Examiners in Clinical Social Work (1989) also produces a directory of its members. These are valuable referral sources, especially for contacts in other cities. The author of this book has also compiled a useful publication called *The Resource Book* (Barker, 1986b), a directory of national organizations, associations, self-help groups, and hotlines. Each organization is briefly described and indexed according to the need that its constituent agencies are organized to fulfill.

THE PERSONALIZED REFERRAL GUIDE

One of the most important activities of every social worker is to help clients reach the service providers they need. The best guidebook of all will be the personalized referral guide produced over time as the practitioner gets to know what services are available from whom. The format of the guidebook can be the same as that of the printed resource guides.

To compile this guide, the worker lists all the agencies to which a client might be referred, as well as all the other professionals in the community with whom some working relationship has been or might be established. Every time the worker contacts another agency or professional, a notation should be made in the personal guide, along with information about the professional and ways to get clients to connect with that person.

Keeping a loose-leaf notebook near the worker's telephone is a good way to begin. The notebook may contain page dividers for the different types of service. For example, one section could list information about all the people who have made referrals to the worker, including what information they want in response to their referral. Another section could list information about all the physicians, psychiatrists, nurses, psychologists, and other helping professionals in the area to whom one might refer a client or with whom one might consult, collaborate, or otherwise exchange information.

Another section in the notebook would contain lists of useful agencies and service providers, including private practice lawyers, special consultants on tenant rights or consumer grievances, adoption agencies, volunteer agencies, or nursing care facilities. A useful source of this information could be the clients themselves. It is sometimes useful to indicate on such pages what the clients have to say about such facilities and their own rating of the efficacy and value of the services.

Of course, this personal guidebook would have to be constantly updated. As a personal work, it need not be shared with others, although if the worker is in a group practice it can be useful to colleagues, too. If it is prepared properly and kept current, it will undoubtedly be the practitioner's most popular and often-used reference resource.

7 MANAGING THE FINANCES

Recently, a social worker established a private practice after working in a social services agency for many years. In the agency, money matters had always been dealt with by other members of the staff. The agency budget and bookkeeping system was someone else's department, and clerical staff dealt with the client fees. As she had always done at the agency, the worker was eager to let the clients in her new practice know that her primary concern was for their well-being.

In the first meeting with one client, the discussion centered on the presenting problem, goals, symptoms, and the current overall situation. But nothing was said about fees. By the end of the second interview, the social worker still had not mentioned her charges. The client, naturally concerned that his bill might be excessive, raised the subject. The social worker became somewhat uncomfortable. She had no staff members to take care of the financial arrangements. She mumbled something about her rates. Her manner, body language, and tone of voice conveyed that the money issue was virtually irrelevant, a minor consideration compared to her interest in the client's resolution of his problem.

The worker hoped to bill the client at the end of the month, receive the check in the mail a few days later, and never have to communicate about it thereafter. But consciously or unconsciously perceiving that money was of minimal importance, her client did not get around to paying the bill. Months went by. The social worker became well aware of the growing unpaid bill. The work continued, but the practitioner's reticence still kept her from bringing up the issue. But finally she asked the client about the bill.

His response could have been predicted after the second interview. He minimized its importance, saying he had not gotten around to it but that he would do something about it as soon as his next paycheck came in. The therapy continued, but the worker's increasing anxiety and irritation interfered with her ability to be effective with the client.

Eventually, the client terminated therapy when the goals were reached. As he departed, he promised to pay soon and asked if he could pay a part of the bill each month since it was so large. The relieved social worker assured him that that would be no problem. Monthly statements were sent, but there was no response. The worker's anxiety and irritation began to grow again. The choices available to her were all unpleasant. She could either call her former client and confront him, or she could get specialists—lawyers, bill collectors, or credit bureaus—to do it. She realized that whatever she did would undermine her ideal of total altruism toward the client. And she began to see that if she intended to stay in private practice, she would need to learn much more about how to manage the financial aspects of her new field.

NEEDED KNOWLEDGE AND SKILLS

What does the private social work practitioner actually need to know about money management to have a successful practice? Many financial consultants would answer that the more information one has, the greater is the likelihood of success. But such an answer is not entirely accurate. An endless amount of information is available about this subject, and practitioners could (and some do) devote nearly all their time to acquiring it. When they do, they have less time to devote to enhancing their professional knowledge and skills.

It is better to find a balance; acquiring some knowledge about business management and more about professional practice is the best way to achieve an enduring practice. In other words, one should learn the basics about practice management before starting the practice and then build on that knowledge gradually in the future so as not to interfere too much with the time spent on building professional knowledge.

Essential knowledge about management takes some time to acquire but is not very complicated. The worker should know how to establish an accurate budget as well as a financial record-keeping system that is separate from his or her personal financial system. The worker should be able to establish a ledger or spreadsheet that records all practice receipts and expenses. Each client's case record should include a separate set of entries for fees, payments, insurance reimbursements, and other financial matters.

The worker also needs to know how to estimate start-up costs for a new practice and how to minimize these costs. In managing the ongoing practice, the worker needs to know how to estimate future earnings for income tax purposes as well as for planning future purchases and expenses. Financial management also requires knowledge about taxes, retirement, insurance, and salaries for employees.

Knowledge alone is not sufficient to manage the financial aspects of the private practice. It is also necessary to act on that knowledge. Maintaining a private practice in social work sometimes requires behaviors that might seem crass, mercenary, or unprofessional. For example, workers often must directly ask their clients to pay or remind clients that their bills are overdue. They sometimes have to employ bill collectors and credit bureaus and thus acknowledge that their concern for the clients is not solely altruistic. Other necessary actions include keeping careful, accurate, and contemporaneous financial records in which every penny received and spent on the practice is accounted for, and sticking to the budget so as to avoid the many financial hazards to which practices are vulnerable.

SOME FINANCIAL HAZARDS

A starting point for acquiring this knowledge and skill is a realistic assessment of the financial problems that the practitioner might encounter. The risk of economic problems is usually the first and greatest worry facing anyone who contemplates private practice, and well it might be. A worker could easily spend thousands of dollars attempting to establish a practice before receiving one penny of income. The worker could borrow heavily to finance the high starting costs and then have to begin repaying the loan immediately. The practitioner has to be prepared to meet the monthly operating costs of a private practice without any immediate assurance of enough clients and income to cover obligations, much less provide for living needs.

Many young private practitioners think that their only financial problem will be getting enough client referrals. Referrals are necessary, but it is not enough to get clients to come; they must also pay for their services. Getting them to do this is more complicated than it seems and requires as much advance planning as anything else the practitioner does. Many clients are not inclined to reimburse the private social work practitioner promptly and docilely. Many who are willing to pay expect the fee to be less than that for the services of other professionals (Whittington, 1988). This impression is often shared by insurance companies and other third-party financing institutions. Many of them will not help clients pay for social work services (Jewitt & Thompson, 1989; Belser, 1989). The private practitioner also has to contend with unpredictable variations in the national and local economies that influence the ability of clients to use the worker's services (Barker, 1983).

Many social workers in private practice get into financial difficulty when they are not realistic about the spendable income they receive from their practice. As the social worker begins to see more and more clients, the increasing income may lead the practitioner to develop a more opulent life-style than is justified. Experienced private practitioners have learned, sometimes the hard way, that their actual earnings are less than they thought, even when the practice is successful.

Clients and agency-based social workers sometimes think private practitioners must be wealthy because of the seemingly high fees they charge. They compare their own hourly earnings with the private practitioner's hourly fee and see an immense difference. But the private practitioner is generally paid only for direct services to clients, not for the number of hours on the job. To keep a practice viable, the private practitioner must devote considerable time to activities that are not compensable.

No private practitioner could maintain the pace of seeing 40 clients a week, 52 weeks a year. Even if that were possible, it is unlikely that the worker would collect 100 percent of the billings; always keep a full schedule; and never have to take time away from the office for educational, administrative, or professional activities. When a private practitioner attends a professional conference, as is necessary to maintain credentials and professional competence, income stops. Vacations, consultations with other professionals, and bookkeeping are all without reimbursement.

The fees charged are often further diminished by third parties. Many insurance companies, if they pay for social workers' services at all, do not cover the full amount of the charge. Furthermore, they will pay nothing to providers who ask the client to make up the difference. Some insurance companies still refuse to reimburse for social work services unless the services are supervised by a physician. Many social workers in private practice deal with this unsatisfactory requirement by employing the services of a physician, usually a psychiatrist. The worker and the doctor meet for supervision and consultation, perhaps weekly or monthly. The doctor is paid for the amount of time taken. The worker's spendable income is reduced not only by the cost of the doctor's time, but also by the time lost from seeing clients.

Another factor to consider in estimating spendable income is indirect services. Unlike psychiatrists or psychologists, who typically retain some clinical detachment from the client's social setting, the conscientious social worker does much valid social work in the client's surroundings with friends, associates, fellow employees, and neighbors. If such activities are ignored, the social worker is engaged in a narrow and limited version of the profession. However, with no agency to pay for this work and little opportunity to charge the client for these indirect services, the worker's income is reduced commensurate with the time thus spent.

When all these factors are considered and deducted from what appears to be a high hourly fee, the private practitioner does not seem nearly as well paid as first imagined. Those who are in high income brackets are there mostly because they work far more than 40 hours a week. But high earnings alone do not make for affluence—careful financial planning and budgeting are just as important.

START-UP COSTS

Most full-time private practitioners find their costs of opening a practice to be roughly comparable to those of beginning lawyers and accountants self-employed in the same geographic area. Start-up costs for private practitioners are estimated to be a little more than half the annual salary of a beginning social worker in agency employment. These costs usually include the first month's rent on the office lease; a security deposit equal to two month's rent; and the purchase of basic furniture and office equipment, carpeting, and necessary alterations to the office structure. Also included are costs for telephone installation, answering services or machines, stationery, announcements of the opening of the practice, malpractice and business insurance, and the many other supplies described in chapter 6.

To economize, it might be tempting to set up a spartan office with the intention of upgrading it later. But new clients and potential referral sources look at the office as an indication of the worker's capability. There are other, more satisfactory ways to reduce start-up costs. Many social workers minimize the problem of initial expenses by renting space in the office of an existing private practice and working when the established professional is away.

Another option is to establish a private practice with other professionals so that many of the expenses can be shared. However, the expenses of shared offices are never directly proportionate to the number of workers involved. In other words, it costs more than half a solo practitioner's start-up costs apiece for two workers to open an office. Even so, the expenses are less than those borne by the worker who practices alone.

Leasing, rather than buying, the necessary equipment and furniture is another way to cut down on the costs of starting the practice. There are two advantages: First, a considerable initial outlay does not have to be made, even though rental fees will add to the monthly operating expenses. Second, the practitioner will not be stuck with furniture and equipment later found to be nonessential or inappropriate to the particular practice. Leasing makes experimentation and change possible. Also, leasing companies usually allow the customer to apply a portion of the rental costs toward purchase.

Another way to reduce start-up costs is to buy an existing private practice. This possibility is rarely thought of as a way to reduce costs.

Why pay someone a substantial amount when it is possible to build one's own practice for free? The answer, of course, is that one never builds a practice for free—it is a costly process. The actual cash outlay for marketing, meeting the public and referral sources, and equipping the facility is considerable. Moreover, there is a hidden cost. In the beginning, many available hours go unfilled, and unfilled hours mean lost income.

The purchaser of an existing practice usually acquires the seller's office lease; some of the furniture and equipment; and, most importantly, the referral resources (Samuels, 1983). The seller agrees to introduce the purchaser to those who have made the referrals in the past, and records of former clients are kept on hand in case they call for additional services or have their own referrals to make. The seller also introduces the purchaser to the existing clients and may recommend that they transfer to the purchaser (Weitz, 1983).

Depending on how the sale of the practice is negotiated, the purchaser could begin by paying nothing or a minimal amount. The purchaser agrees to pay over time a portion of the net income from the practice. If the income is low, the seller's proceeds are low. Thus, the seller has an incentive to help the practice stay healthy and thrive. So the seller may perform added services, such as providing ongoing consultation for the existing clientele, writing letters of introduction to clients and community leaders, and maintaining a presence in the office for a time.

The price of an established practice is highly flexible and negotiable. Because psychotherapy is such an intimate process and because it is so difficult to transfer the primary asset—the referral base—a fair price cannot be determined until sometime after the practice changes hands. For this reason the price is usually based on a percentage of the practice's average net receipts for a period of three years or so. This sum is paid gradually, so the purchaser's start-up costs are spread out.

MONTHLY OPERATING COSTS

The start-up costs are, of course, just the beginning. To stay in private practice, the worker must make regular payments for the rent, telephone and utility bills, secretarial and maintenance services, office supplies, postage, continuing education, and insurance. Most full-time workers calculate that between 20 and 30 percent of their gross income goes for operating and overhead expenses if they maintain a full caseload. Some practitioners spend up to 50 percent of their gross receipts on overhead.

This percentage increases if the caseload is less than full. It decreases to some extent if the practice is shared. It also varies according to such individual circumstances as the amount of time a worker takes from practice because of illness, vacations, or classes. Naturally, the operating expenses continue whether or not the worker is seeing clients.

Other expenses private practitioners must face are taxes and funds for retirement. Some private practitioners get into financial trouble because they are unable to set aside funds for these expenses. Unlike the worker employed in an institution that withholds money for taxes and retirement without effort on the worker's part, the private practitioner must set aside or save part of the money already received. It is all too easy, especially for the hard-pressed beginning worker, to postpone this savings program. One can omit paying for a retirement fund altogether, but it would be far better at the outset to get in the habit of setting aside something each month, no matter how small.

Setting aside funds for retirement may be optional, but income taxes to the federal and most state governments are not. As explained in chapter 5, the Internal Revenue Service requires all self-employed workers to estimate their annual earnings and make appropriate quarterly tax payments. Failure to do so results in being closely scrutinized by the IRS thereafter; having to pay a fine for the amount not paid in the quarter; and, of course, having to pay the tax, too. Many people who are self-employed find it difficult to set aside funds for this purpose and hope to be able to make up the difference before the quarterly payment is due in January, April, June, or September. A better approach is to make a savings program for taxes a priority.

FINANCIAL MANAGEMENT SYSTEM

Developing a system to manage the finances of the practice is crucial. This system should be put into effect before the first client is seen—even before any efforts are made to get referrals. A financial system is as important for agency-employed social workers who want to see only a few clients privately as it is for social workers contemplating full-time private practice. Fortunately, it takes little time, effort, or money to develop a good system, which will prove to be of inestimable value once the practice is established.

Every financial management system should include at least four elements: (1) a business checking account, (2) a financial ledger or spreadsheet, (3) a separate tax record, and (4) a procedure for keeping track of payments due from and payments made by each client. This system can take many forms, and as long as this information is recorded and accessible, each practitioner can organize the system in the most personally suitable way (Nickerson, 1986).

1. *The business checking account.* A checking account solely for practice expenditures and receipts should be established before the first purchase

is made. Having the complete record of all receipts and expenditures in one account provides a valuable cross-reference for the practitioner's financial record and is also useful to tax auditors and accountants.

Although it is tempting to wait until the address of the office is known so that it can be placed on the check, the establishment of an account should not be delayed for this reason. Money will be spent to establish the practice long before clients are seen and fees collected, and these early expenses should be handled through the permanent business account.

Before any income is received, expense money for the practice is "loaned" to the business account from personal funds or a bank. It is expected that revenues will eventually be sufficient to cover overhead, provide an income for the practitioner, and repay the initial "loan."

The business checking account should be kept separate from the worker's personal checking account. The only checks written on it directly relate to running the practice; the only money placed in the account, apart from the clearly designated initial loan, is from clients' payments. The amount left in the account after all practice expenses have been met is the practitioner's "salary." A check should periodically be drawn on these funds (if any) for the practitioner.

2. *The financial ledger or spreadsheet.* The first check written should be to buy a financial ledger or a spreadsheet program for a computer. A ledger can be as simple as a tablet of columned accounting sheets or as elaborate as a personally designed accounting system or computer program developed by a management consultant. Many beginning and well-established private practitioners still use a standard loose-leaf notebook to record all pertinent financial records for the practice. Increasingly, private practitioners are keeping these records on their computers, taking care to keep current printouts, or "hard copies," of this information (Kreuger, 1987).

Whether the financial records are handwritten in a ledger or entered onto a computer, the data to be retained are the same. On the first page of the record, all the income is recorded. Whenever a payment is received, by check or in cash, by or in behalf of the client, an entry is made on this page. (Clients should always be given receipts for cash payments.) The entry should indicate the date the money was received, the name of the client, and the amount of the payment. Every line on this page must eventually be filled, in ink, leaving no blank space. This practice helps assure tax auditors that receipts are not being omitted.

The periodic deposits to the business checking account should also be listed on the first page. The amount shown on the ledger or printout should be the same as the amount deposited; this is even more reassuring to the IRS.

The next page of the record is for disbursements. Again, each line must be filled in ink, showing when the bill was paid, who was paid, and the amount. If possible, every expenditure for the practice—including the social worker's salary—should be paid by check from the business checking account so that the account and the disbursement page are the same. For tax purposes, an item is considered paid when a valid check for it is written, rather than when the bill comes in.

3. *The separate tax record.* At tax time, the practitioner should have a clear record of all financial activity. To this end, the income and disbursement sheets are totaled and filed at the end of each month or when they are filled. In this file also goes all other financial information that pertains to the practice for the tax year. If a ledger is used, these sheets should be removed from the notebook and photocopied, and originals and photocopies should be placed in separate file folders. If a spreadsheet is used, two hard copies are printed and placed in separate file folders. The two folders are exact duplicates and should be kept in separate places. This can be valuable in case of fire, theft, vandalism, misfiling, computer glitches, or any other loss of information from one file.

4. *Financial records for individual clients.* The ledger book also contains, in alphabetical order, a separate sheet for each client detailing all financial transactions with the practitioner. If the record is on computer, all popular programs for private psychotherapy and other small businesses make it convenient to keep separate hard copies for each client.

The financial record for each client should have a heading with at least the following information: name, address, place of work, home and work telephone numbers, Social Security number, insurance company number, date of first appointment, source of referral, and names of others seen collaterally. A ledger sheet for each client may be kept in the looseleaf notebook with this information at the top. Then the sheet can be lined and columned and can indicate such things about the client as the following: date seen, coded type of service provided, and charge for service. Some practitioners also indicate on these sheets how much the client owes, how much the insurance company paid, and when these payments were made.

These sheets are updated after every client meeting or financial transaction. If this system is computerized, the program can make it possible to easily record these data by entering a minimal amount of information, such as the date seen. The program then calculates the amount of the charge, the amount to be paid by the client, and the amount due from the insurance company.

A copy of this record can be used as a bill for the client. When the client's case is closed and outstanding amounts paid, these sheets may be removed from the notebook or computer file and the hard copy included in the client's case record file. This method makes it possible to keep client financial information on separate pages from the case record. This step should be taken, lawyers say, to minimize malpractice complications and other legal problems.

The double entries described above on the income sheet and on the client's financial sheet help reduce the chance of mistakes. Some practitioners also have a third entry in the form of notations in their appointment book. They keep this book with them at all times and record when a payment was made beside each client's name and the date seen. They also note on the appropriate date when a practice expense was paid. All this may seem overly cautious, but it is actually very simple, takes little time, and keeps the accounts in order.

Social workers thinking about entering private practice should read one or more of the many available guides to accounting for small businesses to become familiar with basic principles. One of the most useful of these guides is the IRS's (1991) *Tax Guide for Small Businesses.*

DISCUSSING FEES WITH THE CLIENT

No matter what policy is used for charges and insurance, the private social work practitioner must disclose this information to the client at the first contact. Before the first interview—possibly by phone, letter, or brochure—the worker should clearly state what the fees are for all available services and how and when they are to be paid.

Failure to be clear and explicit about fees can lead to many unnecessary problems (Jacobs, 1986). For example, some clients might expect no charge for the first appointment, somewhat like a free estimate from a contractor, auto mechanic, or lawyer. Some helping professionals advertise, "No charge for the first appointment." But unless they say otherwise in the beginning, virtually all helping professionals charge the same fee for the initial session as for all subsequent ones. The first appointment should not be made unless this is clear and agreeable to the client.

At some point during the first session, if it is determined that subsequent meetings are in order, the social worker and client should spend a small amount of time discussing the fee arrangement. The client has the right to be told what the cost is for each subsequent session and the procedure and time by which it should be paid.

If the practitioner uses a formal, written contract with the client, it should include fee information. (Examples of such contracts appear in appendix A.) Even if a written contract is not used, it is still useful to provide the client with a small pamphlet that describes the practitioner's fee system, as well as his or her qualifications and treatment methods, to reduce the likelihood of misunderstanding.

A printed explanation of the fee system is also helpful for those who are loath to discuss money with their clients. Many social workers are like the private practitioner described at the beginning of this chapter; they want to say nothing to their client that could be construed as crass commercialism. They send the bills out and hope to receive checks by return mail, without ever having to discuss this aspect of the relationship. This attitude is unrealistic; it is confusing to the client, and it confuses the nature of the relationship.

DECIDING HOW MUCH TO CHARGE

The fees social workers charge vary considerably; there is no legal or professional requirement about the maximum or minimum amount. All practitioners are essentially free to set whatever fees they want. Of course, they are influenced by competitive factors and many other considerations.

Five factors usually enter into the decision: (1) how much other social workers in the area charge, (2) how much other helping professionals charge for similar services, (3) what the practitioner's own level of experience and education is, (4) what the third-party financing organizations say are "reasonable and customary charges" for that profession in that area, and (5) what the worker thinks will be the most attractive rate to the clientele he or she hopes to attract.

In most areas in the United States, licensed MSW social workers have recently been charging somewhat more than half the amount charged by local psychiatrists who have equal experience. Licensed master's-level social workers charge about 30 percent less than psychologists with doctorates. Social workers with doctoral degrees, and many of those with MSWs and considerable experience, charge about the same as psychologists with doctorates. There is wide variation among practitioners within and between professions because of changes in insurance coverage and eligibility, marketplace factors, and the general economy.

Third-party organizations are now a major influence in the pricing structure. Third-party organizations, including managed health care providers and health maintenance organizations, keep records of the rates charged by the various local professionals for the services covered. This provides them with the "reasonable and customary" delineation. Practitioners who charge above these limits will not receive reimbursement for the amount that exceeds the organization's guidelines. Nevertheless, most fee-for-service professionals consider these amounts to be too low. So they charge their clients more than these amounts, and the clients are not reimbursed by their health insurance program to cover all the actual charges.

Social workers are also influenced in their fee structures by the knowledge that they cannot charge too little and maintain professional credibility. Clients often see higher fees as a signal of higher quality (Hass-Wilson, 1990). Conversely, fees that are much lower than those of other professionals indicate not that the practitioner is caring and altruistic, but that he or she is less competent. Unfortunately, clients tend to refer others to those practitioners who charge higher fees because they think higher fees are an indication of better service.

One other influence in fee setting comes from the professional association and the philosophical position of the social work profession. Many social workers consider it unethical to charge clients high fees. They say all the fees should be low to afford maximum accessibility from client groups or that, at the least, the fee should be individualized based on each client's ability to pay.

Fees for Groups and Families

Some workers charge different rates for family, couple, or group therapy. A few social workers charge 25 to 50 percent more for an hour with a couple or family than for an hour with an individual. They justify this by saying that they devote that much more time in study, paperwork, and attention to the individual needs of the family members. However, most professionals do not charge different rates for family units seen together.

The charges for clients in group therapy meetings are figured differently. Groups usually are 50 to 100 percent longer than individual sessions, and each group member is charged about half the fee for a one-hour individual session. For example, if a social worker charged $80 for an individual client in a one-hour session, the charge for each group client would usually be $35 to $40 for a session that was 1 1/2 to two hours long. The rationale is that, unlike the couple or family, which is a single economic unit, the group members are economically autonomous. Financial records for each group member are separate, as are case records. Many private practitioners could charge much smaller fees for group clients but tend not to do so; in fact, many professionals consider group therapy to be a highly lucrative aspect of their practice.

Fees for Nonclinical Services

There is even more variation in the amount charged for nonclinical services. Such services include consulting for social services agencies, providing expert testimony in divorce and custody hearings, leading workshops, providing educational services to profit-making organizations, and writing reports for educational or public interest groups. The fees vary so much because the types of service are so disparate and because the health insurance companies do not usually reimburse for such activities. Yet because nonclinical activities are such an important part of the social worker's professional activity, every practitioner should have a specified fee-charging procedure.

The most straightforward procedure is simply to charge the same rate for the time devoted to the activity as is charged for an individual therapy session. So, for example, if that fee is $80 per hour, the charge for presenting a workshop is $80 times the number of hours, including preparation and travel time, devoted to it. Of course, travel expenses should also be covered. Obviously, there is ample room for negotiation on these charges, but a consideration of the hourly rate schedule is a place to start these negotiations.

Charging Extra for Special Considerations

Sometimes a social worker might want to charge more than the standard fee to see clients at preferred times or less to see clients at less desirable times. Many clients want sessions in the evenings or on weekends because of their own jobs. Thus, the worker sometimes has many hours available at midday but turns people away in the evenings or on Saturdays. It might seem logical therefore to charge more for the hours in greatest demand and less for the other times.

Although this procedure might work for some, it is ill-advised for most practitioners. It requires complicated bookkeeping to keep clients in different financial tracks. Third-party financing organizations would be suspicious. The procedure would have to be discussed with clients, and whenever they changed times or called for special sessions it might have to be renegotiated.

DILEMMAS INVOLVING FEES AND SOCIAL WORK VALUES

Private practitioners who are setting fee policies have to grapple with several social work value issues that do not confront agency-based colleagues with such intensity. Among the most debatable of these are the following questions: Should the practitioner set a flat fee for service or use a flexible fee scale? Should practitioners provide some services for free?

Should clients be charged for indirect services? Should the client be charged for missed appointments? Should practitioners share receipts from clients? How can the worker ethically enforce payment of fees?

Many social workers feel so strongly about one side or another of these issues that consensus remains elusive. But although theoretical debate continues, every one of these issues comes up frequently for practitioners in their day-to-day work. It is essential therefore that each practitioner make a decision about each of these issues and implement an explicit policy.

Flexible Fee Scales or Flat Rates?

Social workers in private practice do not agree about whether to have flat or flexible fee scale policies. More private practitioners use flexible, or sliding, fee scales than use flat rates (Barker, 1987d). Both sides think the other side is wrong and perhaps engaging in an act that borders on the unethical.

Neither NASW nor the National Federation of Societies for Clinical Social Work takes a position on this issue. However, the NASW (1990b) *Code of Ethics* says "when setting fees, the worker should ensure that they are fair, reasonable, considerate and commensurate with the service performed and with due regard for the clients' ability to pay" (p. 6).

Some private practitioners interpret this as requiring them to scrutinize their clients' finances to determine how much should be charged. Others dispute this contention, arguing that charging "commensurate with the service performed" means one should not have different fees for a given service regardless of the client's circumstances.

Without explicit guidelines from those in authority, the policy must be decided individually. In coming to a decision, the practitioner should objectively review the arguments on each side.

The primary argument used by advocates of the flexible fee policy is that it makes the social worker's services more accessible to less affluent people. It is a way that private social work practitioners can fulfill their traditional role of helping the economically disadvantaged. And it is a good marketing device for acquiring more clients.

There are many arguments for flat rate schedules. Such a schedule is consistent with consumer protection laws. For example, there is little difference between a social worker using a sliding fee scale and a store changing its price for an item if a customer seems affluent. Consumers of any product or service are entitled to know its price and to have some assurance that the price will not be changed arbitrarily.

Another argument against flexible fee schedules is that clients must be subjected to a "means test." The *means test* is an evaluation of the client's economic resources to determine eligibility for service. Social workers in public assistance programs have fought for decades against this policy, considering it demeaning, unfair, and inconsistent. In addition, when it is used properly in private practice, the worker must periodically review the client's income and assets and renegotiate the fee. Presumably, as the client's economic circumstances change over time, so would the fee. Knowing this, the client might be reluctant to inform the worker of any improvement in finances because doing so would lead to increased charges.

Another problem with flexible fees is that the system can be confusing to the clients. The most important sources of new referrals are previous clients, and clients compare information about fees. A former client who paid a full fee may wonder why a newer client is being charged less and may become dissatisfied.

Insurance companies and other third-party organizations find the practice unacceptable, too. They say that to provide coverage, they need one consistent fee. They argue that if the fee is low for a less-affluent client, then the amount they must reimburse should be commensurately low.

As managed health care systems, health maintenance organizations, and third-party insurance companies become increasingly influential in the financing of worker-client transactions, the flat fee system will become more common and probably the norm. Only those few social workers who remain outside these systems will be able to continue to use a flexible fee scale.

Free Services

A social worker who uses only the flat fee policy is still free to see some clients at no charge. There are many times when it is ethically impossible to do otherwise. For example, a client might begin treatment at the stated fee and then have a financial reversal. Under such circumstances, it would be unreasonable to terminate. It would also be unethical: The NASW (1990b) *Code of Ethics* says "[the social worker] should withdraw services precipitously only under unusual circumstances, giving careful consideration to all factors in the situation and taking care to minimize possible adverse effects" (p. 5).

Situations like these often happen when clients divorce during treatment or when children or elderly clients unexpectedly lose their sources of support. At such times, social workers and other helping professionals have an obligation to arrange for continued service. At the very least, the worker should arrange for the client to begin treatment in a subsidized agency. Many practitioners, however, would continue to see the person without charge.

Some private practitioners set aside a fixed percentage of their time to see clients free of charge; a waiting list may be established for clients who want those slots. Workers can thus fulfill their sense of professional and personal obligation to help some disadvantaged people without the aforementioned complications.

Fees for Indirect Services to Clients

Social workers in private practice have more difficulty with indirect services than do agency workers. Indirect services—those activities that the social worker does in behalf of the client but not necessarily in the client's presence—are a traditional and important component of the social worker's repertoire. For example, the worker may leave the office and meet with members of the client's community, write reports about the client, or give testimony for the client. When the worker is agency-employed, the salary covers those services.

The private social worker may have difficulty justifying such bills to their clients unless it is made clear at the outset that indirect service is a possibility and that charges will be based on the time spent in such activities. The explanation could liken the situation to that of a lawyer, who charges for all time spent on activities in behalf of the client. This practice is established at the beginning of the lawyer-client relationship, and clients have come to expect it. There is no reason why private social workers cannot do likewise.

Whether to Charge for Missed Appointments

The worker must have an established policy about charging a client who has failed to keep a scheduled appointment. If charges are to be made for missed sessions, the client should always be forewarned. The practitioner should also specify the conditions under which an appointment is considered missed or properly cancelled. Usually, practitioners charge their standard rate for missed sessions unless the client has given ample notice, say 24 hours, of cancellation. The rationale is that the worker has held that time for the client and will need some time to fill it with another client.

This policy is complicated by third parties. Insurance companies take a dim view of the practice. They often refuse to reimburse for an unkept appointment. In this case, the client must be informed that full and unreimbursed payment of the session will have to be made.

Of course, the private practitioner uses discretion in implementing the policy. The worker may find it easier to forgive a client who has always been reliable about keeping appointments when the absence is due to a sudden illness, family emergency, or automobile problem. However, if the client is often absent or seems to be trying to avoid the worker because of an uncomfortable session during the last appointment, the worker might impose the charge.

The policy for group therapy sessions must be less flexible. The client is generally charged for every scheduled group session whether present or not. The only exception some group therapists have to this rule is vacations; clients may miss some meetings (say two or four weeks per year) if vacations are planned and the group is given ample notice. The policy is less flexible because the client's position in the group is available to that client only; another person cannot simply be substituted when the original group member is absent. The group goes on in a person's absence, and on the client's return some group time is usually devoted to reviewing what transpired. Here again, some flexibility may be in order, but all group clients are entitled to know in advance the policy in effect and any exceptions to it.

Sharing Fees

Fee-Splitting. An unethical practice that is becoming all too common among private practitioners is fee-splitting. *Fee-splitting* is the practice of referring a client to another professional, who then pays the referring person for the referral, usually a percentage of the client fee. A version of this system is especially common with inexperienced social workers. An experienced practitioner with too many referrals "hires" a struggling worker to see the overload and keeps a sizable portion of the fee. In this way, experienced practitioners can increase their income beyond what their available work hours would otherwise permit. And the new worker begins to build a practice.

This arrangement seems so simple and reasonable that many new workers do not see anything wrong with it. They forget the client's need. The client is paying for something (the experienced practitioner's services) and not getting it. This practice drives up costs for all who must use health care because lower-priced providers are excluded from the system. And the new worker is locked into the relationship with the experienced practitioner because the newcomer is almost always contractually forbidden to establish a practice in the same community.

The practice is considered unacceptable by authorities in the legal, medical, psychological, and social work professions. For example, the

NASW (1990b) *Code of Ethics* states "the social worker should not accept anything of value for making a referral" (p. 6). Fee-splitting is unethical because it allows practitioners to refer clients not to the professional most suitable for the client but to the person who pays the referral fee or repays with a percent of the fee.

Despite efforts by the various professions to combat it, the practice is becoming more common. Many who practice it do not consider it to be fee-splitting, but rather a collaborative effort for clients. Others do not think about why it is unethical; all they know is they need the work.

Collaboration. The practice of fee-splitting should not be confused with an effective and desirable approach to service delivery, that of collaboration. The worker who sees clients in a co-therapy situation, on a social work team, or in an interdisciplinary approach is engaged in a perfectly appropriate and ethical practice. The professionals then divide the client fees, but in this case both practitioners are actively and continuously involved in the treatment.

Charging clients for collaborative treatments may entail some complications. Clearly, both practitioners have the right to be paid for their services. Often, the practitioners send separate bills to the client; in other instances, a single bill with all the collaborators' names on it is sent. Generally, the fee received is divided by the practitioners equally or in proportion to the amount of their time spent in behalf of the client.

Fee Collection

Some clients avoid paying the worker the agreed fee. Nonpayment is more likely when the worker is not clear about the expectations or lax about encouraging and enforcing payment. But, unfortunately, it happens even when the policy about money has been clearly explicated. One need not be heartless or obsessed about money collection, but being firm with some clients is certainly in order.

There is little variation in the procedures used by most fee-for-service practitioners. Most professionals mail their bills to clients at the end of each month. It is made known to the client, with a notation on the bill, a sign in the waiting room, or a spoken reminder from the practitioner or secretary, that payment is expected within a specified time period, such as 10 days. An increasing number of professionals avoid postage expenses by handing bills to their clients each month.

Many clients want and expect the practitioner to collect from their insurance company first and then bill them for the co-payment or any other remaining amount. This expectation occurs because their family physician and other health care providers follow this method. It is less common in mental health services, however. The insurance companies are slow to reimburse for mental health coverage. If the practitioner agrees to collect from the insurance company first, the client should still be asked to bring in and complete insurance forms. If the practitioner does not agree to waiting for insurance payments before collecting the client's co-payment, the practitioner must tell the client in advance of treatment.

Ethical social workers in private practice are flexible about the terms of payment. They can circumvent the need for a flexible fee scale by spreading expected payments over time. Agreements can be reached to spread low monthly payments over many months or years. Most health care professionals do not charge interest on unpaid balances, but many other professionals, such as lawyers and accountants, do. Social work has not established an ethics policy about interest charges as yet; therefore, workers can use their own judgment.

If the client does not pay in the agreed time and manner, the worker has to act promptly and forcefully. The client is asked about payment during the next personal encounter. If treatment has concluded and payment has not been made, the worker must write or call. The monthly statements can also contain messages about late payment; stickers can be attached to bills warning of consequences. Most clients will pay at some point, but some will not, despite all these efforts.

If a former client will not pay after a reasonable time, then the worker must either write the amount off as a loss or take legal action. Losses of this sort cannot be deducted from income taxes. If the worker decides to take more forceful action, the choices are small claims court, engaging an attorney, hiring a professional bill collector, or using a collection agency. The collection agency is by far the most common choice; the other means are time-consuming and expensive and usually not all that successful.

The collection agency takes little time and results in a minimum of unpleasantness, at least for the worker. The disadvantage is that it usually leaves the client with some bad feelings about the worker. Another disadvantage is that the collector retains about half the amount collected as a fee for the service.

INSURANCE FRAUD

Social work practitioners are commonly engaged in several types of insurance fraud. These frauds are usually committed with honorable intentions—to enable their clients to be reimbursed by the insurance company. Even so, they are illegal and unethical, and the perpetrator could easily be convicted of a crime and removed from the profession.

"Signing off" is a common fraud, wherein private practitioners get other professionals to submit their insurance claims. The practice occurs when the client's insurance company will not reimburse for the services of a particular provider. It might be because the provider is not qualified to perform the service; is not licensed; or, most commonly, belongs to a profession that the insurance company does not reimburse. Although more and more social workers are becoming eligible for reimbursement by insurance companies, many companies still pay only for psychiatrists and sometimes psychologists.

The practitioner in this position must forgo reimbursement from third parties—a competitive disaster—or get someone who is qualified to sign the insurance form. In signing the form, the other professional may be implying that he or she is the primary provider or the practitioner's supervisor. If the form represents the wrong person as providing the service, it is insurance fraud. All the parties involved are committing an illegal act and can be prosecuted (Hait & Tyrell, 1991). Many practitioners have been convicted of this crime; even so, it is still a common practice and is not taken seriously enough by those who commit it.

In another type of fraud, the worker puts a wrong diagnosis on the claim (for example, dysthymic disorder) because it is likely to be covered, whereas the actual diagnosis (for example, marital conflict) would not be. In a similar action, the worker uses a less serious diagnosis (for example, seasonal affective disorder) instead of a more accurate one (for example, explosive disorder) so that the actual problem will not appear on the patient's record. The practitioner may have noble motives, but the action is illegal (Kirk & Kutchins, 1988).

An even more common form of insurance fraud occurs when practitioners waive the client's part of the fee but claim full payment from the insurance company. For example, the bill for five sessions at $80 each is $400. In the insurance policy contract, the client is obliged to pay 25 percent of the bill. The practitioner forgives the client's $100 fee but bills the insurance company for its full $300 share. Dismissal of co-payments (the amount the client is required to pay under the agreement with the insurance company) is being prosecuted by insurance companies and peer review committees (AAMFT Ethics Committee, 1991). One must also wonder about the effect on the worker-client relationship when the practitioner engages in improper collusion with the client to defraud an organization. If the client sees the practitioner doing this to an insurance company, why would the client not feel free to do it to the practitioner?

8
LEGAL AND ETHICAL ISSUES

Malpractice is a mounting concern for social workers in private practice, and for good reason. Even those who are unfailingly conscientious, competent, and ethical are vulnerable, as the following actual case illustrates:

Everyone knew she was a capable, well-qualified professional, a dedicated person who could be relied on by her clients and fellow employees. Ironically, her troubles began because she was so highly regarded. Her job was to evaluate people who were hospitalized with emotional disturbances. Prompt decisions about them were required by law: Should they be retained voluntarily, released to outpatient treatment, or committed? Usually, the worker interviewed the client and family members before preparing her reports. The reports were used by the judges and court-designated psychiatrists who made the final decision.

One day the worker interviewed a young man and his family. Her report suggested that he was not likely to be dangerous. The psychiatrist in charge had no time to give an intensive examination to the young man before the case had to go before the judge. So on the basis of the worker's report, he recommended discharge. Soon after the man was released, he shot several people and then himself.

Eventually, the victims and their families sued both the psychiatrist and the social worker for malpractice—the doctor for the improper recommendation and the social worker for providing the information that led to it. The malpractice suit took years to resolve; it would have taken longer except that the defendants finally agreed to settle out of court. The social worker faced substantial legal expenses and was unable to earn an income during the long hours she had to spend in courtrooms and law offices. The incessant questioning of her professional competence took a stressful, painful toll. Ultimately, she felt she had little choice but to settle despite her continued belief and assertion that she had committed no wrong.

LITIGATION WORRIES

Lawsuits can be brought against any social worker inside or outside agency auspices, no matter what the level of skill or quality of work has been. There are no fail-safe formulas that guarantee against malpractice suits. Social work litigation exists because the laws and standards pertaining to professional practice have been interpreted inconsistently and unpredictably by judges, lawyers, juries, clients, and workers. One recent case involving a social worker went through numerous courts and appeals until it finally reached the U.S. Supreme Court; even there, the outcome was inconclusive, and the judges suggested that in the future plaintiffs might prevail if states enacted more lenient malpractice laws (Bullis, 1990). Only confusion prevails.

Some helping professionals, for example, have been sued for confining patients in institutions. Others have been sued for not confining patients in institutions (as in the case above). Sometimes professionals have lost court actions for not breaking confidentiality and failing to warn people who were subsequently endangered by the client. Other practitioners have been sued for divulging confidences. Many suits have occurred over the issue of incorrect diagnosis; others have been based on the claim that the practitioner devoted excessive and costly resources to diagnostic testing at the expense of treatment (Green & Cox, 1978). The list of reasons for malpractice liability is endless, and the public predisposition to sue is now being accompanied by an oversupply of underemployed lawyers who take cases on contingency. It is little wonder that workers worry about being sued for malpractice (Broadsky, 1988).

Private practitioners may have even less protection from litigation than practitioners in agencies and thus even more cause for worry. The private practitioner has less professional supervision, no other workers with whom to share the burden or blame for problems, and little help from other professionals in making the many professional decisions regarding client's well-being (Barker, 1989). Agencies sometimes diffuse the focus of attention from an individual worker in a possible malpractice incident, and they often assume some of the responsibility for the problem. Some writers have argued that agency-based social workers are less vulnerable to lawsuits because they are more oriented to altruistic service to others (Jones & Alcabes, 1989).

HOW TO LOSE A MALPRACTICE SUIT

For a private social work practitioner to lose a malpractice suit, the plaintiff must prove four elements: (1) that the private practitioner owed the client a duty to conform to a particular standard of conduct, (2) that this duty was not fulfilled owing to some act of omission or commission in the practice, (3) that the client suffered actual damage, and (4) that the worker's professional conduct was the direct or proximate cause of the damage (Bernstein, 1978).

In private practice, the "duty" owed to a client to meet a standard is established if there is a therapeutic relationship, and it is reaffirmed if fees for the services have been paid. The "client suffering damage" element is established by health records, tests, testimony of health and mental health experts, and testimony of other witnesses about the client's condition before and after the intervention.

To establish element 2, that the worker's care did not meet established standards, experts are called to explain the appropriate treatment for the type of case. They discuss the worker's professional code of ethics and note any violations of the code. The worker will lose unless it can be shown that his or her actions were in accord with professional standards or that the choices of treatment came from a range of acceptable alternatives.

Once it is established in court that the worker had a duty to the client, that he or she failed in that duty, and that damages to the client occurred thereafter, it is theoretically necessary to show that the damage was caused by the failure. Actually, attorneys regularly convince juries that such connections exist, even though they do not really prove it (Barker & Branson, in press). One can lose the suit, or (as more often happens) settle on a payment to the injured client, without such proof.

HOW TO WIN A MALPRACTICE SUIT

The practitioner's best hope of winning a malpractice case is to demonstrate complete adherence to professional standards of conduct. To do this requires knowing those standards completely. Ignorance of the standards is itself an indication of a substandard level of practice. The worker must also choose to meet those standards. Most claims against social workers have occurred in situations where the worker knew what was appropriate but chose the inappropriate action anyway.

Unfortunately, one cannot really win a lawsuit. Even a completely favorable judgment resulting in full vindication is a costly, time-consuming, and never entirely conclusive process. The worker's reputation remains somewhat besmirched, and recovery from the economic and emotional trauma is slow. Most plaintiff's lawyers know this and work toward getting the defendant to agree to pay out of court. The worker avoids this situation by convincing the plaintiff and the plaintiff's attorney that they have no chance of winning. To achieve this goal, the worker must have an appropriate rationale for every action taken, and this rationale must appear in writing in the client's case record. Of course, this documentation should be done while working with the client, and absolutely not after the legal action has been initiated (Barker, 1987e). When the plaintiff's lawyer finds in the record a full justification for the action taken, it becomes difficult to proceed with the case.

ACTIONS LEADING TO LITIGATION

One of the major carriers of social work malpractice insurance periodically issues statistics delineating the types of malpractice cases they have processed (American Home Assurance Co., 1987). In their findings, the following types of problems have led to the number of malpractice cases indicated to date: incorrect treatment, 78: sexual impropriety, 69; breach of confidentiality, 46; improper child placement, 41; improper diagnosis or faulty assessment, 31; defamation, 28; improper death of a client, 26; failure to supervise client properly, 23; bodily injury of clients, 22; violation of civil rights, 21; suicide, 21; countersuit due to fee collection, 19; assault and battery, 17; false imprisonment, 13; breach of contract, 11; failure to warn of client's dangerousness, 9; and failure to cure/poor results, 6. The company indicates that many other isolated activities have also resulted in malpractice actions against social workers.

Many of these actions are more relevant for private practitioners than others. Private practitioners have relatively fewer cases involving improper child placements, bodily injury and death of clients (other than through suicide), breach of confidentiality, and defamation. However, they have relatively more cases involving incorrect treatment, sexual impropriety, fee collection disputes, and breach of contract. For the other issues, agency-based and private practitioners are proportionately equal.

Sexual Misconduct

Unfortunately, one action by social workers in private practice leading to litigation is sexual misconduct. Perhaps this is because the private practice worker–client contact occurs in relative isolation and privacy. There is no question that this is a breach of professional ethics. The NASW (1990b) *Code of Ethics* says "the social worker should under no circumstances engage in sexual activities with clients" (p. 5). Some social workers have tried to defend their actions by claiming that they ended the formal therapy sessions before actually engaging in such liaisons. This is not a valid argument. The benefits of therapy are intended to be lifelong; the influence of the therapist exists equally as long. Thus, a client remains a client indefinitely.

Misuse of Influence

In some malpractice cases, workers are accused of inducing client behavior that serves the professional's rather than the client's interests. For example, workers have tried to convince older clients to include them in their wills. Or they have sold or bought property from clients without giving proper remuneration or other adequate consideration. There is a specific prohibition against this in the NASW (1990b) *Code of Ethics,* which says, "the social worker should avoid relationships or commitments that conflict with the interests of clients" (p. 4). This prohibition also remains in effect permanently, because the worker's influence might remain for the rest of the client's life.

Incorrect Treatment

The type of incorrect intervention that private practitioners are most likely to be involved in litigation over is intervention that keeps clients from obtaining more appropriate treatment (Watkins & Watkins, 1989). For example, a social worker treats a client for anxiety; later it is shown that the client had a physical disorder that resulted in the anxiety symptoms. If the social work treatment had not occurred, then more appropriate medical treatment could have prevented further injury. Merely talking with a client will not reveal whether a symptom is due to inner conflict or to a medical disorder. The prudent worker therefore should always advise clients to get physical exams before starting treatment.

Faulty Diagnosis

If the worker incorrectly diagnoses a client and harm results, the likelihood of a malpractice lawsuit is great. This is true even if the worker only provides faulty information that another professional uses to arrive at an incorrect and harmful diagnosis. To protect against this type of action, the worker should maintain accurate records and obtain the widest sources of information possible. It is unwise to write reports or insurance claims with inaccurate diagnoses. Studies show that deliberate misdiagnosis in mental health practice, usually to meet insurance company criteria, is widespread (Kirk & Kutchins, 1988). Diagnostic judgments involving the incarceration of clients are especially risky and must be made with as much input as possible from colleagues, other professionals, the client, those in the client's social environment, and those in the environment where the client may be sent.

Failure to Refer to Other Professionals

Closely related to cases involving faulty diagnosis and treatment are those in which workers fail to send clients to other professionals who can better provide for their needs. Private practitioners are sometimes accused of holding onto clients even though they require medical or other help that the worker cannot provide. Referrals should be made to reputable professionals who are properly trained to provide the services needed. Otherwise, malpractice litigation may occur.

If their forms of treatment will not or might not be effective, all professionals are ethically obliged to disclose this information to their clients and to inform them that more effective treatments are available. Furthermore, if a social worker treats a client who requires medical care in collaboration with therapy, the worker must be careful not to encroach on the physician's activity.

In 1990, one private social work practitioner learned through legal action how important it is to respect this boundary. The worker shared offices with a psychiatrist and helped with the psychiatrist's patients. Following an initial visit by the physician, the worker would often virtually take over the case, writing prescription renewals and ordering medical tests in the physician's name. Both the worker and the physician lost their licenses, were placed on probation and professionally sanctioned, and had to pay heavy fines for their actions.

Wrongful Death or Client Suicide

Even when workers are not closely connected with cases of client death or suicide, their vulnerability to lawsuits is high. The authorities and attorneys for the family want to determine the degree, if any, to which those involved might have precipitated the results. Workers will feel saddened by the client's death, and possibly somewhat guilty, even if there is little connection between the therapy and the death. The dilemma facing professionals is that although they are expected to prevent clients from death and suicide, they are forbidden by the threat of a malpractice suit from telling others or incarcerating the client for self-protection. All that a worker can do in a case like this is closely monitor the client and try to get the family involved in this monitoring process.

Breach of Confidentiality and Defamation

Private practitioners are vulnerable to malpractice problems when they disclose information about clients to others, especially information that proves harmful to the client. The principle of confidentiality has always been regarded seriously by social workers, and they rarely disclose information carelessly to outsiders. However, every private practitioner has been asked to provide information about clients to potential employers, vehicle operators' administrators, military recruiters, law enforcement officers, and the like. When they do, and when the information is considered detrimental to the client's interests, the claim of defamation might well be issued.

The worker can defend against this accusation by demonstrating that the statements were not lies and that they had been solicited by the plaintiff. Unfortunately, many plaintiffs seek to have these cases settled before they reach court. Litigation is less likely to occur if the worker obtains the client's written permission for anything disclosed. Keeping derogatory opinions and unsubstantiated negative information about clients out of case records is also important.

Premature Termination

Social workers and other professionals in private practice are far more likely to engage in the unethical behavior of premature or precipitous termination than are agency-based professionals. Practitioners sometimes want to discharge clients who are still in need simply because the client's funds or insurance coverage has been exhausted (De Berry & Baskin, 1989).

If the client's need continues and the client is adhering to the contract, the worker has an ethical obligation to continue treatment or facilitate a suitable referral regardless of the financial circumstances. When the termination is appropriate, and not based on financial considerations, the worker should include a note in the case record providing the rationale; the record should also include a final summary letter or a termination of treatment notice.

There are times when clients want to continue even though termination is more appropriate. For example, sometimes the client forms a transference-based attachment to the therapist, or vice versa. These feelings compromise the effectiveness of the treatment. In such cases, the worker should use caution so as to terminate without making the client feel rejected or personally abandoned (Barker, 1987b).

Treatment without Informed Consent

When one of the above actions leads a plaintiff to take action, the issue of informed consent is likely to become part of the argument. Clients must willingly and explicitly consent to any treatment they are offered. Only when a client is institutionalized, a minor, or judged incompetent to make decisions is there an exception. Even then, consent must be obtained from the person legally responsible. The private practitioner is unlikely to have trouble about consent because clients come of their own volition.

There is, however, some risk when the client is not sufficiently informed to consent. For example, in one case, a couple sought marital therapy from a private practitioner, and they were not informed that divorce could be an outcome of treatment. Soon they came to understand that their marriage was surviving largely because of their feelings of insecurity and fear of the economic consequences of divorce. The treatment enhanced their ego strengths and restored their self-confidence, and one of the partners eventually sought a divorce. The other felt the action was the result of the marital therapy and sued the therapist. The case was not won by the litigant, but the therapist had to defend herself against the action.

Since then, many court cases have established the principle that any professional who offers treatment is obliged to warn the client of potential adverse effects or dangers from the treatment. It is therefore in the interest of both the practitioner and the client that the risks inherent in the therapy relationship be made clear and explicit before there is an agreement to begin work (Reamer, 1987b).

Countersuits in Fee Disputes

Some malpractice claims grow out of disputes about fees and the way those fees are collected. When clients fail to pay the agreed-on fees to private social work practitioners, workers feel sometimes forced to take strong actions to collect. They hire lawyers to sue for payment or employ collection agencies to impose constant pressure for payment. Sometimes clients feel that these tactics are inappropriate and issue counterclaims. Such actions most commonly are taken when the collector contacts the client's employer or discloses confidences about the client. These cases are nearly always settled out of court, but rarely to the worker's satisfaction. Most often they result in agreements to forget the whole thing; thus, the worker not only does not receive payment but also has to pay legal and collection costs.

To guard against such countersuits, the private practitioner can take two precautions. Collectors should always be instructed to be very cautious, especially about confidentiality issues, and the worker should keep the bill from getting very high by extracting payment throughout the ongoing therapy.

Failure to Warn

Closely related to confidentiality and defamation problems is the requirement in many states that workers warn potential victims whenever a client makes threats in the practitioner's hearing. This requirement was imposed retroactively when it was first instituted in California in *Tarasoff vs. Regents of the University of California* (1976). In this case, a student at the University of California, Berkeley, was in treatment in the campus mental health clinic. He told the therapist of his plan to kill a young woman, Tatiana Tarasoff, because she broke off her relationship with him.

The therapist and his supervisor took the threat seriously and informed the campus police, and the young man was detained. However, the man convinced the authorities that he was harmless. Soon after the police released the man, he murdered Tarasoff. Her family sued the therapist and the university for failing to warn them of her peril. Eventually, the state supreme court upheld the decision that the therapist should have warned them.

This interpretation now has the force of law in California and most other states (Kerman & Drob, 1987). Such a ruling could be made in any jurisdiction in the United States and thus puts the social worker in an impossible dilemma. If the worker warns someone every time a client makes a threat, the client could be justified in suing the worker for defamation if no harm was actually done. Yet if the worker does not issue the warning and the threat is carried out, litigation is possible (Barker, 1984).

What can the practitioner do to resolve such a dilemma? None of the choices are completely satisfactory. Not long after the *Tarasoff* case was resolved, psychiatrists Roth and Meisel (1977) researched the issue and made several recommendations for all therapists.

First, they said, the practitioner should not issue warnings unless the client's dangerousness is unequivocally certain. Threats are seldom carried out, and workers can always be more helpful to such clients if the working relationship is maintained. The worker must, however, inform the client that the confidentiality provision has exceptions, including threats to others. Second, if the client still seems intent on harming someone, the social worker may tell the client what the law requires the worker to do if the threats persist. Third, a social worker can sometimes modify the client's surroundings to vitiate the client's dangerousness. For example, the worker might convince the client to get rid of any weapons or call on the client's family for support in looking after the client. Finally, if the worker has no choice but to warm the potential victim, the worker should inform the client of the intent and, if possible, obtain permission to divulge the information. The worker should also attempt to reveal the information to the intended victim in the client's presence (VandeCreek & Knapp, 1989).

Obviously, these measures are not completely satisfactory to the worker and are not likely to delight the client, either. However, they are an expedient. The worker must above all consider the effect on the client and weigh the odds.

WHAT TO DO IF SUED

Being named as a defendant in a malpractice or other lawsuit is distressing but need not be ruinous if the right responses are made. The first response is to remain calm on being notified of the action. It helps to remind oneself that most actions are resolved long before they reach the courtroom; of those that do come to trial, the outcomes tend to favor the professional, especially when no claim of physical harm is made. Next, one should not admit any wrongdoing to the plaintiff or the plaintiff's representatives. If such admissions are made, the plaintiff's chances of a favorable settlement improve dramatically.

The next response is to contact one's malpractice insurance agency. These organizations specialize in such cases. They do not want their policyholders to lose and so can be expected to provide effective assistance. In some cases, they can provide or recommend appropriate legal counsel.

Then it is crucial to hire a lawyer as soon as possible. In most jurisdictions, an attorney has 30 days to answer a civil complaint, so it is important to act in time to prepare an effective response. If the worker is named as a co-defendant, as is the case more often than not, then one must decide whether to share counsel or retain one who is independent. The co-defendants should talk this over with their own attorneys first, and if they agree that a joint defense is in their best interests, then only one attorney is retained. Otherwise, the worker should retain separate counsel, because the interests of the other co-defendants will not necessarily be the same as those of the worker.

In choosing an attorney, it is important to find an expert in malpractice litigation. This is done by asking each prospective attorney the following questions: Do you ordinarily handle this type of case? What kind of experience have you had with malpractice suits? How many malpractice cases have you handled? When was the last time you handled one? What were the outcomes of these cases? Will you be the one actually working on my case, or will it be one of your assistants? If an assistant, what is that person's experience with malpractice? What legal and procedural advice do you offer right now?

If these questions are answered satisfactorily, the worker should then contact the state and local bar associations to verify the attorney's good standing. The state bar association in particular would be able to let the worker know of any formal reprimand, censure, or disbarment proceedings that might have an impact on the decision to retain that attorney.

After the retainer is in effect, it is important to "educate" one's lawyer about social work. The lawyer will ask for much relevant information, but he or she cannot know everything that is helpful in understanding social work practice. Information relevant to therapeutic techniques, professional norms, and standard procedures will be useful to the lawyer.

From then on, the worker should follow the attorney's advice to the letter. This includes refraining from any communication with the plaintiff or plaintiff's representatives. All questions from them should be referred to the worker's attorney.

Before going to court, the worker may want to review the case records to refresh his or her memory about all aspects of the case. One should never alter case records in any way, however, even if some entries seem damaging to one's case. If the case goes to court, it is likely to be a long, drawn-out affair. Thus, the worker should continue in practice and be patient. Once the case is resolved, in settlement or in court, the worker will most likely be able to resume a normal professional life.

PROFESSIONAL ADJUDICATION

Social work and the other helping professions have established procedures in their associations to help resolve professional disputes outside of courtrooms. Social workers do this through their committees on inquiry. Every NASW local chapter maintains such a committee, and the national headquarters has a "supercommittee" to review any appeals. NASW has specific procedures for administering these committees, including criteria for case adjudication, composition of committees, procedures for conducting the hearings, and sanctions to be made against the professional when the committee finds in favor of the complainant.

When private practitioners are involved in such cases, the action has usually been initiated by the client. The client calls the NASW office, states the problem, and then participates in the hearing. Lawyers are not present, and the stakes are mostly limited to professional censure or banishment from the association. The procedure has been criticized by some as suspending due legal process (Zastrow, 1991), but others see it as a fair system for resolving disputes without expensive, time-consuming legal procedures (Berliner, 1989).

9 WORKER–CLIENT CONTRACTING

Should the working agreement between the private social work practitioner and the client be implicit or in writing? So far, the great majority of social workers have not elected to write such agreements. According to a survey of 430 clinical social work practitioners that the author conducted at several seminars on private practice, only 44 (10.1 percent) had ever used written contracts.

Few workers use contracts, even though there are increasingly good reasons to use them. The contract has been shown to be an effective tool in facilitating the therapeutic process (Seabury, 1979). It can reduce the likelihood of misunderstandings about what is to be expected in the relationship by both the worker and the client (Wilcoxon, 1991). It can remind clients of their agreement to get a physical examination before starting therapy and to contact insurance companies if they expect to be reimbursed for professional services. Malpractice risks can be minimized, and both the worker and the client have a reminder of the goals they seek to achieve together (Bernstein, 1978).

ARGUMENTS AGAINST CONTRACTS

Not everyone agrees that contracts are beneficial. P. Miller (1990) argued that the use of a contract interferes with the traditional social work relationship, which should be based instead on the "covenant." This covenant is an implicit obligation, which the social worker assumes in the therapeutic relationship, to do everything possible to help. It is a one-way process in which the worker offers a "gift" to the client. The contract, according to this view, involves a "minimalist" form of helping, in which all therapeutic activity is restricted to achieving explicated goals. The covenant orientation, on the other hand, supposedly accommodates the ever-expanding range of goals that will become apparent only during the course of the relationship.

A different kind of argument against contracts was offered by Croxton (1988). As a lawyer–social worker, he claims that the term "contract" is misused by social workers and helping professionals. The legal concept of contract, which is what clients think of when they hear it, has little applicability to the professional relationship. The social worker's responsibilities come from the public and professional sanctions that oversee the practice, rather than from anything in a contract. Moreover, even though contracts state the expectations made of clients, the law cannot enforce compliance.

Most social workers have different reasons for not using written agreements. One is that they do not learn about them in school or in field placements, and they do not see examples of them in the literature. Most of the material written about them consists primarily of discussions about their general value without specific delineation of their contents.

Some social workers do not like the idea of contracts because they think contracts contradict their humanistic-psychosocial orientation (Barker, 1986c). Some incorrectly think of contracts as being part of the task-centered, behavioral model of intervention. Some worry that their clients might be offended because contracts suggest to many that there is little trust and mutual respect and much need for formal protections. Some workers think that the contract actually might add to malpractice risks by placing the relationship in a legalistic orientation rather than a trusting one. And finally, many do not use them because they have done just fine without them so far.

ARGUMENTS FOR CONTRACTS

Proponents of formal contracts dispute these claims and worries. They point out that written agreements do not compel professionals to limit their efforts to what is written (Corcoran, 1991). Nor does a contract keep the work from going beyond specific goals. If the stated goals have been reached, or if new problems or symptoms emerge, it is easy to revise the contract or prepare a new one.

The worker-client relationship is a "fiduciary relationship" (Kutchins, 1991), one founded on trust. The client trusts that the worker will fulfill certain specified obligations. A contract provides assurance for the client by spelling these obligations out in writing. It also reiterates the worker's obligation to adhere to the professional code of ethics. The code itself precludes premature termination of services—that is, termination before fulfillment of obligations—so the contract is simply telling clients what is already known to the worker.

Those who have used contracts find that clients like them. Clients are not as sure as professionals seem to be that a "gift covenant" exists in the relationship. Clients may have read how some mental health professionals exploit their clients. They may be understandably reluctant to enter into a therapeutic relationship that is based solely on a "you-can-trust-me" attitude and that has no specific goals, the prospect of an endless series of expensive and time-consuming meetings, and no specification of the mutual obligations. To enter such a relationship is no more sensible than making payments on the purchase of a house for years with no deed, mortgage papers, or documentation.

Third parties may have some influence on the use of contracts with clients. None of the insurance programs require professionals to use written contracts, but they do require many of the elements found in written contracts. They now require that professionals specify treatment goals and procedures, the reasons for the procedures, and the estimated time frame within which goals are expected to be achieved. They require the professional to make this assessment at the beginning of the treatment, or at least when reimbursements are supposed to begin. Furthermore, third parties will not pay for services unless the professional is licensed or certified in the relevant jurisdiction and adheres to ethical professional standards. If a private social work practitioner meets all these conditions, most of the elements that go into the written contract will have already been fulfilled.

In the absence of a written contract, third parties get more of this information than clients do. Practitioners do not always tell the client what the diagnosis is or confer about the treatment plan. The "trust-me" orientation does not disclose much about the professional's credentials and background. Some workers justify this by saying that such information gets in the way of the needed transference, can cause the client to lose confidence in the professional, or tends to focus the client's attention on such a narrow range of issues that the whole problem cannot be addressed.

Private social work practitioners can significantly reduce their risk of legal problems with written contracts. Croxton's (1988) argument that the written contract would not help much in malpractice situations might have more validity with involuntary clients and those in public settings, because they are not in a position to agree to the terms of the relationship anyway. But the situation is very different in private practice. The clients come of their own volition and freely agree to partake of the services rendered. They meet the "informed consent" criterion because it can be shown in writing that they were told what the conditions of the relationship would be.

If a social worker is sued for malpractice, the first thing a good defense lawyer looks for is some written substantiation of the terms of the relationship. The written contract contains a statement about the explicated goals and procedures that would be crucial to the defense. It also shows that the professional specified procedures to which the client agreed.

Contracts reduce problems about confidentiality and premature termination, too. Now that confidentiality is no longer an absolute and can be suspended in certain situations, the client has the right to know that before starting to divulge possibly deleterious information. The contract can delineate the conditions under which confidentiality would be limited to obey the law. Only if the client agreed to these conditions would there be much defense for the worker in a dispute about a breach of confidentiality.

Problems about premature termination are minimized when the client and worker establish in the contract an orderly procedure by which termination can take place. Any discussion at the beginning of treatment of the possibility of premature termination is likely to be forgotten at the end, especially if there is any disagreement at the end about the procedure.

Finally, when a private social work practitioner is called before a court of law or peer review committee, the allegations usually involve violations of standards or the code of ethics. These authorities are trying to determine whether the practitioner has engaged in unethical practices, made false claims about expertise, or impugned the integrity of the profession. The contract spells out the worker's claims about credentials and procedures, and thus it is clear at the beginning what claims have been made and what have not.

ARE ORAL CONTRACTS ADEQUATE SUBSTITUTES?

Most private practitioners say that, at the least, they use oral contracts. In their first meetings, they establish agreements with clients as to the goals, procedures, financial terms, and conditions for termination. But discussing these matters in the beginning session may be useless; clients and workers are not always able to "hear" one another while negotiating these conditions (Kenemore, 1987). Clients may not be able to understand what the terms of the contract are in the beginning session. Usually they seek help at the time they are distressed; they focus on their problems, not on the future of the therapeutic relationship. If the first session is taken up with a discussion of the presenting problem, no time is left to discuss the terms of the contract. On the other hand, if all the elements that must be considered in the therapy transaction are reviewed in the first session, there is scant time to look at the problem.

Most practitioners would not argue that oral contracts are subject to misunderstanding and misinterpretation. Oral contracts require clients to remember what was said during the stressful initial interview about such things as confidentiality, the worker's credentials, how to get insurance reimbursement, and the goals and ways of reaching them. And even if the client could remember, in times of dispute, malpractice claims, or peer review issues, there still would be no back-up documentation.

The therapeutic relationship is clearly established and defined when the relevant parties sign a written contract; the ongoing relationship concludes in an orderly process when all the terms and obligations of the contract have been fulfilled. The contract is useful in keeping the relationship focused on defined goals that are consented to by the client. And if properly drawn and implemented, the contract will have considerable legal weight in malpractice or other lawsuits or in peer review committees on inquiry (Weinrach, 1989). Few of these virtues of written contracts occur in oral agreements.

ELEMENTS OF THE WRITTEN CONTRACT

The written agreement should be a simple and concise document that the client can understand without a lawyer's interpretation, although a lawyer should be able to interpret it, too. The agreement need not even be called a contract; the use of another term (such a "letter of agreement," "list of conditions," "mutual obligations") would avoid some of the connotations of distrust and potential legal action.

Whatever it is called, it should contain information about what is to be generally expected in the therapeutic relationship. It should delineate the worker's obligations to the client and vice versa. It should explain the required methods of payment and should say something about how to facilitate reimbursement from third-party institutions. The written agreement should tell the client what to do when the worker is unavailable. It should describe the procedures for terminating treatment when the goals have been reached, changed, or abandoned. It should give the client some knowledge about the qualifications of the worker or agency.

Written agreements nowadays must disclose the limits of confidentiality. They should require clients to get medical examinations to rule out physical problems as the cause of the presenting symptoms. Finally, they should list the agreed-on goals that will be the focus of the treatment relationship. Both parties should sign and keep copies of this agreement. The client should be asked to keep it where it is easily accessible, and the worker's copy should remain in the client's case file permanently.

Private social work practitioners use several different kinds of written agreements, depending on the situation. Different agreements may be used for adult therapy clients, couples in marital therapy, members of group psychotherapy programs, families, or children. Even though the agreement letters are intended as information pamphlets and reminders of goals and not as binding legal documents, workers should show them to their lawyers before using them. Varying state laws and new court rulings might necessitate some modifications.

The author of this book has used written letters of agreement with his private practice clients, with good results, for over 20 years. Several versions of these contracts are given in appendix A. Any social worker who has this book is welcome to use them after modifications to suit the particular situation.

These contracts have been presented at many conferences and symposia for private practice social workers and have been adapted and modified by other workers for use in their own practices. They are printed on both sides of a plain sheet of legal-sized (8 1/2" x 14") white paper. The contents are printed in eight columns, four to a side, about three inches wide each. The sheet is then folded in half and then folded in half again, with the folds occurring in the spaces between the columns. This produces an eight-panel document that is 3 1/2" x 8 1/2".

The fourth panel on side 2 (this panel will be the front cover when folded) contains only the worker's name, degree, address, telephone number, and a line indicating whom the client may contact in emergencies when the worker is unavailable. The third panel on side 2 (which will be the back cover when folded) is blank except for the heading "Goals." Here the client and worker can spell out the objectives of the intervention. The other two panels on side 2 and all four panels on side 1 contain the content of the contract; appendix A provides sample language.

REACHING AGREEMENT WITH THE CLIENT

The letter of agreement is presented to the client during the last few minutes of the initial meeting. Some writers suggest it should come at the beginning of the first meeting, but this may take up the time available to the client for problem-focused discussion (Seabury, 1979). Without commenting much about it, the worker hands the statement to the client and explains that it spells out what is to come if they decide to continue working together. The worker simply asks the client to read it carefully sometime before the next session. This exchange can take less than 30 seconds. And the client can examine the paper during a calmer, more private time. So far, no pressure has been imposed on anyone.

At the beginning of the next session, possibly shortly after the worker and client have discussed the week's events, the worker asks if the client has read the contract. Whether or not the answer is yes, the worker spends a few minutes going over its most important points. This is important to make sure every element is understood. Once the worker is sure the client understands, the goals of the helping relationship are discussed. Together, the worker and client spend part of the session deciding on these goals and writing them in specific and doable terms on the contract in the space provided.

The worker and client have identical copies of the contract and the explicated goals, both of which are signed by both participants. During the ongoing therapeutic work, the goals can be periodically reviewed. So, too, can any of the contract's other elements. Periodic reviews help define, focus, and minimize misunderstandings.

THE VALUE OF WRITTEN AGREEMENTS

Any tool that will help private social work practitioners and clients achieve their goals in a purposeful, systematic manner should be in more common use. No one claims that written agreements will resolve all possible misunderstandings or supersede the professional obligation of competent and ethical service to the client. What is claimed is that the written agreement is an effective tool for the worker to use in providing services. Like all tools, it can be either misused or not used when it could have helped. Like all tools, when used properly, it can enhance the abilities of its users to get the job done.

10 MARKETING AND BUILDING A CLIENTELE

Social workers enter private practice at a disadvantage compared with many other fee-for-service professionals. The other professionals can develop clientele more easily because the public has a better understanding of what they do and what services they perform. Most people still are not sure what social workers do, especially social workers in private practice. And although there has been some increase in the public's overall estimation of social work and increased use of its psychotherapy services, its vague image persists (Andrews, 1987; Goleman, 1985).

Obviously, this vague image poses a significant problem for social workers in private practice. Their vocational survival depends on recognition of their skills and function by the public. The fact that they are well trained, highly skilled, competent, honest, and well-regarded by their colleagues is a necessary but insufficient factor in their professional success. What is necessary to overcoming this handicap and building a clientele is a marketing strategy.

TRENDS IN SOCIAL WORK MARKETING

Marketing has not been a high priority in the social work profession until recent years. Because most social workers have been employed in non-profit, noncompetitive public service jobs, there has been little need for self-promotion. In addition, many social workers have resisted efforts to promote the profession in the media, because they feared that client confidentiality would be compromised or that they would be depicted unfavorably (Brawley, 1985–86). Most of the profession's marketing and public relations activity has sought to educate the public about the various social problems; little has been done to show the public what social workers can do about these problems.

In recent years, however, this resistance to the idea of promotion has been breaking down. Social workers have emulated the techniques of political campaigners and product sales promoters (Bynum, 1991). Public interest campaigning, known now as "social marketing," is being used with as much success in the private, profit-making sector of the economy as in the public sector (Bailis et al., 1990). Marketing and public relations courses and workshops for workers in private practice are being developed. Professionals are seeing similarities between social workers and salespersons, both groups being people who exert influence on others (Zastrow, 1990b).

Private social work practitioners think marketing should be used more often to tell the public about social work and about the individual practitioner (Belser, 1987). Many private practitioners have written that because too little attention has been given to the first goal and the public remains in the dark about social work, they have been forced to devote more of their efforts to the second goal, self-promotion. In so doing, they are often accused by their social work colleagues of downplaying their professional identities.

DO PRIVATE PRACTITIONERS CONCEAL THEIR PROFESSION?

Many social workers in private practice do not emphasize their professional identity. This is true even of some who maintain membership in social work professional associations and use social work licenses. On their business cards, signs on doors, Yellow Page listings, and other identifiers, they list such things as "psychotherapist," "marriage counselor," "individual and group therapy specialist," and "stress management consultant." Nowhere do they indicate "social worker."

Naturally, this tendency has not been favorably received in the profession; it has long been cited as a reason why private practice should not be considered part of social work (Smalley, 1954). The number of private practitioners who avoid the social work designation is unknown. Helen Perlman once estimated that there were few, if any, private practitioners who acknowledge their social work roots. "To my knowledge," she wrote, "the title is never used by [the private practitioner trained in social work] as his professional designation. It may have too little meaning for his prospective clients—or too much" (Perlman, 1955).

If this estimate was true in 1955, it is not now. Increasingly, private practitioners are displaying their "social work" designation. One need only look in the Yellow Pages under "social workers" to see that many practitioners are comfortable using the name.

But others still are not. One of the most influential private social work practitioners, Arnold M. Levin, who once chaired the NASW Committee on

Private Practice, explained why. For years he downplayed the title for himself and wrote that he could not recommend that anyone in private practice use the label of social worker, at least not without further description. He believed that, for most people, the designation brings to mind the "image of a public assistance, bureaucratic functionary shuffling papers, interpreting rules and regulations and guarding or disbursing the taxpayers' moneys in miserly amounts" (A. M. Levin, 1976). He has subsequently modified his view, as the social work image has changed, and now comfortably identifies himself as a social worker (A. M. Levin, 1983).

VAGUENESS IN THE "SOCIAL WORK" DESIGNATION

At the present time, most social workers in private practice are also comfortable with the designation and do not think of it as a liability. The public is indifferent about it at worst, for they do not have a clear understanding of what it is. Indeed, social work is still trying to define its specific domain and expertise to its own members.

If the members are not yet clear, one can hardly expect the public to be. As long as social work is ill defined to the public, the private practitioner cannot consider membership in social work to be as great an asset in building a clientele as is membership in their own professions for other professionals. The private practitioner's concern could be not that the "social worker" appellation would lose business, but only that it might not bring any.

Thus, many social workers in private practice identify themselves properly, but with additional explanations for what they do. One private practitioner answered the author's questionnaire this way:

I list my professional affiliation as "social worker" but not with enthusiasm. It simply isn't a good way to draw clientele. The public doesn't know what social workers do. I have to be more specific about the work I do. My name and MSW degree are right on my door and below that is "psychiatric social worker." But I also put "psychotherapist" on that door. People know what a psychotherapist does.

Another social worker in full-time private practice wrote,

People don't think they should have to pay a social worker much. So I guess it's a financial thing. But it's more too. A lot of doctors or lawyers would refer someone to a psychologist or a teacher or a physical therapist, but they don't have the foggiest notion of what a social worker is so they aren't going to refer anyone to them.

Potential clients obviously do not seek a professional's services unless they understand what services are being offered and believe

be of value. Usually, a consumer knows which professional or occupational group to consult when they need help. If they want to learn something, they go to a teacher. If they want to sue someone, they consult a
lawyer. If someone has a toothache, or a sick dog, or a stopped-up sink,
they know whom to consult. The consumer might wonder which individual is best within that field but is less likely to question whether that is
the best field to provide their service. Most people, therefore, still do not
think about seeking the services of a social worker. Many think social
work is for someone else, perhaps poor people, or those with disabilities,
or disadvantaged people. Yet even those groups do not always look to
social workers for help. When these people have a choice, they want to be
served by the same professionals who serve the affluent or nondisadvan-
taged or nondisabled.

As long as the professional image problem remains, the private social
work practitioner will have to rely more on personal self-promotion than a
mere identification with the profession to build a successful practice.

HOW TO BUILD A CLIENTELE

One of the skills to be developed for success in private practice is that of
building a clientele. This process includes the tested marketing strategies
of specializing, targeting potential consumers (referral sources), and becoming known in the community (to build referrals) (Foreman & Foreman, 1983).

The essence of building a clientele is, of course, getting regular
referrals. Most referrals come from former clients who have been treated
well by the professional in previous encounters. To get such referrals, the
worker must be competent and ethical. Practitioners who exploit their
clients—by such behaviors as encouraging their return long after their
need for service has ended—obtain short-term gain and long-term
problems.

Most private practitioners get referrals (in order of importance) from
former clients, physicians, social services agency staff members, client self-
referrals, psychiatrists and psychologists who seek social services in
collaboration with their own cases, lawyers, school counselors, the
clergy, and miscellaneous others (Barker, 1982). Clientele building involves identifying those in the community who make referrals and then
showing the influential members of the targeted audience that the service
offered is of value. Because the potential referral sources are not likely to
know what services social workers provide, the practitioner can usually
draw more attention and referrals by demonstrating unique skills and
specialized knowledge with specific populations or problems.

[handwritten notes: work w/ children + adolescents - ADHD behavioral problems - depression social skills groups]

Specializing

Perhaps the most common and successful marketing strategy used by private practitioners is specialization. Practitioners tell the public that they are social workers who work with certain target populations or use specific treatment methods.

For example, all social workers are familiar with the experience of introducing themselves to strangers and saying, "I'm a social worker," only to be met with polite nods and blank stares. People are probably not being unfriendly, but because they are vague about the role of social work, they just do not know how to respond. However, if the social worker said instead, "I'm a social worker in private practice, and I specialize in working with teenagers who have alcohol or drug abuse problems," the worker would be remembered and possibly contacted if there was a future need.

The specializing process includes providing a specific service that people need and referrers remember. Many social work writers have described successful private practices specializing in work with identifiable population groups. Examples include work with Asian Americans (Dhooper & Thanh, 1987), adolescents and children (Frisman, 1990), older people (Stoesz, 1989), black people (Brown, 1990b), rural clients (D. Cohen, 1987; Enright, 1988; Peirce, 1986), obese adults (Weiss, 1989), cancer patients and their families (Royse & Dhooper, 1988), and clients who are terminally ill (van Wormer, 1990). Other social work writers describe specialties in providing specific treatment methods. Examples include such methods as hypnosis (Knight, 1991), biofeedback (Long, Machiran, & Bertell, 1986), neurolinguistic programming (Zastrow, Dotson, & Koch, 1986), and existential intervention (Lantz, 1987).

Once the professional develops a special knowledge or skill, word gets around to potential consumers. Newspaper reporters find out about the professional's expertise and seek quotes when working on a story on that topic (Royse, 1988). The members of the special population group, being more independent and communicative among themselves, will soon discuss the specialist's services. The worker is not necessarily confined, thereafter, to such work, but he or she has a steady referral base from which to branch out to the extent desired.

Although specialization is a useful tool for private practitioners, some social work colleagues criticize it. They might see the practice as a guise to disavow one's social work identity by becoming too focused. Some workers are "weeping for the lost profession" because of a possible trend toward specialization (Lee, 1983). This view is understandable, even if debatable.

The distinctiveness of social work, and its proudest tradition, has always been its determination to see the "big picture." Its expansive and generic approach to social problems and its goal of enhancing the well-being of people in society are noble. However, it is unrealistic to think that one person can do everything well. Some social workers are better suited to being generalists, whereas others make better specialists. It is no more disloyal to be one thing than the other. The profession has room for both.

Once social workers have become identified with a specialty, it becomes easier to promote themselves to potential consumers. They make clear to the public what it is they are selling and that their services are attractive and worthwhile, and they show that their particular services are competitive with the similar offerings of others. Social workers should make services convenient and accessible to the potential consumer. Once they have built a reputation for quality service, they can expect return business and word-of-mouth recommendations from their referral sources. These techniques are the foundation of any reputable business.

Referral Sources

The most important source of referrals is, of course, a satisfied client and the people close to the client. The client who is happy with the outcome of the work is the best advertisement there can be. Many of the client's associates who know about the treatment are also going to become advertisers, if not clients themselves.

The second most important referral source is physicians who care about their patients but do not always have the time, skill, or inclination to meet their social services and mental health needs. Physicians are more likely to refer their patients to psychiatrists because they are more familiar with the techniques of fellow medical doctors. However, when they have first-hand knowledge of social work and the techniques used, they are also likely to send their patients to social workers. Private practitioners can readily demonstrate to physicians that because of their training, experience, and skill they are more focused toward helping people with family, marital, and social relationship problems than are most psychiatrists. The first referrals from the doctor to the social worker will probably be followed carefully; if the results are poor or even equivocal, the doctor will be reluctant to make additional referrals.

The staffs of social services agencies, especially if the worker was affiliated with the agency before entry into private practice, are the third most important referral source. For many social workers entering private work, this is the major, if not sole, source. Private practitioners sometimes get an agency's "client overload," or at least get their names on the list of the agency's referral resources for those clients whom the agency cannot serve. Many social workers keep in close contact with several agencies for this purpose.

Psychiatrists, psychologists, lawyers, school counselors, and the clergy can also be important referral sources. However, referrals come from them only in certain cases. These professionals will probably refer only if they know the worker directly or know the worker's special expertise indirectly. They must see the worker as offering some unique skill or knowledge and some form of treatment that does not duplicate the services other professionals provide. When social workers target members of these professions as potential referral sources, they usually find it effective to cultivate a personal or working relationship with them in which they can demonstrate their ethics and competence first-hand.

Referral-Building Activities

Whatever the referral source, the chances for referrals increase if the worker is known personally or because of expertise. Thus, the fundamental referral-building activity consists of becoming known by those who may recommend clients. Private practitioners have concentrated on six basic activities to accomplish this: (1) communicating with those who have already made referrals, (2) following up with former clients and referrers, (3) contacting those who have not referred clients but who have a professional interest in a client, (4) "prospecting" for clients, (5) advertising, and (6) participating in community activities. Of course, not all private practitioners take part in all these activities or even approve of their colleagues who do.

The first three of these techniques assume that the worker already has some clients and can build a practice and caseload on this foundation. Workers who have no clients at all, and thus have no foundation on which to build a practice, are forced to rely on the others. Many professionals have negative feelings about techniques 4 and 5, but virtually everyone endorses the appropriate use of technique 6.

Communicating with Referrers. The best way to become known by referrers is to communicate with them. The first communication occurs as soon as the worker learns that someone has made the referral. The referral is then acknowledged by phone or letter. A brief note on the worker's stationery might simply say, "Thank you for recommending my services to Mrs. _____. She called for an appointment today, and we will meet on _____. With her permission, I will keep you informed about the findings and treatment."

After the assessment is completed, if the client gives permission a more complete letter is sent to the referrer. If the referrer is sional, such as the family physician, the letter may include a sui the presenting problem, the social work assessment, the recon treatment, the prognosis, and the worker's plan for helping solve the problem. If the practitioner plans to continue working with the client, the letter concludes by saying that subsequent progress notes will be sent. If the letter goes to the physician, it is marked at the top, "CONFIDEN-TIAL: FOR FILE ONLY." The letter is usually kept in the physician's file on the patient, so the worker's name and telephone number are available thereafter. As treatment continues, less formal and less detailed progress notes may be sent. They might say "Mrs. _____ has been attending our weekly group therapy sessions regularly. She seems motivated and appears to be progressing. I'll notify you if there are any changes. Again, thank you for recommending me to her."

When the goals of the intervention are reached or when termination takes place, the referrer is given a more detailed summary. A letter, again marked "CONFIDENTIAL: FOR FILE ONLY," summarizes the intervention process and indicates which goals have been reached and which have not. It includes a prognosis and indicates what to look for in the future in case some regression occurs. The letter also indicates that the worker will continue to keep in touch with the client and concludes with another "thanks for the referral."

If the referral source is not a professional but a personal acquaintance or family member, there are significant differences in the way communication takes place. Usually, a brief informal note or call saying the person made the contact is enough. It is, of course, inappropriate to provide any substantive information to such persons about the nature of the problem or intervention plan. They do deserve, however, the courtesy of acknowledging their effort.

The client must always give permission before any substantive information is sent. Clients are usually amenable to this communication, and some even expect it. Many private practitioners find it useful to let clients read any information to be sent out, so that changes can be made in advance. In such cases, the client might be asked to initial the copy kept in the worker's file to indicate approval. If more detailed information is requested by relevant others, it is essential to get the client to sign a written release-of-information form.

There are many advantages to communicating in this way. Most important, it provides some coordination between those who are trying to help the client. It is consistent with the social work orientation of involvement in the client's environment, and it minimizes problems that can occur with referrers who might want to stay involved in the intervention process or second-guess the worker's efforts with the client. The more these others are kept informed and made to feel a part of the helping process, the less they will interfere. Finally, communication keeps the social worker in the mind of the referrer. Showing that the worker is conscientious, organized, and goal-oriented does a great deal to improve the chances of subsequent referrals.

Following Up with Former Clients and Referrers. Clients who never again hear from their worker may think the worker is not interested in them, or they forget the successful results they achieved during treatment. It is almost always worthwhile to stay in some contact with clients who have terminated. The worker might occasionally call or write a brief note. A handwritten note on office stationery might say something like "It's been over a year since we last met, and I was just thinking about you. I hope all remains well with you and your family." The worker can also do this with the source of referral, indicating that there has been no word from the client for many months and the worker is hoping that all is well. In both instances, such contact demonstrates continued interest, is professional, and is a reminder that the worker is still there.

Although brief follow-up activities are to be encouraged, involvement of the worker in the client's life outside treatment is, of course, not at all desirable. There may be times when the former client wants to invite the worker to a party or have some other social contact. The worker would be unwise to have any such involvement; the basis of the relationship was, and always shall be, the client's therapeutic interests, and any socializing, regardless of how long after termination, is dubious practice.

Contacting Relevant Others. One way some private practitioners meet potential referrers is by contacting them about or in behalf of existing clients. For example, if a client is referred by friends, the worker may ask the new client the name of his or her physician. Then, with permission, the worker writes to the doctor, saying that the client is being seen. The letter can indicate who referred the client and for what reason. It can have a sentence or two stating the worker's qualifications for seeing the client, and then it can present the social work assessment, prognosis, and intervention plan. The worker may also promise to keep the physician informed about the client's progress. When goals are reached, a final summary letter is sent. At this point, the procedure is the same as for a referring physician.

This procedure is appropriate for many professionals in the client's helping network. If the client is having some educational difficulties, school counselors may be contacted; if there are marital problems, the client's clergy may be notified; if there is some potential conflict about financial problems or legal difficulties, a letter might go to the client's attorney.

Clients often appreciate this kind of attention and easily give permission for such contacts to be made. Nevertheless, it should not be done unless the client gives permission, and in most cases it is advisable to let the client read and initial any letters first. This way, no information goes out that the client wants concealed.

This activity is beneficial to all concerned. The client receives more input from those in the helping network, and the professionals involved are informed about the intervention. Practically, it enhances the chances of referrals from new sources because the worker becomes known to those who had been unaware of the worker's existence or professional expertise. The worker is seen as one who is concerned about clients and capable of recognizing the client's problem and providing appropriate services to correct it. Finally, it is consistent with social work values and norms, for it shows that the worker does not see clients as existing only in a clinical setting, completely detached from external considerations.

Prospecting for Clients. Many business people call on potential customers at random in the hope that a percentage of those contacted will use their services or products. For example, insurance and real estate salespeople call or knock on doors looking for potential customers. Some lawyers dispense their business cards at accidents to offer their services.

Most professional people who attempt to get referrals by the "prospecting" process, however, use more subtle techniques. A common and acceptable form is to send out announcements and letters of introduction to those who might become referral sources. Announcements are typically 3" x 5" printed cards that say something like "Sylvia Lee, ACSW, DSW, announces the opening of her office for the practice of social work treatment of children and adolescents."

The address and available hours are also indicated. The cards, while traditional, are not very effective by themselves. Few professionals are likely to refer clients to someone they do not know, and especially not to someone whose profession is not well-known to them. If cards have any worth at all, it is one step in a whole procedure for becoming known to referral sources. They will be forgotten unless they are soon followed by additional contacts.

Another step, which can follow the announcement card, is the letter of introduction. This letter would be useless, and perhaps even harmful, as an impersonal form letter. It should be written specifically for the addressee and should call attention to mutual interests, concerns, and goals. It should not solicit referrals. It merely says that the social worker is opening a private practice in the area and will specialize in working with certain kinds of problems or client groups. It briefly states the worker's credentials and experience.

The letters are also not effective unless some additional contact is made soon after they are received. Ideally, the contact is in the form of a personal visit or a message about a client who has started to work with the social worker.

Some workers prefer a personal follow-up. They state in their letter of introduction that they might informally drop in at the addressee's office in the near future. A few days later, they go to the office and ask if the employer is available to say hello. If not, the worker can simply leave a card and more information about his or her practice and background. It is unwise to spend more than a few minutes, for it indicates that the worker has nothing better to do than visit. It is also unwise to schedule a formal meeting: This can be an irritating intrusion, and the worker would have to be very clear about the nature of the call or take the chance of being billed for the time.

Advertising. Many private practitioners now see merit in advertising as a way to reach initial referrals, although others still find the practice abhorrent. The conflict about advertising exists among all fee-for-service professionals. Until recently, the practice had been considered unethical because of the abuses that had been rampant in the 19th century, in which practitioners would make unsubstantiated claims to attract clientele. Reputable professions could combat this by keeping members from advertising. Their premise was that clients would get to the practitioner by referrals from other reputable professionals or not at all. However, the consumer movement and Federal Trade Commission regulations took a different stance in the 1960s; at that time, the professional organizations that forbade their members from advertising were seen as attempting to restrict fair trade and uphold high fees. Now it is illegal for any profession to prevent members from advertising, and ads in the media for professionals, including social workers, have become commonplace (Woody, 1989). Professional associations now try to provide assurance that the advertised claims are truthful and reflect the integrity of the member and the profession.

Whether or not the private practitioner should advertise is now an individual decision rather than a professional one. There are many advantages and disadvantages for each practitioner. Ads can clarify for the public what the social worker is qualified to do and interested in doing for potential clients and what the charges are. Social work's role and expertise are not very well known to the public, but advertising can help to erase that disadvantage. On the other hand, professionals who do no advertising often have an unfavorable impression of those who do, and they are not likely to become referral sources.

Advertising also may not be cost-effective. It is expensive, and the well-established worker does not really need to reach more than a few new clients each month to maintain a full caseload. The newer professional will find it cost-inefficient at best, unless it is pinpointed to specific target groups. And, of course, it is pointless to advertise in those places where large numbers of people are reached far beyond the location of the practitioner's office.

One of the most common places used by practitioners to notify potential clients is the Yellow Pages. It is not usually necessary or effective for the social worker to purchase a large display ad in these pages, regardless of claims about its effectiveness. In the helping professions, the Yellow Page listing is considered a supplement to various forms of public exposure; it is a way to let clients who have heard about the worker find a telephone number. Therefore a simple line or two is sufficient.

However, if the worker feels dependent on the listings in the Yellow Pages, arrangements for inclusion should be made well in advance of entry into private practice. The telephone companies have deadlines for new listings of about six months prior to publication, so a worker who just misses a deadline might have to wait as long as 1 1/2 years for the listing to appear. To avert this, workers can notify the telephone company as soon as they know they are going to enter private practice. Their home phone number goes into the ad, and when their office phone is established, the telephone company records a change of number announcement.

Under what Yellow Page heading is the best place to be included? Many practitioners choose to be listed under "marital and family counselors," "consultants," "psychotherapists," or "guidance clinics" if it is legal in that jurisdiction. They believe that few people will look up "social workers" when they have a problem. Nevertheless, the practitioner should also be listed under "social workers." As workers become known to clients, referral sources, and third-party financers, their numbers and addresses will be sought in that listing.

The Yellow Pages, as well as other forms of advertising, are impersonal, and referral sources and potential clients are more often attracted to practitioners they have met or heard about. Ads should be considered no more than a supplement to activities designed to keep the practitioner in the public eye. They will always be more costly and less effective than community activities.

Participating in Community Activities. Social workers, more than any other professional group, are supposed to be involved in the community and in its resources. They are supposed to be aware of the consequences of social problems affecting individuals, and they are oriented to changing those problems as well as personal problems. Private practice does not excuse a social worker from this responsibility. Even if it did, there are many rewards for such involvement. It is an effective way for the worker to practice social work ideals. Practically speaking, working in the community is an excellent way for the social worker to get into the public eye and is the private practitioner's best single means of getting new referrals. To achieve these goals, seven community activities in which workers have been engaged have been identified as being particularly effective:

1. *Providing free consultations.* One community activity is offering services to one or more social services agencies or self-help groups as a free consultant. Such organizations abound, and they often have little money to pay for professional advice. Many social services agencies are now struggling to keep afloat; because they have serious financial problems, they are increasingly staffed by volunteers or less well-trained professionals. To retain their credibility and maintain their valuable public services, they require (but can ill afford) professional expertise. Self-help groups are also grateful for occasional input from professionals, but they have scant resources to hire them.

When a private practitioner meets periodically with such agencies and groups to answer questions or provide feedback, the time spent is mutually rewarding. Such contacts help the worker keep on his or her toes as well as help refine skills and increase knowledge. Contacts with others outside the isolation of the office also help reduce vulnerability to burnout. And, of course, the exposure makes the worker known to a larger group of potential referrers.

2. *Serving on agency boards.* Agencies that are better funded and more formally organized need community leaders to serve on their boards. A board determines an agency's policy and priorities and oversees its functions. Social workers often take on such roles, and they have much to offer in such capacities. They can interpret for their fellow board members the ethical and value bases for actions taken by agency staff. They can help set agency policy in ways more consistent with social work values and orientations. Agency workers seldom are able to do this, as they are ineligible to serve on their agency's board, but private social workers are in an ideal position to serve. The private practitioner is aware of the needs of the agency as well as the community. On a board, the practitioner often works with members of other professions, including doctors, lawyers, clergy, and business leaders, affording ample opportunity for a demonstration of knowledge and skill. The worker's fellow board members often become referral resources, as do agency staff members.

3. *Public speaking.* Social workers only need to hint at their willingness to speak before civic groups, educational associations, church groups, and fraternal organizations to be given the opportunity. Almost every organization has regular formal programs in which the membership is eager to learn

about a community problem or professional solution to a problem. If the worker proves to be informative and interesting for the group, other groups will hear about it and extend invitations as well. In these talks, the worker might show an interest in and knowledge about an issue that is of particular concern to the group. The worker might describe how professionals address such problems and provide examples from his or her own experience. The audience would then identify the speaker as one who might provide such services on a fee-for-service basis. Some members of the audience might think about using or recommending the worker's services.

4. *Participating in panel discussions.* A similar but less demanding activity that accomplishes results similar to those of public speaking is to participate in panel discussions or act as a resource person for community workshops. Letting groups know of an interest in being a discussant at a formal speech made by another professional will lead to invitations. The worker's credentials are usually described, and he or she is called on as an expert. Panel discussions are less structured and formal than are speech presentations, so it is easy for the worker to mingle with the audience during the evening and to be seen as one who might be able to help. It is not at all uncommon for workers to receive telephone calls following these presentations from someone who attended the meeting and wants an appointment.

5. *Campaigning for public office.* There are two parts to this activity, and it is not for every social worker in private practice; however, those who campaign find considerable public exposure and personal satisfaction. One part is to campaign for and hold elective office; the other is to lead or participate in a public crusade to change some social norm or law.

Social workers are often encouraged to become more political. This is not always possible for those who work in publicly funded social services agencies that frown on certain political activities. The private practitioner is under no such constraints and, in fact, should be in a very good position to engage in such activities.

Social workers are as well-qualified as other professionals to administer public programs and set public policy. Even if they do not win the election or accomplish the cause they fought for, the workers have still established themselves as leaders in the community and, as such, are in a better position to influence the community.

6. *Appearing in the media.* The last activity is to reach the public through the media, and a number of possible approaches can be used. One is to appear on local radio or television programs. Public interest programs abound on all stations (they are required by the Federal Communications Commission), and problems in the community are often the subject of

concern. If the worker is able to speak clearly, with some humor and irreverence and in a jargon-free way, the worker will be welcome on many of these programs. The worker then has a vehicle for expressing concern, interest, and skill in dealing with the problem under discussion. Having been identified on the program as a local private practitioner who works with the specific problem, the worker is likely to be called by some listeners who seek additional advice.

Practitioners can accomplish something of the same thing by writing articles and columns for newspapers and magazines. Often these works are in the form of advice-giving columns using a question-and-answer format. The larger magazines and newspapers usually have professional writers write such materials, but there are numerous neighborhood newspapers, advertising fliers, newsletters, and other printed matter where the practitioner can find a vehicle for this form of expression. Workers can also call attention to themselves, their views, and their skills by writing letters to the editor in response to articles on issues of their own concern.

Writing for professional journals is another way of expanding the referral base. Even though the audience is more limited, other professionals in the area will take the writer more seriously as an expert. Writing for journals can lead to contacts with other professionals and thus to the possibility of more referrals, especially when the journal appears to members of more than a single profession.

7. *Being a role model.* The last possibility for expanding the referral base is the most important: to present oneself in a positive, ethical, and knowledgeable way to whatever public sector is being addressed. All the public relations activities one can think of are fruitless if the worker is dishonest or engages in behaviors that discredit the individual or the profession. If ethical business practices are performed at all times and if the worker is a good citizen, the good will achieved is worth all the other public relations activities put together.

Clearly, the worker cannot engage in all these community relations activities, or there would be no time to work with fee-paying clients. It is equally clear that the private social work practitioner will find it necessary and useful to engage in some of them. The vague image of the profession requires that the individual worker in private practice communicate with the public to clarify individual skills as well as those of the profession. Some workers are obviously not well-equipped to participate in one or another of these activities, but there are enough possibilities that some will appeal to any private practitioner. Each worker has the opportunity to choose those that might be most useful and effective given the worker's particular personality, expertise, and community.

11

THE FUTURE OF SOCIAL WORK IN PRIVATE PRACTICE

T his book began with a glimpse of the past, of the inauspicious, bastardlike origins of private practice, whose social work parents wanted to disown it, whose growth continued without much nurturing or guidance, and whose size and influence now make it hard to disavow. It ends with a look at the future, at a time when private practice is entering promising maturity, a time when its social work progenitor has been enfeebled by decreased public support for the programs, methods, clients, and agencies that had once been the reason for its existence.

Although social work has overcome considerable adversity many times in the past, private practice has not yet had to prove its durability. Private practice might appear strong and vital to some, but it has three serious vulnerabilities, any one of which could lead to its premature senescence or demise. It is vulnerable because of changing social and economic conditions, the trend toward managed health care programs, and problems within the social work profession itself. The degree to which the profession solves or circumvents these problems will largely determine the fate of its private practice.

SOCIOECONOMIC VULNERABILITIES

The growth of social work in private practice in the past 30 years has been largely due to an economic and political climate that fostered its development. An ever-increasing number of consumers wanted the service. The national economy was relatively healthy and oriented toward spending its resources on personal growth and development. Politically and socially, the trend was toward increased privatization of health and human service delivery systems (Abramowitz, 1986). Many people who had no serious emotional or social problems simply wanted to understand themselves better. Many clients sought private help because they were being turned away from social services agencies or put on long waiting lists owing to social work personnel shortages. Third-party financing organizations were increasingly willing to pay for the professional services of private practitioners. To a great extent, U.S. social welfare systems were being transformed into for-profit ventures (Perlmutter & Adams, 1990).

Obviously, if such conditions were to continue indefinitely, the prognosis for private practice would continue to be optimistic. But change is the very nature of economic conditions. The socioeconomic factors that once stimulated the growth of private practice are now undergoing transformation.

For example, the demand for the services of private practitioners in all helping professions may be diminishing. This is because of changing demographics, changing value priorities, and cost factors. The demographic change is easily seen in U.S. Bureau of the Census data: In the 1990s, there are fewer people in the age and socioeconomic categories that have been the most likely consumers of private psychotherapy services, the affluent 25 to 45 year olds.

Regarding changed values, there is a clear shift away from the self-preoccupied orientations of previous years. The 1970s were called the "culture of narcissism," and the 1980s were called the "me decade." These appellations partly referred to the desire of many people to explore their psyches, a desire that for a while had reached almost fad-like proportions. Those who went to private practice social workers and other mental health therapists were not only people with serious mental illnesses or social dysfunction problems, but also people ("the worried well") who wanted to enhance their potential as human beings, to become self-actualized, or simply to get someone to listen to them. Fewer people now see psychotherapy or psychosocial intervention as the primary device by which to achieve such objectives. The value and efficacy of therapy and social services in private practice have still not been clearly demonstrated to the public or to the third parties who help pay the bills.

Finally, costs have become an even greater obstacle for many. Health care prices stay high even during economic slowdowns, even with increased professional competition. Costs were less important to consumers when their insurance companies and government programs paid for most of the service provider's charges. However, escalating costs borne by the third parties have led them to find ways of getting consumers to share their costs. As a result, co-payments are higher for the consumer, and limits on costs that insurers pay have been reduced. The number of people insured has declined by more than 7 million in recent years (Health Insurance Association of America, 1990). And cuts are being made in insurance coverage of specialized areas such as mental health (Barker, 1988c). The continued trend is toward managed health care programs—health maintenance organizations, preferred provider organizations, and utilization review programs—which control client access to services and service providers (Leon, 1990).

These trends inevitably result in reduced demand, but the supply of mental health care workers continues to grow. Over 1.5 million American professionals provide some form of counseling, guidance, or therapy (U.S. Department of Health and Human Services, 1989). All of the traditional mental health care professions have been growing dramatically, with social work in the lead (Goleman, 1985). There are an estimated 200,000 people in the labor force who have social work degrees and over 440,000 people who hold nonadministrative social work jobs (Williams & Hopps, 1990).

These professions, thus far, have not addressed the possibility of an oversupply of mental health care providers; instead, they tend to pay more attention to increasing the demand and improving their competitive position with respect to the other professions. In several states, representatives of various professional associations have testified against each other's applications for licensing and third-party eligibility.

VULNERABILITIES CAUSED BY THE MANAGED HEALTH CARE TREND

Private social work practitioners are in an increasingly precarious position with regard to third-party financing systems. If these systems were to start excluding social workers, then few workers could survive in private practice.

The influence of third parties in mental health care has been limited until recent years (Walfish & Janzen, 1988). Before then, many private practitioners were able to prosper, even though neither they nor their clients received any third-party funds. Many clients did not expect their health insurance to cover mental health problems. Now they do. Over 60 percent of Americans are currently covered through managed health care programs, and unless there is a national health insurance program, over 90 percent of Americans will be by the end of this decade (Leon, 1990; Robertson & Jackson, 1991). This trend has helped sap the vitality from the publicly funded community mental health centers and social services agencies (Dumont, 1990). Managed health care is an industry that is booming despite many internal problems (Stevens, 1991). Virtually every potential client will seek only the services of those providers in the managed health care system.

It is already apparent that becoming eligible for third-party reimbursement makes a great difference to social work in private practice (NASW, 1990a). It affects where practitioners locate, what type of services they provide, what kinds of clients they see, how long they see them, and how much they charge (A. A. Lieberman & Turner, 1991; Shatkin et al., 1986; W. Turner, 1987). If insurance companies reimbursed members of all professional groups on an equal basis using the same criteria for all, or if they did not reimburse any outpatient mental health care providers, then consumers could choose for themselves which ser- vices and providers to seek. No doubt, social work, or at least its most competent practitioners, could hold their own and compete effectively. But when vendor eligibility changes and an insurance company says it will help pay for services rendered only by members of designated profes- sions or for specified forms of treatment, those excluded will be at a competitive disadvantage, no matter how worthwhile their work.

So far, social work has been successful in establishing itself as a profession to be included in these systems; most of the third parties are agreeing to employ or reimburse for the services of licensed, profession- ally certified social workers in private practice (NASW, 1991b). However, there are great pressures on the managed health care systems to exclude some provider groups. The continued efforts of social work professional groups will be necessary to maintain and enhance their current position.

Some private social work practitioners may want to stay apart from the professional associations' efforts to keep within managed health care systems. Perhaps they think that they do not need to be part of such systems or that they can remain within them through their individual efforts. Both views are incorrect. Private practitioners cannot, by them- selves, prevent their exclusion from these systems. No third-party system could exclude an entire profession while making an exception for one specific practitioner. Their hopes lie in the group efforts of the profession; if the professional association remains effective in showing that private practice is of value, then the third parties will continue to reimburse for social work services.

PROFESSIONAL VULNERABILITIES

With increased competition from members of other disciplines for the shrinking population of potential clients and with constant pressure to eliminate social work from managed health care groups, private practitio- ners must hope that their profession remains viable. Although some practitioners seem to think otherwise, the profession and its organiza- tions are necessary to the visibility of private practice.

Without a social work affiliation, private practitioners would have no more influence and credibility than do the many self-proclaimed "psychotherapists" and unregulated counselors that now abound. In addition, they would find it difficult to convince potential clients, third parties, or the public that they have special expertise and high ethical and professional standards.

Unfortunately, many private practitioners do not seem convinced that their careers are intertwined with the fortunes of the profession. Their personal efforts are devoted more to convincing potential clients that they have worthwhile services to offer; they have little concern for the well-being of the profession as a whole. A high proportion are not NASW members, and many do not belong to any other social work organization. Some private practitioners who retain NASW membership contribute little more than their annual dues. In the long run, this isolation is self-defeating. Their lack of support diminishes the profession's potential. This in turn weakens the profession's clout with licensing boards and third-party groups and minimizes some of the marketability of the individual private practitioner. Even with the support of every private practitioner, the profession will have a difficult time achieving its goals.

GOALS FOR THE FUTURE OF PRIVATE PRACTICE

No matter how weak or strong a professional association is, the profession's services would have little appeal to private consumers and third parties unless the profession could show that its members adhered to high standards. Social workers in private practice would have little incentive for remaining in the profession if its standards were minimal or unenforced. Therefore, private practitioners, working through the professional association, have a great stake in further upgrading professional standards, improving quality controls, and developing the way their practice is publicly regulated.

As these goals are achieved, there is greater likelihood that consumers will continue to seek private practitioners' services and that third parties will be inclined to help finance them. There is a bright future for social work's private practice sector, especially if it can effectively demonstrate to consumers and insurers that it has reached its goals of improved standards and quality controls. Great efforts have been made, and many successes have already been achieved by the profession in the past few years toward this end. However, there is still much to be done. Consumers and those who pay for professional services will question any practitioner who cannot demonstrate that such standards exist. From the private practitioner's viewpoint, five major quality assurance objectives must still be accomplished. Implicit in each objective is the belief that their achievement will benefit the profession as well as private practitioners.

Objective 1: Strengthen Existing Licensing Laws

The elusive goal of meaningful public regulation for social work practice in every state still must be reached. Even though every state but Wisconsin provides for legal regulation of social workers, the requirements are neither uniform not universally mandatory. If their deficiencies remain, consumers and third parties will not continue their endorsement. Members of NASW and the National Federation of Societies for Clinical Social Work have been active in every state in trying to improve the existing licensing statutes. They have developed a model statute that is clear, useful, and enforceable. Some state lawmakers have used it, or many of its provisions, with good results.

However, many of the state licensing laws that now exist were written before such a model was available, or they were developed before the profession and its practice were clearly defined. Thus some of these statutes are poorly written, unenforceable, and virtually useless, except as public relations devices (Hardcastle, 1990). Many need to be clarified and strengthened. They need to include requirements for competency testing, reexaminations, mandatory continuing education, and explicated sanctions for those who violate these statutes. Private practitioners probably have a higher stake in achieving this goal than agency-based colleagues. Therefore, private practitioners have a greater obligation to work on improved licensing standards.

Objective 2: Use Competency Exams

Many state regulations to license social workers have no provision for testing whether applicants have the knowledge to do the job or not. If a profession is to have much credibility, it must tell the public that it distinguishes between those who are qualified for membership and those who are not. The licensing provisions of most other professions use competency tests as well as education and experience to qualify for membership. These requirements permit them to make the claim, whether or not it is valid, that all their members have proved to have a certain type and degree of knowledge. To get a social work license in many states, a social worker who has graduated from an accredited school of social work need only apply, pay the fee, and perhaps provide a letter of recommendation from a supervisor or colleague. Some people who have held social work jobs for many years can even be excused from the requirement to graduate from an accredited school of social work.

One historical reason for the delay in getting exams built into licensing requirements has been that the profession has had a disparate membership. There are so many different kinds of social workers—with various levels of training and experience and various areas of expertise—that one test for all of them seemed to some to be unfair.

By now, this argument should be vitiated by the exams and procedures that have been developed under the sponsorship of the American Association of State Social Work Boards. These exams are now in use in most of the states that formally test social workers. They use the multiple-choice question format, the same format used to test all the other human services professions (Biggerstaff & Eisenberg, 1990). Thyer (1990) pointed out these tests have not been empirically validated by objective investigators yet. Nevertheless, they hold more promise for achieving their goal than anything the profession has had to date.

Objective 3: Eliminate "Grandparenting"

Another deficiency in nearly all of the state licensing laws is their inclusion of some people who may not be qualified to be licensed social workers. Many social workers who had established themselves in the profession before a certain date were not required to fulfill all the criteria for membership that were applied to newer members. Such "grandparent" social workers were excused from competency exams. The rationale—that veteran social workers have proved their knowledge through years of past experience—is unconvincing. If social workers actually believe this (and it is hard to believe that many do), it certainly does not mean that consumer groups do.

So why do grandparent exclusions exist? One suspects that a latent reason for grandparenting is to protect more experienced social workers from the embarrassment of failing the exams. Some advocates of the grandparent exclusion have argued that competency tests are not valid indicators of a worker's actual competence. If this is a valid concern, it should be equally valid for newer social workers. However, most grandparented social workers seem to want the tests to remain, but only for others (Barker, 1988a). The profession's leadership is still dominated by social workers who have been grandparented, so they may not want to change this requirement. But as long as it continues to exist, it makes it that much more difficult for social workers to claim rigor in their quality controls.

Objective 4: Require Continuing Education

The fact that a private social work practitioner once met qualifications for a license does not demonstrate that the worker is currently up-to-date on new social work knowledge. Most other professions have long demonstrated their members' continuing competence and knowledge through mandatory continuing education. Continuing education may not necessarily prove continuing competence. Nevertheless, it is a tangible sign that the professional wishes to keep current with the available knowledge (Seelig, 1990). These other professions require their members (through membership rules and licensing laws) to take a certain number of qualified courses within a specified time.

Some professional groups keep computerized records of the number of formal continuing education unit (CEU) credits each of their members has acquired; when a member applies for renewal, their CEU credits are scrutinized. If they have not obtained sufficient credits, they are put on probation until they have fulfilled the requirement. This record keeping is not expensive for a professional group because its costs are covered by the member's renewal fees.

There is little that is equivalent in social work. Few states require continuing education as part of their licensing requirements. Fewer still require it and are able to enforce the requirement. NASW requires its clinical members to maintain continuing education; however, it keeps no records of a worker's CEUs and takes the worker's word for it that the proper amount of continuing education has been achieved.

Objective 5: Establish Periodic Reexaminations

Whether or not a professional can demonstrate that the prescribed amount of continuing education has been achieved, there also needs to be a way to show that the material was actually learned. All dynamic professions have an expanding knowledge base and improved technology, and the credibility of the profession is largely contingent on the ability to show that its members are current. If there is no way to demonstrate that a member is still competent, the consumer may assume that the profession is stagnant.

Periodic reexaminations are the customary way to prove that one has retained competence. Even people who want to keep driving their cars must demonstrate continued competence in most states. Other professions, through their professional associations as well as through state licensing, require proof of continued competence and use exams every five to 10 years after the first competency tests have been passed.

In most states, there is no social work equivalent. Yet there is no reason why the same tests for initial entry into the profession or the specialty could not be given to experienced social workers at least once every decade. Obviously, passing the exam does not in itself prove that the person is competent to do social work—and failing it or not retaking it does not prove the person is no longer competent—but it has some value in providing assurances for the consumer.

Other Objectives

There are, of course, many other objectives that private social work practitioners could seek and have sought in order to improve their position. Many have advocated that private practice be restricted to those with advanced social work degrees or special additional training. This requirement would counter the argument raised by some competing professionals that social workers should not be patronized or reimbursed by third parties because they lack the high level of training that is required of other professional groups.

Many practitioners have advocated that the profession develop fairly autonomous subspecialties for practitioners who want to provide particular clinical services. They argue that they have no way at present to demonstrate that they are competent to provide valuable services. Many private practitioners advocate a closer, more mutually supportive relationship with agency-based colleagues than now exists. They argue that the well-being of private practitioners and that of all other social workers will be improved with more mutual support and respect.

These objectives, however, are controversial, and efforts to achieve them will distract from the far more immediate ones listed above. The five objectives deserve priority because failure to achieve them in the near future could seriously impair the prospects for social work and its private practice.

CONCLUSION

Exciting and challenging days lie ahead for social work and its private practitioners. The excitement will come from effectively competing with other professions so that social work can continue to provide its valuable services in private as well as agency practice. The challenge will be in finding ways to upgrade quality assurances so that competition can occur. It is, of course, always easier to say what ought to be done than to do it. But it seems likely that quality assurance efforts—upgraded licensing, better competency testing, elimination of grandparenting, continuing education requirements, and periodic reexaminations—will receive more serious attention by all social workers as the competition continues to intensify. If social workers redouble their efforts to demonstrate the value and quality of their services, the prospects for the profession are encouraging, and social work can continue to provide worthy and effective assistance for the problems that plague the natural and human environment.

BIBLIOGRAPHY

Abell, N., & McDonell, J. R. (1990). Preparing for practice: Motivations, expectations and aspirations of the MSW class of 1990. *Journal of Social Work Education, 26*(1), 57–64.

Abramowitz, M. (1986). The privatization of the welfare state: A review. *Social Work, 31,* 257–264.

Alexander, C. (1976). *Testimony to Subcommittee on Comprehensive Coverage.* New York: Health Insurance Association of America.

Alexander, M. P. (1987). Why social workers enter private practice: A study of motivations and attitudes. *Journal of Independent Social Work, 1*(3), 7–18.

American Association for Marriage and Family Therapy, Ethics Committee. (1991). *Third party insurance guidelines.* Washington, DC: Author.

American Association of Social Workers. (1926). *American Association of Social Workers.* New York: Author.

American Board of Examiners in Clinical Social Work. (1989). *1989/90 Diplomate directory.* Silver Spring, MD: Author.

American Home Assurance Co. (1987). *Malpractice claims against social workers.* Amityville, NY: American Professional Agency.

American Psychiatric Association. (1987). *Diagnostic and statistical manual of mental disorders* (3rd ed., rev.). Washington, DC: Author.

American Psychological Association. (1989). *Ethical principles of psychologists.* Washington, DC: Author.

Andrews, J. (1987). Social work public image building: "East Side/West Side" revisited. *Social Service Review, 61,* 484–497.

Antler, S. (1987). Professional liability and malpractice. In A. Minahan (Ed.-in-chief), *Encyclopedia of social work* (18th ed., pp. 346–351). Silver Spring, MD: National Association of Social Workers.

Arches, J. (1991). Social structure, burnout, and job satisfaction. *Social Work, 36,* 202–207.

Association assists members in litigation on right to practice. (1981, November). *NASW News,* p. 10.

Bailis, S. S., Stone, S. P., & Bailis, L. N. (1990). Marketing social work services. In L. Ginsberg, S. Khinduka, J. H. Hall, F. Ross-Sheriff, & A. Hartman (Eds.),

Encyclopedia of social work (18th ed., 1990 suppl., pp. 203–217). Silver Spring, MD: NASW Press.

Barker, R. L. (1982). *The business of psychotherapy: Private practice administration for therapists, counselors, and social workers.* New York: Columbia University Press.

Barker, R. L. (1983). Supply side economics in private psychotherapy practice: Some ominous and encouraging trends. *Psychotherapy in Private Practice, 1,* 71–81.

Barker, R. L. (1984). The Tarasoff paradox: Confidentiality and the duty to warn. *Social Thought, 10*(4), 3–12.

Barker, R. L. (1986a). Fee splitting: A growing ethical problem. *Journal of Independent Social Work, 1*(2), 1–5.

Barker, R. L. (1986b). *The resource book: Directory of organizations, associations, self-help groups, and hotlines for mental health and human services professionals and their clients.* New York: Haworth.

Barker, R. L. (1986c). Spelling out the rules and goals: The worker-client contract. *Journal of Independent Social Work, 1*(2), 67–78.

Barker, R. L. (1987a). The affiliations of independent social workers: How much is too much independence? *Journal of Independent Social Work, 1*(4), 1–7.

Barker, R. L. (1987b). "Client dumping": Some ethical and legal considerations. *Journal of Independent Social Work, 2*(1), 1–7.

Barker, R. L. (1987c). Private and proprietary services. In A. Minahan (Ed.-in-chief), *Encyclopedia of social work* (18th ed., pp. 329–333). Silver Spring, MD: National Association of Social Workers.

Barker, R. L. (1987d). Sliding fee scales: A return to the means test? *Journal of Independent Social Work, 1*(3), 7–18.

Barker, R. L. (1987e). To record or not to record: Now it's a question. *Journal of Independent Social Work, 2*(2), 1–6.

Barker, R. L. (1988a). It's time to retire grandfather! *Journal of Independent Social Work, 3*(2), 1–9.

Barker, R. L. (1988b). Just whose code of ethics should the independent practitioner follow? *Journal of Independent Social Work, 2*(4), 1–6.

Barker, R. L. (1988c). Obstacles to obtaining health insurance following social work treatment: The spectre of the M.I.B. *Journal of Independent Social Work, 2*(3), 1–4.

Barker, R. L. (1989). Independent social workers and legal training. *Journal of Independent Social Work, 3*(3), 1–6.

Barker, R. L. (1990a). Are MSW degrees sufficient for today's psychotherapy practices? *Journal of Independent Social Work, 5*(1), 1–9.

Barker, R. L. (1990b). Continuing education: A neglected component of competent practice. *Journal of Independent Social Work, 4*(3), 1–6.

Barker, R. L. (1991). *The social work dictionary* (2nd ed.). Silver Spring, MD: NASW Press.

Barker, R. L., & Branson, D. L. (in press). *Forensic social work.* New York: Haworth.

Bartlett, H. M. (1958). Toward clarification and improvement of social work practice. *Social Work, 3*(2), 3–9.

Baumback, C., & Lawyer, K. (1989). *How to organize and operate a small business* (8th ed.). Englewood Cliffs, NJ: Prentice Hall.

Belser, E. (1987). Marketing: A survival tool for private social work practitioners. *Journal of Independent Social Work, 2*(2), 47–56.

Belser, E. (1989). *Insurance reimbursement manual for licensed clinical social workers in California.* Sacramento, CA: National Association of Social Workers, California Chapter.

Bentrup, W. W. (1964). The profession and the means test. *Social Work, 9,* 10–17.

Berliner, A. K. (1989). Misconduct in social work practice. *Social Work, 43,* 69–72.

Bernstein, B. E. (1977). Privileged communications to the social worker. *Social Work, 26,* 239–244.

Bernstein, B. E. (1978). Malpractice: An ogre on the horizon. *Social Work, 23,* 264–268.

Besharov, D. J. (1985). *The vulnerable social worker: Liability for serving children and families.* Silver Spring, MD: National Association of Social Workers.

Besharov, D. J., & Besharov, S. H. (1987). Teaching about liability. *Social Work, 32,* 517–521.

Biegel, J. K., & Earle, R. H. (1990). *Successful private practice in the 1990s.* New York: Brunner/Mazel.

Biggerstaff, M., & Eisenberg, R. (1990). *Summary report: Job analysis verification study.* Culpeper, VA: American Association of State Social Work Boards.

Blumenstein, H. (1988). Survival issues challenging family agencies. *Social Casework, 69,* 107–115.

Bogolub, E. R. (1986). Tape recorders in clinical sessions: Deliberate and fortuitous effects. *Clinical Social Work Journal, 14,* 349–360.

Borenzweig, H. (1977). Who passes the California licensing examinations? *Social Work, 22,* 173–177.

Borenzweig, H. (1981). Agency vs. private practice: Similarities and differences. *Social Work, 26,* 239–244.

Borys, D. S., & Pope, K. S. (1989). Dual relationships between therapist and client: A national study of psychologists, psychiatrists and social workers. *Professional Psychology: Research and Practice, 20,* 283–293.

Brawley, E. A. (1985–86). The mass media: A vital adjunct. *Administration in Social Work, 3,* 337–348.

Briggs, T. L. (1961). *Private practice* (Memorandum to chapter chairmen, Document No. 3832/1/5). New York: National Association of Social Workers.

Briggs, T. L. (1975). A critique of the NASW manpower statement. *Journal of Education for Social Work, 10*(1), 5–19.

Broadsky, S. (1988). Fear of litigation in mental health professionals. *Criminal Justice and Behavior, 15,* 492–500.

Broman, C. L., Neighbors, H. W., & Taylor, R. J. (1989). Race differences in seeking help from social workers. *Journal of Sociology and Social Welfare, 16*(3), 109–123.

Brooks, D. K., & Gerstein, L. H. (1990). Counselor credentials and interprofessional collaboration. *Journal of Counseling and Development, 68,* 477–484.

Brown, P. M. (1989). Goals and goal attainment: Differences between private practice and agency workers. *Journal of Independent Social Work, 4*(1), 19–35.

Brown, P. M. (1990a). Black social workers in private practice: Challenges and dilemmas. *Journal of Independent Social Work, 5*(1), 53–68.

Brown, P. M. (1990b). Social workers in private practice: What are they really doing? *Clinical Social Work Journal, 18*(4), 56–71.

Browning, C. H. (1989). *Private practice handbook: The tools and techniques for successful practice development* (2nd ed.). Los Alamitos, CA: Duncliffs.

Bullis, R. K. (1990). Cold comfort from the Supreme Court: Limited liability protection for social workers. *Social Work, 35,* 364–366.

Butler, A. C. (1990). A reevaluation of social work students' career interests. *Journal of Social Work Education, 26*(1), 45–51.

Butler, B. B. (1990). Job satisfaction: Management's continuing challenge. *Social Work, 35,* 112–117.

Bynum, P. (1991). Marketing social service programs using political campaign technology. *Computers in Human Services, 8*(1), 67–72.

Cherry, A., Rothman, B., & Skolnick, L. (1989). Licensing as a dilemma for social work education. *Journal of Social Work Education, 26,* 268–275.

Chodorkoff, B. (1990). Providing psychotherapy in private practice. *Generations, 14*(1), 27–30.

Cloward, R., & Epstein, I. (1965). Social welfare's disengagement from the poor. In M. Zald (Ed.), *Social welfare institutions* (pp. 623–644). New York: John Wiley & Sons.

Cohen, D. (1987). Rural area private practice. *Psychotherapy in Private Practice, 5*(4), 41–52.

Cohen, M. (1966a). The emergence of private practice in social work. *Social Problems, 14,* 84–93.

Cohen, M. (1966b). Some characteristics of social workers in private practice. *Social Work, 11*(4), 69–77.

Cohen, N. (1956). A changing profession in a changing world. *Social Work, 1*(4), 12–19.

Committee on Professional Standards, National Federation of Societies for Clinical Social Work. (1987). Clinical social work code of ethics. *Clinical Social Work, 15*(1), 4–6.

Consumer Reports. (1991). *Guide to income tax preparation*. Mt. Vernon, NY: Consumers Union.

Conte, H. R., & Karasu, T. B. (1990). Malpractice in psychotherapy: An overview. *American Journal of Psychotherapy, 44,* 252–256.

Corcoran, K. (1991). In defense of contracts and the caveats of covenants. *Social Work, 36,* 183–197.

Coulton, C. (1987). Quality assurance. In A. Minahan (Ed.-in-chief), *Encyclopedia of social work* (18th ed., pp. 443–445). Silver Spring, MD: National Association of Social Workers.

Croxton, T. A. (1988). Caveats on contract. *Social Work, 33,* 169–172.

Cunningham, G. (1990). Social work and employee assistance programs. *Social Thought, 16*(1), 34–40.

De Berry, S., & Baskin, R. (1989). Termination criteria in psychotherapy: A comparison of private and public practice. *American Journal of Psychotherapy, 43*(1), 45–53.

Demeo, W. J. (1990). *A comparative study of differences in personal style of social workers in independent practice and social workers in organizational settings.* Unpublished doctoral dissertation, Catholic University of America, Washington, DC.

Deutch, J. A. (1987). Mary E. Richmond: A compassionate scholar was in our midst. *Journal of Independent Social Work, 2*(1), 45–56.

Dhooper, S. S., Royse, D. D., & Wolfe, L. C. (1990). Does social work education make a difference? *Social Work, 35,* 57–61.

Dhooper, S. S., & Tranh, V. T. (1987). Social work with Asian Americans. *Journal of Independent Social Work, 1*(4), 51–62.

Dressel, P., Waters, W., Sweat, M., Clayton, O., & Chandler-Clayton, A. (1988). Deprofessionalization, proletarianization and social welfare work. *Journal of Sociology and Social Welfare, 1,* 113–131.

Drucker, R., & King, D. (1973). Private practice services for low-income people. *Social Work, 18,* 115–118.

Dubin, S. S. (1981). Obsolescence or lifelong education: A choice for the professional. *American Psychologist, 36,* 486.

Dumont, M. P. (1990). Managed care, managed people, and community mental health. *American Journal of Orthopsychiatry, 60,* 166–168.

Edwards, R. L., & Green, R. K. (1983). Mandatory continuing education: Time for reevaluation. *Social Work, 28,* 43–48.

Enright, M. F. (1988). Small town independent practice: New professional opportunities. *Psychotherapy in Private Practice, 8*(1), 3–10.

Farber, B. A. (1990). Burnout in psychotherapists: Incidence, types and trends. *Psychotherapy in Private Practice, 8*(1), 35–44.

Feldman, D. (1977). Debate on private practice. *Social Work, 22,* 3.

First, M. B., Williams, J.B.W., & Spitzer, R. L. (1988). *DTREE: The electronic DSMIIIR.* Washington, DC: American Psychiatric Association.

Fizdale, R. (1959). Formalizing the relationship between private practitioners and social agencies. *Social Casework, 40,* 539–544.

Fizdale, R. (1961). The rising demand for private casework services. In *Social welfare forum, 1961* (pp. 194–204). New York: National Conference on Social Welfare/Columbia University Press.

Flanzraich, M. J. (1985). *The importance of social origins in preprofessional experiences in determining whether social workers become private practitioners.* Unpublished doctoral dissertation, Columbia University, New York.

Flynn, J. P. (1987). Licensing and regulation of social work services. In A. Minahan (Ed.-in-chief), *Encyclopedia of social work* (18th ed., pp. 43–47). Silver Spring, MD: National Association of Social Workers.

Foreman, B., & Foreman, K. (1983). Market concepts for psychotherapists. *Psychotherapy in Private Practice, 1,* 24–31.

Freudenberger, H. (1983). Hazards of psychotherapeutic practice. *Psychotherapy in Private Practice, 1,* 83–91.

Frisman, L. K. (1986). *Private practice and the mental health professional: An analysis of factors influencing career opportunities and decisions of clinical social workers.* Unpublished doctoral dissertation, Brandeis University, Waltham, MA.

Frisman, L. K. (1990). Social workers and private practice opportunities. *Administration and Policy in Mental Health, 18*(1), 65–78.

Gerhart, U., & Brooks, A. (1985). Social workers and malpractice: Law, attitudes and knowledge. *Social Casework, 66,* 411–416.

Gillespie, D. (Ed.). (1986). *Burnout among social workers.* New York: Haworth.

Ginsberg, L. (1990). Selected statistical review. In L. Ginsberg, S. Khinduka, J. Hall, F. Ross-Sheriff, & A. Hartman (Eds.), *Encyclopedia of social work* (18th ed., 1990 suppl., pp. 256–288). Silver Spring, MD: NASW Press.

Gitlin, M. J. (1990). *The psychotherapist's guide to psychopharmacology.* New York: Free Press.

Goldmeier, J. (1986). Private practice and the purchase of services: Who are the practitioners? *American Journal of Orthopsychiatry, 56*(1), 89–102.

Goldmeier, J. (1990). Combining agency and private practice. *Families in Society, 71,* 614–619.

Goleman, D. (1985, April 30). Social workers vault into a leading role in psychotherapy. *New York Times,* p. 1.

Golton, M. A. (1971). Private practice in social work. In R. Morris (Ed.-in-chief), *Encyclopedia of social work* (16th ed., p. 952). New York: National Association of Social Workers.

Goodman, N. (1960). Are there differences between fee and nonfee cases? *Social Work, 4*(4), 46–52.

Goodman, N. (1971). Fee charging. In R. Morris (Ed.-in-chief), *Encyclopedia of social work* (16th ed., pp. 467–473). New York: National Association of Social Workers.

Green, R. K., & Cox, G. (1978). Social work and malpractice: A converging course. *Social Work, 23,* 100–105.

Grosser, R., & Block, S. (1983). Clinical social work practice in the private sector: A survey. *Clinical Social Work, 11,* 245–262.

Hahn, A. P. (1989). Private social work practice in a legal setting: A feasibility study. *Journal of Independent Social Work, 3*(3), 17–35.

Hait, J., & Tyrell, K. N. (1991). Are we ethical: Avoiding third party fraud. *WAMFT [Washington Association of Marital and Family Therapists] News, 9*(3), 1.

Hardcastle, D. A. (1977). Public regulation of social work. *Social Work, 22,* 14–20.

Hardcastle, D. A. (1990). Legal regulation of social work. In L. Ginsberg, S. Khinduka, J. Hall, F. Ross-Sheriff, & A. Hartman (Eds.), *Encyclopedia of social work* (18th ed., 1990 suppl., pp. 203–217). Silver Spring, MD: NASW Press.

Hardcastle, D. A., & Brownstein, C. D. (1989). Private practitioners: Profile and motivations for independent practice. *Journal of Independent Social Work, 4*(1), 7–18.

Hardman, D. G. (1978). Mr. Pringle's shingle. *Social Work, 23,* 3–4.

Hartman, A. (1990). A profession chasing its tail—Again. *Social Work, 35,* 99–100.

Hass-Wilson, D. (1989). Employment choices and earnings of social workers: Comparing private practice and salaried employment. *Inquiry, 26,* 182–190.

Hass-Wilson, D. (1990). Quality signals and patient referrals in the market for social workers' services. *Administration and Policy in Mental Health, 18*(1), 55–64.

Health Insurance Association of America. (1990). *1988–89 Sourcebook of health insurance data.* Washington, DC: Author.

Hellman, I. D., & T. L. Morrison. (1987). Practice setting and type of caseload as factors in psychotherapist stress. *Psychotherapy, 24,* 427–433.

Himle, D. P., Jayaratne, S., & Thyness, T. (1991). Buffering effects of four social support types on burnout among social workers. *Social Work Research and Abstracts, 27*(1), 22–27.

Hines, M. H. (1988). How to fail in private practice: 13 Easy steps. *Journal of Counseling and Development, 67,* 253–254.

Holland, T. P., & Petchers, M. K. (1987). Organizations: Context for social service delivery. In A. Minahan (Ed.-in-chief), *Encyclopedia of social work* (18th ed., pp. 204–216). Silver Spring, MD: National Association of Social Workers.

Howe, E. (1980). Public professions and the private model of professionalism. *Social Work, 25,* 179–191.

Internal Revenue Service. (1991). *Tax guide for small businesses.* Washington, DC: U.S. Government Printing Office.

Iverson, R. R. (1987). Licensure: Help or hindrance to women social workers? *Social Casework, 68,* 229–233.

Jackson, J. A. (1987). Clinical social work and peer review: A professional leap ahead. *Social Work, 32,* 213–220.

Jacobs, D. H. (1986). On negotiating fees with psychotherapy and psychoanalytic patients. In D. Kreuger (Ed.), *The last taboo: Money as symbol and reality in psychotherapy and psychoanalysis* (pp. 35–72). New York: Brunner/Mazel.

Jayaratne, S., & Chess, W. (1984). Job satisfaction, burnout, and turnover: A national study. *Social Work, 29,* 448–453.

Jayaratne, S., Davis-Sacks, M. L., & Chess, W. A. (1991). Private practice may be good for your health and well-being. *Social Work, 35,* 224–229.

Jayaratne, S., Siefert, K., & Chess, W. A. (1988). Private and agency practitioners: Some data and observations. *Social Service Review, 62,* 324–336.

Jewitt, D. R., & Thompson, L. E. (1989). *The private practitioner, the client, and the insurance company: A handbook for clinical social workers.* Salem, OR: National Association of Social Workers, Oregon Chapter, Clinical Council.

Johnson, D. A., & Huff, D. (1987). Licensing exams: How valid are they? *Social Work, 32,* 159–162.

Johnson, D. A., & Huff, D. (1988). Testing: How important is it to licensing for social work practice? *Journal of Independent Social Work, 3*(2), 9–23.

Jones, J. & Alcabes, A. (1989). Clients don't sue: The invulnerable social worker. *Social Casework, 70,* 414–420.

Karger, H. J. (1989). Private practice: The fast track to the shingle. *Social Work, 34,* 566–567.

Kelley, P., & Alexander, P. (1985). Part-time private practice: Practical and ethical considerations. *Social Work, 30,* 254–258.

Kelley, P., Alexander, P., & Cullinane, M. A. (1986). Ethical issues in private practice. *Journal of Independent Social Work, 1*(2), 5–18.

Kenemore, T. K. (1987). Negotiating with clients: A study of clinical practice experience. *Social Service Review, 61*(1), 132–143.

Kerman, E. J., & Drob, S. L. (1987). Tarasoff decision: A decade later dilemma still faces psychotherapists. *American Journal of Psychotherapy, 41,* 20–42.

Kettner, P. M., & Martin, L. L. (1988). Purchase of service contracting and private practice. *Journal of Independent Social Work, 3*(2), 77–92.

Kirk, S. A., & Kutchins, H. (1988). Deliberate misdiagnosis in mental health practice. *Social Service Review, 62,* 225–237.

Knight, B. M. (1991). Using hypnosis in private social work practice. *Journal of Independent Social Work, 5*(2), 43–52.

Koeske, G. F., & Koeske, R. D. (1989). Work load and burnout: Can social support and perceived accomplishment help? *Social Work, 34,* 243–248.

Kreuger, L. W. (1986). Microcomputers in private practice. *Journal of Independent Social Work, 1*(2), 55–66.

Kreuger, L. W. (1987). Microcomputer software for independent social work practice. *Journal of Independent Social Work, 1*(23), 45–58.

Kurzman, P. A. (1976). Private practice as a social work function. *Social Work, 21,* 363–368.

Kutchins, H. (1991). The fiduciary relationship: The legal basis for social workers' responsibility to clients. *Social Work, 36,* 106–113.

Kutchins, H., & Kirk, S. A. (1987). DSM-III and malpractice. *Social Work, 32,* 205–211.

Land, H. (1988). The impact of licensing on social work practice: Values, ethics and choices. *Journal of Independent Social Work, 2*(4), 87–96.

Lantz, J. (1987). The use of Frankl's concepts in family therapy. *Journal of Independent Social Work, 2*(2), 65–80.

Lechnyr, R. J. (1984). Clinical social work psychotherapy and insurance coverage. *Clinical Social Work Journal, 12*(1), 69–77.

LeCroy, C. W., & Rank, M. R. (1986). Factors associated with burnout in the social services: An exploratory study. *Journal of Social Service Research, 10,* 23–29.

Lee, J. (1983). Weeping for the lost profession: Social work in transition. *Jewish Social Work Forum, 19,* 20–32.

Leon, J. (1990). Health care financing and service delivery. In L. Ginsberg, S. Khinduka, J. Hall, F. Ross-Sheriff, & A. Hartman (Eds.), *Encyclopedia of social work* (18th ed., 1990 suppl., pp. 135–158). Silver Spring, MD: NASW Press.

Lesse, S. (1990). Psychiatrists: Don't look behind you; someone may be catching up. *American Journal of Psychotherapy, 44*(4), 1–4.

Levenstein, S. (1964). *Private practice in social casework: A profession's changing pattern.* New York: Columbia University Press.

Levin, A. M. (1976). Private practice is alive and well. *Social Work, 21,* 356–362.

Levin, A. M. (1983). *The private practice of psychotherapy.* New York: Free Press.

Levin, A. M. (1988). How do you know if you're ready to become a private social work practitioner? *Journal of Independent Social Work, 2*(4), 7–18.

Levin, R., & Leginsky, P. (1989). Independent social work practice in Canada. *The Social Worker/Le Travailleur Social, 57*(3), 155–159.

Levin, R., & Leginsky, P. (1990). The independent social worker as entrepreneur. *Journal of Independent Social Work, 5*(1), 89–100.

Lewis, K. N., & Lewis, D. A. (1985). Pretherapy information, counselor influence, and value similarity: Impact on female clients' reactions. *Counseling and Values, 29,* 151–163.

Lieberman, A. A., & Turner, W. M. (1991). Assessing the effect of vendorship on fee setting for social workers: An empirical test. *Social Work Research and Abstracts, 27*(1), 28–33.

Lieberman, F. (1987). Psychotherapy and the clinical social worker. *American Journal of Psychotherapy, 41,* 369–383.

Long, J. M., Machiran, N. M., & Bertell, B. (1986). Biofeedback: An adjunct to social work practice. *Social Work, 31,* 476–478.

Longres, J. F. (1987). Mary Ellen Richmond (1861–1928). In A. Minahan (Ed.-in-Chief), *Encyclopedia of social work* (18th ed., p. 937). Silver Spring, MD: National Association of Social Workers.

Lorish, C. C. (1977). Examining quality assurance systems. *Health and Social Work, 2,* 20–41.

Luborsky, L., Crits-Christoph, P., McLellan, A. T., Woody, G., Piper, W., Liberman, B., Imber, S., & Pilkonis, P. (1986). Do therapists vary much in their success? Findings from outcome studies. *American Journal of Orthopsychiatry, 56,* 501–503.

Lubove, R. (1965). *The professional altruist: The emergence of social work as a career: 1890–1930.* Cambridge, MA: Harvard University Press.

Mackey, R. A., Burek, M., & Charkoudian, S. (1987). The influence of setting on clinical practice. *Journal of Independent Social Work, 2*(1), 33–44.

Magill, R. S. (1989). Working for private business: The experience of eight social agencies. *Social Casework, 70,* 51–56.

Magner, D. K. (1989, January 4). Graduate schools of social work enjoying new boom as adults seek career changes and advanced degrees. *Chronicle of Higher Education,* pp. A33–34.

Mathews, B. (1989). Terminating therapy: Implications for the private practitioner. *Psychotherapy in Private Practice, 7*(3), 29–39.

Matorin, S., Rosenberg, B., Levitt, M., & Rosenblum, S. (1987). Private practice in social work: Readiness and opportunity. *Social Casework, 68,* 31–37.

Meloche, M. (1988). Private practice, or how to go from being an orchestra musician to a soloist. *The Social Worker/Le Travailleur Social, 56*(3), 123–126.

Merck and Co. (1991). *The Merck manual.* Oradell, NJ: Author.

Merle, S. (1962). Some arguments against private practice. *Social Work, 7*(1), 12–17.

Middleman, R. R. (1989). *A study guide for ACSW certification.* Silver Spring, MD: National Association of Social Workers.

Miller, I. (1987). Supervision in social work. In A. Minahan (Ed.-in-Chief), *Encyclopedia of Social Work* (18th ed., pp. 748–756). Silver Spring, MD: National Association of Social Workers.

Miller, P. (1990). Covenant model for professional relationships: An alternative to the contract model. *Social Work, 35,* 121–124.

Minahan, A. (Ed.-in-Chief). (1987). *Encyclopedia of social work* (18th ed.). Silver Spring, MD: National Association of Social Workers.

Moldowsky, S. (1989). Is solo practice really dead? *American Psychologist, 45,* 544–546.

Morris, H. (1991). *Motivations for private practice: An analysis of social workers.* Unpublished doctoral dissertation, Catholic University of America, Washington, DC.

Myers, D. W. (1984). *Establishing and building employee assistance programs.* Westport, CT: Quorum Books.

National Association of Social Workers. (1974). *Handbook on the private practice of social work.* Washington, DC: National Association of Social Workers.

National Association of Social Workers. (1980). *NASW chapter guide for the adjudication of grievances* (rev. ed.). Silver Spring, MD: Author.

National Association of Social Workers. (1982). *Standards for continuing professional education* (Policy Statement No. 10). Silver Spring, MD: Author.

National Association of Social Workers. (1987). *Salaries in social work: A survey report on the salaries of NASW members.* Silver Spring, MD: Author.

National Association of Social Workers. (1990a). *A brief look at managed health care: 1990 Practice update.* Silver Spring, MD: Author.

National Association of Social Workers. (1990b). *Code of ethics.* Silver Spring, MD: Author.

National Association of Social Workers. (1991a). *NASW register of clinical social workers* (6th ed.). Silver Spring, MD: Author.

National Association of Social Workers. (1991b). *Professional social work recognition: Vendorship report.* (No. A41). Silver Spring, MD: Author.

Neale, N. K. (1983). Private practice. In A. Rosenblatt and D. Waldfogel (Eds.), *Handbook of clinical social work.* San Francisco, CA: Jossey-Bass.

Nickerson, C. B. (1986). *Accounting handbook for nonaccountants* (3rd ed.). New York: Van Nostrand Reinhold.

Noll, J. (1974). Needed—A bill of rights for clients. *Professional Psychologist, 5,* 3–12.

Osman, S., & Shueman, S. A. (1988). A guide to the peer review process for clinicians. *Social Work, 33,* 345.

Pardeck, J. T. (1987). Microcomputer technology in private social work practice. *Journal of Independent Social Work, 2*(1), 71–82.

Pawlak, E. J., & Bays, J. (1988). Executive perspectives on part-time private practice. *Administration in Social Work, 12*(1), 1–11.

Peek, J., & Plotkin, C. (1951). Social caseworkers in private practice. *Smith College Studies in Social Work, 21,* 165–197.

Peirce, F. J. (1986). It's scary but I have a night light: Private practice in a small town. *Journal of Independent Social Work, 1*(2), 45–54.

Perlman, H. H. (1955). Psychotherapy and counseling. *Annals of the New York Academy of Sciences, 63,* 319–432.

Perlmutter, F. D., & Adams, C. T. (1990). The voluntary sector and for-profit ventures: The transformation of American social welfare? *Administration in Social Work, 14*(1), 1–14.

Physicians desk reference. (1991). Oradell, NJ: Medical Economics.

Piliavin, I. (1968). Restructuring the provision of social services. *Social Work, 13,* 34–41.

Pines, A., & Aronson, E. (1988). *Career burnout: Causes and cures.* New York: Free Press.

Pines, A., & Kafry, D. (1978). Occupational tedium in the social services. *Social Work, 23,* 499–507.

Pinker, R. (1990). *Social work in an enterprise society.* London: Routledge.

Pruger, R. (1973). The good bureaucrat. *Social Work, 18,* 26–32.

Ranieri, R. F. (1990). Private practice: Readers respond [letter]. *Social Work, 35,* 188.

Reamer, F. G. (1987a). Ethics committee in social work. *Social Work, 32,* 188–192.

Reamer, F. G. (1987b). Informed consent in social work. *Social Work, 32,* 425–429.

Reamer, F. G. (1989). Liability issues in social work supervision. *Social Work, 34,* 445.

Reeser, L. C. (1988). Specialization, professionalization, and social activism. *Journal of Independent Social Work, 2*(4), 43–58.

Reynolds, J. (1987). Social work, survival and the commercialization of health care. *Health and Social Work, 12,* 231–232.

Richmond, M. (1899). *Friendly visiting among the poor.* New York: Macmillan.

Richmond, M. (1917). *Social diagnosis.* New York: Russell Sage Foundation.

Richmond, M. (1922). *What is social casework?* New York: Russell Sage Foundation.

Robertson, H. W., & Jackson, V. H. (1991). *NASW guidelines on the private practice of clinical social work.* Silver Spring, MD: National Association of Social Workers.

Robinowitz, C., & Greenblatt, M. (1980). Continuing certification and continuing education. *American Journal of Psychiatry, 137,* 292–299.

Rockmore, M. (1948). Private practice: An exploratory inquiry. *Survey, 84,* 109–111.

Rosenblatt, A., & Waldfogel, D. (Eds.). (1983). *Handbook of clinical social work.* San Francisco: Jossey-Bass.

Rosenman, L. (1989). Privatisation of social welfare services and social work practice: An overview of the issues. *Australian Social Work, 42*(4), 5–10.

Roth, H. (1983). Independent practice. *Family Therapy News, 14,* 8.

Roth, L., & Meisel, A. (1977). Dangerousness, confidentiality, and the duty to warn. *American Journal of Psychiatry, 134,* 508–511.

Royse, D. (1988). Newspaper exposure, community knowledge of services and marketing: Implications for the private sector. *Journal of Independent Social Work, 2*(4), 19–29.

Royse, D., & Dhooper, S. S. (1988). Social services with cancer patients and their families: Implications for independent social workers. *Journal of Independent Social Work, 2*(3), 63–72.

Rubin, A., & Johnson, P. (1984). Direct practice interests of entering MSW students. *Journal of Education for Social Work, 20*(2), 5–16.

Ryerson, R., & Weller, E. (1947). The private practice of psychiatric social work. *Journal of Psychiatric Social Work, 16,* 110–116.

Samuels, R. (1983). I bought his private practice. *Psychotherapy in Private Practice, 1,* 105–108.

Sancier, B. (1987). Continuing education. In A. Minahan (Ed.-in-Chief), *Encyclopedia of social work* (18th ed., pp. 331–339). Silver Spring, MD: National Association of Social Workers.

Saxton, P. M. (1988). Vendorship for social work: Observations on the maturation of the profession. *Social Work, 33,* 197–201.

Schultz, K. (1988). Money as an issue in therapy. *Journal of Independent Social Work, 3*(1), 7–22.

Seabury, B. A. (1979). Negotiating sound contracts with clients. *Public Welfare, 37*(2), 33–38.

Seabury, B. A. (1987). Contracting and engagement in direct practice. In A. Minahan (Ed.-in-chief), *Encyclopedia of social work* (18th ed., pp. 339–345). Silver Spring, MD: National Association of Social Workers.

Seelig, J. M. (1988a). Drafting a partnership agreement. *Journal of Independent Social Work, 2*(3), 73–80.

Seelig, J. M. (1988b). Social workers in legal partnerships. *Journal of Independent Social Work, 3*(1), 97–102.

Seelig, J. M. (1988c). Tax issues in partnerships. *Journal of Independent Social Work, 3*(2), 107–112.

Seelig, J. M. (1990). Mandatory continuing education. *Journal of Independent Social Work, 4*(3), 75–80.

Seligman, L., & Dougherty, W. (1987). Establishing and maintaining a private practice. *Counseling and Human Development, 19*(5), 1–11.

Shatkin, B. F., Frisman, L. K., & McGuire, T. G. (1986). The effect of vendorship on the distribution of clinical social work services. *Social Service Review, 60,* 437–448.

Sherraden, M. (1990). The business of social work. In L. Ginsberg, S. Khinduka, J. Hall, F. Ross-Sheriff, & A. Hartman (Eds.), *Encyclopedia of social work* (18th ed., 1990 suppl., pp. 51–59). Silver Spring, MD: NASW Press.

Siporin, M. (1961). Private practice of social work: Functional roles and social control. *Social Work, 6,* 52–60.

Skinner, J. (1953). Standards for the private practice of psychotherapy by psychiatric social workers. *Journal of Psychiatric Social Work, 22,* 67–68.

Smaller, M. D. (1985). *Tension amidst commitment: Social workers' perceptions and attitudes toward private practice.* Unpublished doctoral dissertation, University of Chicago.

Smaller, M. D. (1987). Attitudes toward private practice in social work: Examining professional commitment. *Journal of Independent Social Work, 1*(4), 7–19.

Smalley, R. (1954). Can we reconcile generic education and specialized practice? *Journal of Psychiatric Social Work, 23,* 207–214.

Sourcebook 1991–92: Social and health services in the greater New York area. (1991). New York: United Way of New York City and New York Department of Social Services.

Steiner, L. R. (1936). Hanging out a shingle. *Newsletter of the American Association of Psychiatric Social Workers, 6,* 1–8.

Steiner, L. R. (1938). Casework as a private venture. *Family, 19,* 188–196.

Stevens, C. (1991, April 22). An industry that's booming in spite of itself. *Medical Economics,* pp. 47–50.

Stoesz, D. (1989). The gray market: Social consequences of for-profit eldercare. *Journal of Gerontological Social Work, 14*(3/4), 19–34.

Stone, A. (1954). The private practice of social casework. *Social Work Journal, 35,* 61–65.

Tamkin, A. (1976). Adaptability: A paramount asset for private practice. *Professional Psychology, 7,* 661–663.

Tarasoff vs. Regents of University of California. (1976). *California Law Reporter, 14,* 551, p2d 334.

Thyer, B. A. (1990). [Letter to the editor.] *Journal of Social Work Education, 26,* 210–211.

Thyer, B. A., & Biggerstaff, M. A. (1989). *Professional social work, credentialing, and legal regulation.* Springfield, IL: Charles C Thomas.

Turner, F. J. (1978). *Psychosocial therapy: A social work approach.* New York: Free Press.

Turner, F. J. (Ed.). (1984). *Adult psychopathology: A social work perspective.* New York: Free Press.

Turner, F. J. (Ed.). (1989). *Child psychopathology: A social work perspective.* New York: Free Press.

Turner, F. J. (Ed.). (in press). *Mental health in older people: A social work perspective.* New York: Free Press.

Turner, W. (1987). *The private practice of psychotherapy: An example of the impact of social work vendorship in two New England states.* Unpublished doctoral dissertation, Brandeis University, Waltham, MA.

U.S. Department of Health and Human Services. (1989). *Health resources studies: Report on health personnel in the United States.* Washington, DC: U.S. Government Printing Office.

VandeCreek, L., & Knapp, S. (1989). *Tarasoff and beyond: legal and clinical considerations in the treatment of life-endangering patients.* Sarasota, FL: Professional Resource Exchange.

van Wormer, K. (1990). Private practice with the terminally ill. *Journal of Independent Social Work, 5*(1), 23–39.

Walfish, S., & Covert, D. L. (1989). Beginning and maintaining an independent practice: A delphi poll. *Professional Psychology: Research and Practice, 20*(1), 54–55.

Walfish, S., & Janzen, L. (1988). Financial outpatient mental health care: How much does insurance actually help? *American Journal of Orthopsychiatry, 58,* 470–481.

Wallace, M. E. (1982). Private practice: A nationwide study. *Social Work, 27,* 262–267.

Walsh, J. A. (1987). Burnout and values in the social service profession. *Social Casework, 68,* 279–283.

Walter, C. A., & Greif, G. L. (1988). To do or not to do: Social work education for private practice. *Journal of Independent Social Work, 2*(3), 17–24.

Watkins, S. A., & Watkins, J. C. (1989). Negligent endangerment: Malpractice in the clinical context. *Journal of Independent Social Work, 3*(3), 35–50.

Webster, B., & Perry, R. L. (1990). *Complete Social Security handbook* (2nd ed.). New York: Dodd, Mead.

Weinrach, S. G. (1989). Guidelines for clients of the private practitioner: Committing the structure to print. *Journal of Counseling and Development, 67,* 299–300.

Weiss, F. (1989). Private social work practice with obese adult clients. *Journal of Independent Social Work, 5*(2), 65–72.

Weitz, R. (1983). I sold my private practice. *Psychotherapy in Private Practice, 1*(1), 101–105.

Whittington, R. (1985). House calls in private practice. *Social Work, 30,* 254–259.

Whittington, R. (1986). The new friendly visitors: A rediscovered role for independent social workers. *Journal of Independent Social Work, 1*(1), 65–74.

Whittington, R. (1988). Pricing, charging, collecting. *Journal of Independent Social Work, 3*(1), 83–92.

Wilcoxon, S. A. (1991). Clarifying expectations in therapy relationships: Suggestions for written guidelines. *Journal of Independent Social Work, 5*(2), 65–71.

Williams, L. F., & Hopps, J. G. (1990). The social work labor force: Current perspectives and future trends. In L. Ginsberg, S. Khinduka, J. Hall, F. Ross-Sheriff, & A. Hartman (Eds.), *Encyclopedia of social work* (18th ed., 1990 suppl., pp. 289–306). Silver Spring, MD: NASW Press.

Woody, R. H. (1989). *Business success in mental health practice: Modern marketing, management, and legal strategies.* San Francisco: Jossey-Bass.

World Health Organization. (1990). *International classification of diseases* (11th ed.). New York: Author.

Zastrow, C. (1990a). Mental health issues in the 1990s. *Journal of Independent Social Work, 5*(1), 9–22.

Zastrow, C. (1990b). Social workers and salesworkers: Similarities and differences. *Journal of Independent Social Work, 4*(3), 7–16.

Zastrow, C. (1991). Safeguarding rights in NASW adjudication of grievances. *Journal of Independent Social Work, 5*(2), 31–42.

Zastrow, C., Dotson, V., & Koch, M. (1986). The neuro-linguistic programming treatment approach. *Journal of Independent Social Work, 1*(1), 29–38.

APPENDIXES

APPENDIX A: SAMPLE CONTRACTS

On the following pages are samples of contracts (or "letters of agreement") that private social work practitioners use with their clients. They include contracts for (1) individual adult clients, (2) couples, (3) clients who are adolescents or children, (4) parents of children in treatment, (5) families, and (6) individual members of therapy groups.

Although modified versions of these contracts have been in extensive use by social workers for years and have been reviewed by attorneys in several states, they are presented here not as final documents but as rough guidelines and catalysts for thought. Social workers in private practice may want to modify these contracts to meet their individual circumstances. Varying state laws and unique needs suggest that periodic review of the contracts with one's lawyer is not only prudent but essential.

SAMPLE CONTRACT FOR INDIVIDUAL ADULT CLIENTS

LETTER OF AGREEMENT

Welcome. I hope your time here is worthwhile. I'm giving you this letter to answer some questions you may have. It will tell you what to expect of our meetings and how we should work together.

Please go over this carefully. Feel free to ask me anything about it whenever you have questions. You are welcome to show it to others in your family or other professionals you trust.

At the end of this letter is a place for us to sign our names. Signing means we agree with all the points in this letter. There is also space for us to write down the goals we hope to accomplish together. We can review these goals as we go along. We can change them anytime we want if, together, it seems like a good idea. Now, let's discuss what you and I should understand and do to make our meetings worthwhile.

SEE YOUR DOCTOR. Please get a physical examination from your personal physician as soon as possible. This is important to make sure that none of the problems to be discussed are the result of physical health difficulties. Because I am not a physician, I cannot know if you have physical conditions that might be related to our work.

Please tell your family doctor you are going to be working with me as soon as possible, and ask your doctor to send me information about any health problems you have have as soon as possible.

I think information about your work with me should be included in your doctor's medical record. Therefore, unless you say otherwise, I'll write to your doctor to describe your progress. These letters can be included in your medical file if your doctor wants. You will be given copies of these letters before they are sent. That way, any possible corrections, additions, or deletions that you want can be made before they are sent.

TIME OF APPOINTMENTS. Each of our appointments is scheduled to last 50 minutes. I usually begin promptly at the scheduled time. If I'm ever late I'll try to let you know in advance, even if the delay is just a few minutes. If I cause a late start, we will still be together for the full 50 minutes. If you arrive late for an appointment, we still have to end the meeting 50 minutes after it was scheduled to begin. The charge to you for these shortened meetings will be for the full amount. You will not be charged for a session if you cannot keep it and let me know at least 24 hours in advance. You will be charged if you fail to keep a scheduled appointment or do not notify me 24 hours ahead of time.

EMERGENCY MEETINGS. I will try to be available to you as much as possible. The telephone numbers on the front of this letter are attached to 24-hour answering machines, and I monitor them closely. I will try to return your calls promptly. If I am away from town during vacations or professional meetings, I will let you know how to reach me by long-distance telephone. Or I will have a qualified professional in the area return your call. Your case record will be available to that professional, unless you indicate otherwise. If you feel the need for help and cannot reach me or the other professional, please contact your family doctor.

STOPPING OUR SESSIONS. We should agree together when it is time for our meetings to end and for therapy to stop. We can do this in two ways. If you prefer, we can specify as we get started when our last session will be. Then, when the time comes, we will stop, unless we make a new agreement and set new goals. If we end this way, our last meeting will include a final summation and discussion about things to do in the future. Of course, we can resume sessions after that if you want. The second way we might stop is to decide as we go along. We might decide together to stop because we have reached our goals. Or we might decide we are not going to reach them. This is a possibility, because I cannot guarantee that we will reach all of the goals we establish together.

You may tell me you wish to stop, for whatever reason at any time. I'd prefer it if you came in for one final session after that so we can sum up and discuss your future. If you stop coming without letting me know in advance, I cannot assume responsibility for your care and well-being after that.

COSTS. The charge for each of these 50-minute meetings is $_____. This amount is the same if you attend the meeting alone or with other members of your family. The charge to you is the same if, with your consent, I see other members of your family in your behalf. If we agree in advance to have meetings that are longer or shorter than 50 minutes, the charge will be based on the amount of time we are together. For example, if you have a 25-minute session, the charge will be half that of a 50-minute session.

METHOD OF PAYMENT. You may pay by cash, credit card (VISA or Mastercard), check, or money order. You may pay me or my secretary directly at the time of each visit. If this is not convenient, we can discuss other possibilities, such as monthly billing. If your bill has not been paid before the end of the month, you will be sent a statement itemizing the charges and showing the total balance due. This amount should be paid within 10 days after the month begins. If you are having any financial problems that keep you from paying in this way, let's discuss it. We can make special arrangements if necessary.

INSURANCE. Your health insurance may help to pay these charges. You should find out by contacting your insurance company or agent as soon as possible. If they will help you pay my fees, please obtain the proper forms from them and give them to me. I will complete my portion of the form and return it to *you,* not to your insurance company. After that, it is your responsibility to submit the forms to your company. Ask them to send the money to you and not to me.

Your payment to me should be made on time even if your insurance company delays in reimbursing you. Many health insurance companies generally do not reimburse expenses they consider to be unrelated to health. That means some companies do not pay for things like marriage counseling, family relationship therapy, and vocational and educational counseling. Some companies will reimburse you only when your physician has referred you to me and is involved in your treatment. It is important that you find out about these things from your insurance company if you plan on getting reimbursed.

CONFIDENTIALITY. My profession and my professional ethics require me to keep everything you discuss here in the strictest of confidence. I have no intention of giving information about you to anyone unless you ask me to. I have no objection, however, to your revealing anything you want to anyone you want about our meetings.

I will audiotape or video-record some of our sessions only with your permission. If you permit me to record a session, you may have a copy of the tape if you supply a blank cassette. I keep a written record of our contacts. These notes help me stick to our goals. It also helps us get started where we left off last time. These notes are confidential, but I believe they are your property as well as mine. You may read these notes whenever you want, and you may have a copy.

There is one possible exception to the principle of confidentiality. It applies to me and all other mental health professionals in this state. In some very rare circumstances, I could be called upon (subpoenaed) to testify about you in court. This could happen if there was reason to believe I knew of certain types of criminal wrongdoing. Also, if you indicate to me seriously that you intend to harm someone, I may be required to take action to prevent that harm from occurring, including alerting the authorities and/or warning the person who is being threatened. My colleagues and I are also required to report any suspected child abuse. In such situations, my records about you could also be reviewed in court. If the law ever required me to do this, I would try to discuss with you beforehand any testimony I might be compelled to present. Again, the likelihood of any of this happening is extremely rare, but you deserve to be informed of the possibility.

MY BACKGROUND. I have been in private practice in this office since _____. Before that, I worked at _____. I am also on the faculty of _____, where I teach courses in _____. My profession is social work, and I specialize in _____. My academic degrees are _____ from _____ University. I have been licensed in this state since _____ and am a member of the following professional associations: _____.

OUR AGREEMENT. You are the boss, and I am working in your interests. You can determine what your goals are, and my role is to help you reach them. I may show you how to define your goals or show you what the consequences of reaching these goals might be, but you have the last word on this. On the back of this letter, we will list the goals we hope to achieve in our work together. We both agree they can be changed at any time. If we change goals, we agree to restate them on another letter like this one.

SIGNATURE. We the undersigned have read this statement, understand it, and agree with its terms. We will comply with all the points in this letter on our personal and professional honor. It is understood that our relationship may be discontinued whenever these terms are not fulfilled by either of us.

_____   _____
        (signature and date)   (signature and date)

SAMPLE CONTRACT FOR COUPLES

LETTER OF AGREEMENT

Welcome. I hope your time here is worthwhile. I'm giving each of you a copy of this letter to answer some question you may have. It will tell you what to expect of our meetings; it will suggest how all three of us should work together.

Please go over this carefully. If you can, discuss it with each other. Then, feel free to ask me anything about it whenever you have questions. You are welcome to show it to others in your family or other professionals you trust.

At the end of this letter is a place for us to sign our names. Signing means we agree with all the points in this letter. There is also space for us to write down the goals we hope to accomplish together. We can review these goals as we go along. We can change them anytime we want if, together, it seems like a good idea. Now, let's discuss how to make these meetings productive.

SEE YOUR DOCTOR. I strongly recommend that both of you get physical examinations from your personal physicians as soon as possible. This is important to make sure that none of the problems are the result of physical health difficulties. Because I am not a physician, I cannot know if you have physical health conditions that might be related to our work.

Please tell your family doctor or doctors, as soon as possible, that you both are going to be working with me. Please ask your doctors to send me information about any health problems either of you may have as soon as possible.

I think information about your work with me should be included in your doctors' medical records. Therefore, unless you say otherwise, I'll write to your doctors to describe your progress. These letters can be included in your medical files if your doctors want. Each of you will be given copies of these letters before they are sent. That way, any possible corrections, additions, or deletions that you want can be made before they are sent.

TIME OF APPOINTMENTS. Our appointments are scheduled to last 50 minutes in my office. Both of you should attend these sessions together, unless we agree to meet for individual sessions. I usually begin promptly at the scheduled time. If I'm ever late I'll try to let you know in advance, even if the delay is just a few minutes. If I cause a late start, we will still be together for the full 50 minutes. If one of you is late but the other is present, we cannot begin until the other arrives, unless we have already agreed to meet individually during that scheduled session. The charge for these shortened meetings is for the full amount. You won't be charged for a session that one of you cannot keep if you let me know at least 24 hours in advance. You will be charged if one of you fails to keep a scheduled appointment or does not notify me 24 hours ahead of time.

COSTS. The charge for each of these 50-minute meetings is $_____. This amount is the same if you attend the meeting alone or with your partner. If we agree in advance to have meetings that are longer or shorter than 50 minutes, the charge will be based on the amount of time we are together. For example, if you have a 25-minute session, the charge will be half that of a 50-minute session.

Each of you will owe half the total amount due, even if one of you had more individual time with me than the other.

METHOD OF PAYMENT. You may pay by cash, credit card (VISA or Mastercard), check, or money order. You may pay me or my secretary directly at the time of each visit. If this is not convenient, we can discuss other possibilities, such as monthly billing. If your bill has not been paid before the end of the month, you will be sent a statement itemizing the charges and showing the total balance due. This amount should be paid within 10 days after the month begins. Unless you request otherwise, each bill will be made out with both your names. If you want, we will make the bills out in the name of one or the other of you; however, both of you are equally responsible for payment. If you're having financial problems, let's discuss special arrangements.

INSURANCE. Your health insurance may help to pay these charges. You should find out by contacting your insurance company or agent as soon as possible. If they will help you pay my fees, please obtain the proper forms from them and give them to me. I will complete my portion of the form and return it to *you*, not to your insurance company. After that, it is your responsibility to submit the forms to your company. Ask them to send the money to you and not to me.

Your payment to me should be made on time even if your insurance company delays in reimbursing you. Some insurance companies will reimburse you only when your physician has referred you to me and is involved in your treatment. Many health insurance companies do not reimburse for marital therapy, family therapy, or other treatments they consider to be unrelated to health. It is important that you find out about these things from your insurance company if you plan on getting reimbursed.

EMERGENCY MEETINGS. I will try to be available to you as much as possible. The telephone numbers on the front of this letter are attached to 24-hour answering machines, and I monitor them closely. I will try to return your calls promptly. If I am away from town during vacations or professional meetings, I will let you know how to reach me by long-distance telephone. Or I will have a qualified professional in the area return your call. Your case record will be available to that professional unless you indicate otherwise. If you feel the need for help and cannot reach me or the other professional, please contact your family doctor.

STOPPING OUR SESSIONS. We should agree together when it is time for our meetings to end and for therapy to stop. We can do this in two ways. If you prefer, we can specify as we get started when our last session will be. Then, when the time comes, we will stop, unless we make a new agreement and set new goals. If we end this way, our last meeting will include a final summation and discussion about things to do in the future. Of course, we can resume sessions after that if you want. The second way we might stop is to decide as we go along. We might decide together to stop because we have reached our goals. Or we might decide we are not going to reach them. This is a possibility, because I cannot guarantee that we will reach all of our goals.

Either of you may, at any time, tell me you wish to stop, for whatever reason. You should come in for a final session after that so we can sum up and discuss the future. If you stop without letting me know in advance, I cannot be responsible for your care and well-being after that. If one of you wants to stop, even though the other wants to continue, both of you should attend a final meeting together. Then we can sum things up and discuss future possibilities. One possibility is for the one who wants to continue to establish a new letter of agreement to begin individual sessions. Both parties will remain equally responsible for any unpaid fees for the sessions up to that point. The person who continues alone in treatment is solely responsible for payment of these new individual sessions.

CONFIDENTIALITY. My profession and my professional ethics require me to keep everything you discuss here in the strictest of confidence. I have no intention of giving information about you to anyone unless you ask me to. I have no objection, however, to your revealing anything you want to anyone you want about our meetings.

I will audiotape or video-record some of our sessions only with your permission. If you permit me to record a session, you may have a copy of the tape if you supply a blank cassette. I keep a written record of our contacts. These notes help me stick to our goals. It also helps us get started where we left off last time. These notes are confidential, but I believe they are your property as well as mine. You may read these notes whenever you want, and you may have a copy. The notes will contain information about both of you. Notes taken for any individual sessions will be given only to the person who attended that session.

There is one possible exception to the principle of confidentiality. It applies to me and all other mental health professionals in this state. In some very rare circumstances, I could be called upon (subpoenaed) to testify about you in court. This could happen if there was reason to believe I knew of certain types of criminal wrongdoing. Also, if you indicate to me seriously that you intend to harm someone, I may be required to take action to prevent that harm from occurring, including alerting the authorities and/or warning the person who is being threatened. My colleagues and I are also required to report any suspected child abuse. In such situations, my records about you could also be reviewed in court. If the law ever required me to do this, I would try to discuss with you beforehand any testimony I might be compelled to present. Again, the likelihood of any of this happening is extremely rare, but you deserve to be informed of the possibility.

MY BACKGROUND. I have been in private practice in this office since _____. Before that, I worked at _____. I am also on the faculty of _____, where I teach courses in _____. My profession is social work, and I specialize in _____. My academic degrees are _____ from _____ University. I have been licensed in this state since _____ and am a member of the following professional associations: _____.

OUR AGREEMENT. You are the bosses, and I am working in your interests. You can determine what your goals are, and my role is to help you reach them. I may show you how to define your goals or show you what the consequences of reaching these goals might be, but you have the last word on this. On the back of this letter, we will list the goals we hope to achieve in our work together. We all agree they can be changed at any time. If we change goals, we agree to restate them on another letter like this one.

SIGNATURE. We the undersigned have read this statement, understand it, and agree with its terms. We will comply with all the points in this letter on our personal and professional honor. It is understood that our relationship may be discontinued whenever these terms are not fulfilled by any of the three of us.

_____
(signature and date)

_____
(signature and date)

_____
(signature and date)

SAMPLE CONTRACT FOR CHILDREN AND ADOLESCENTS

The following is a contract used between the social worker and clients who are older children and adolescents. This contract is used when the young person attends individual (rather than family) therapy sessions. Generally, it is used in conjunction with the contract that follows (for the parents or guardians responsible for the youngster).

LETTER OF AGREEMENT

Hello. I hope the time you spend with me is useful and pleasant. This letter is to explain how we should work together. If you have any questions about it, please ask me. At the end of this letter, there is a place for us to sign our names. Signing means we agree with all the points in this letter. There is also space for us to write down the goals you and I want to reach. We can review these goals as we go along. We can change them anytime we want if, together, it seems like a good idea.

SEE YOUR DOCTOR. First, I'll ask your parent to get you a physical examination from your doctor as soon as possible. We need to make sure you're healthy. I'm not a physician, so your regular doctor should do this for you. I will tell your doctor about our visits so your health record is complete.

TIME OF APPOINTMENTS. We will meet every week at the same time in my office. Each meeting will last 50 minutes. It is very important to be on time. I will let you know beforehand if I'm going to be late. You should also let me know in advance if you are going to be late. I will talk with your parents about helping you get here on time.

COSTS. The cost for each of our 50-minute meetings if $_____. This will be your parent's responsibility. Your parent will have to pay this bill even if you skip a meeting, unless you tell me one day beforehand that you cannot come.

EMERGENCY MEETINGS. I will try to be available to you if you want to talk before our next meeting. Keep my phone number handy, and I'll return your call as soon as I can. Sometimes I will be out of town. If I am, I'll leave word about my long-distance phone number. If I can't be reached and you need to talk, I'll see that another professional is available to return your call.

STOPPING OUR SESSIONS. Our meetings should continue until we reach our goals. When you or I think we've reached the goals, we'll then have a last meeting to discuss the future. If you decide you want to stop before the goals are reached, please don't just stop coming. Let me know you want to stop. Then we can decide together what to do. We can start over again later, if you want.

CONFIDENTIALITY. Everything you say in my office is private. Normally, I will not tell your parents or anyone else what you have said. However, you may tell anyone what we talked about. I sometimes have to tell the authorities if a young person in my office seems in danger of being harmed by others or of harming someone else.

If you say it's okay, I will video-record some of our meetings. You and I will be the only ones to see the tape, unless you permit others to see it. I also keep notes about our visits. You may read these notes if you want.

SIGNATURE. We have read this letter, understand it, and agree with its terms. If we do not follow the points of this letter, we may stop our meetings.

_____   _____

(signature and date)   (signature and date)

SAMPLE CONTRACT FOR PARENTS OF YOUNG CLIENTS

The following is a contract to be used for the custodial parent(s) or guardian(s) of a child who is a client of the worker. It is used in conjunction with the contract for children and adolescents. This contract is not given to the minor children, but it need not be concealed from the child.

LETTER OF AGREEMENT

I hope the time we all spend here in behalf of your youngster is worthwhile. This letter is to answer some questions you may have and to spell out the conditions of our work together. Please go over this carefully. Feel free to ask me anything about it whenever you have questions. You are welcome to discuss it in your family or with others.

At the end of this letter, there is a place for us to sign our names. Signing means we agree with all the points in this letter. There is also space for us to write down the goals you have for your youngster in our meetings. Your child will have a chance to write down the goals for these sessions. We can review these goals as we go along. We can change them anytime we want if, together, it seems like a good idea. Now, let's discuss what we all should understand and do to have productive meetings.

PHYSICAL EXAMS. You should arrange a physical exam for your child as soon as possible. This is important to make sure that none of your child's problems are the result of physical health difficulties. Because I am not a physician, it is not my role to determine if any physical health problems are relevant.

It is a good idea for your child's doctor to know about these sessions. Please tell the doctor as soon as possible. Also, please let me know if the doctor is currently providing any ongoing treatment or medications for your child. Your child's medical record should include information about our sessions. Therefore, unless you say otherwise, I'll write to the doctor to describe these meetings. These letters can be included in your child's medical file if the doctor wants. You will be given a copy of these letters before they are sent. That way, any possible corrections or things you feel should be left out or added can be done before it is sent.

TIME OF APPOINTMENTS. It is your responsibility to see that your child gets to each of our meetings on time. Each of our appointments is scheduled to last 50 minutes. I usually begin promptly at the scheduled time. If I'm ever late, I'll try to let you know in advance, even if the delay is just a few minutes. If I cause a late start, I will still meet with your child for the full 50 minutes. If the child arrives late for an appointment, we still have to end the meeting 50 minutes after it was scheduled to begin. The charge to you for these shortened meetings will be for the full amount. You will not be charged for a session if your child cannot keep it and you let me know at least 24 hours in advance. You will be charged if your child fails to keep a scheduled appointment without 24 hours advance notice.

COSTS. The charge for each of these 50-minute meetings is $_____. This amount is the same if I see only your child or if I see other members of the family, too. If we agree in advance to have meetings that are longer or shorter than 50 minutes, the charge will be based on the amount of time we are together. For example, if you have a 25-minute session, the charge will be half that of a 50-minute session.

METHOD OF PAYMENT. You may pay by cash, credit card (VISA or Mastercard), check, or money order. You may pay me or my secretary directly at the time of each visit. If this is not convenient, we can discuss other possibilities, such as monthly billing. If your bill has not been paid before the end of the month, you will be sent a statement itemizing the charges and showing the total balance due. This amount should be paid within 10 days after the month begins. The statement will be sent to you and will be itemized as "in behalf of [your child's name]." It will be your responsibility to pay this bill, even if you have agreements for child-support payments from others. If you are having any financial problems that keep you from paying in this way, let's discuss it. We can make special arrangements if necessary.

INSURANCE. Your child's health insurance may help to pay these charges. You should find out by contacting your insurance company or agent as soon as possible. If they will help you pay my fees, please obtain the proper forms from them and give them to me. I will complete my portion of the form and return it to *you,* not to your insurance company. After that, it is your responsibility to submit the forms to your company. Ask them to send the money to you and not to me.

Your payment to me should be made on time even if your insurance company delays in reimbursing you. Many health insurance companies generally do not reimburse expenses they consider to be unrelated to health. That means some companies do not pay for things like family therapy, educational counseling, academic testing, or behavioral training. Some companies will reimburse you only when your physician has referred your child to me and is involved in the child's treatment. It is important that you find out about these things from your insurance company if you plan on getting reimbursed.

COLLATERAL SESSIONS. During your child's course of treatment, it is important for you and me to communicate, plan, and coordinate our efforts to help. Therefore, I will ask periodically to see you. And you may ask, anytime, to see me. This may be in the presence of your child or alone. If we meet without your child being present, I will respect your privacy and confidentiality. I will simply say to your child that I did see the parent to discuss general progress. Even though I will not disclose the content of the meeting, you are welcome to do so. You will be charged at the same rate for these visits, and the statement will be itemized as a "collateral session in behalf of _____."

CONFIDENTIALITY. My profession and my professional ethics require me to keep everything you discuss here in the strictest of confidence. I have no intention of giving information about your child or the child's family. As I will tell your child, I won't reveal what we discuss alone. However, I normally encourage youngsters to discuss our meetings with the parents.

Sometimes I audiotape or video-record some of these sessions. I would only do this with your permission and your child's permission. No one will see the tape except me, unless you and your child give permission for its use elsewhere. I'll give a copy of the tape to your child.

There is one possible exception to the principle of confidentiality. It applies to me and all other mental health professionals in this state. In some very rare circumstances, I could be called upon (subpoenaed) to testify about your child in court. This could happen if there was reason to believe I knew of certain types of criminal wrongdoing. Also, if your child gave me the strong impression of being abused, suicidal, or dangerous to others, I might be compelled to reveal this to authorities. If any of these actions had to be taken, I would try to discuss it with you first. Again, the likelihood of any of this happening is extremely rare, but you deserve to be informed of the possibility.

EMERGENCY MEETINGS. I will try to be available to you and your child as much as possible. The telephone numbers on the front of this letter are attached to 24-hour answering machines, and I monitor them closely from wherever I am. I will try to return your calls or your child's calls promptly. If I am away from town during vacations or professional meetings, I will let you know how to reach me by long-distance telephone. Or I will have a qualified professional return your call. The case record will be available to that professional, unless you indicate otherwise. If you feel that your child needs help and cannot reach me or the other professional, please contact your child's doctor.

STOPPING OUR SESSIONS. We should agree together when it is time for the meetings with your child to end and for therapy to stop. We can do this in two ways. If you prefer, we can specify as we get started when our last session will be. Then, when the time comes, we will stop, unless we make a new agreement and set new goals. If we end this way, our last meeting will include a final summation and discussion about the future. Of course, we can resume sessions after that if you and your child want. The second way we might stop is to decide as we go along. We might decide together to stop because we have reached our goals. Or we might decide we are not going to reach them. This is a possibility, because I cannot guarantee that we will reach all of the goals we establish together.

You may tell me you want your child's treatment with me to stop, for whatever reason at any time. I'd prefer it if you and your child came in for one final session after that so we can have a summation and discussion about the future. If you or your child stops coming without letting me know in advance, I cannot assume responsibility after that.

MY BACKGROUND. I have been in private practice in this office since _____. Before that, I worked at _____. I am also on the faculty of _____, where I teach courses in _____. My profession is social work, and I specialize in _____. My academic degrees are _____ from _____ University. I have been licensed in this state since _____ and am a member of the following professional associations: _____.

OUR AGREEMENT. I am working for you, in behalf of your child. Therefore, you and your child have the right to determine what your goals are, and my role is to help you reach them. I may show you and your child how to define the goals or show you what the consequences of reaching these goals might be, but you both have the last word on this. On the back of this letter, we will list the goals you hope we achieve in behalf of your child. If we change goals, we agree to restate them on another letter like this one.

SIGNATURE. We the undersigned have read this statement, understand it, and agree with its terms. We will comply with all the points in this letter on our personal and professional honor. It is understood that our relationship may be discontinued whenever these terms are not fulfilled by either of us.

_____   _____
(signature and date)   (signature and date)

SAMPLE CONTRACT FOR THE ADULTS IN FAMILY THERAPY

This contract is used for adults in family therapy. This contract is not given to the minor children. The worker may or may not use the contract for children when the entire family is involved in these sessions.

LETTER OF AGREEMENT

Welcome. I hope your time here is worthwhile. I'm giving you this letter now to answer some questions you may have. It will tell you what to expect of our meetings and how we should work together. Feel free to ask me anything about it whenever you have questions. You are welcome to discuss it in your family or with others.

At the end of this letter, there is a place for us to sign our names. Signing means we agree with all the points in this letter. There is also space for us to write down the goals we hope to accomplish together. We can review these goals as we go along. We can change them anytime we want if, together, it seems like a good idea. Now, let's discuss what we all should understand and do to have productive meetings.

SEE YOUR DOCTOR. All of you should get physical examinations from your personal physicians as soon as possible. This is important to make sure that none of the problems are the result of physical health difficulties. Because I am not a physician, I cannot know if you have physical conditions that might be related to our work.

It is a good idea for your doctors to know you are working with me. Please tell them as soon as possible. It is also important that I am informed about any work they are doing with you. I especially need to know about any health problems that any of the members of the family may have. This includes any members of the family or household who are not involved in these sessions. Please ask your doctor to send me this information as soon as possible.

I think information about your work with me should be included in your doctors' medical record. Therefore, unless you say otherwise, I will write to your doctors to describe these meetings. These letters can be included in your medical files if your doctors want. You will be given a copy of these letters before they are sent. That way, any possible corrections, additions, or deletions that you want can be made before it is sent.

TIME OF APPOINTMENTS. Each of our appointments is scheduled to last _____ minutes. I usually begin promptly at the scheduled time. If I am ever late I will try to let you know in advance, even if the delay is just a few minutes. If I cause a late start, we will still be together for the full _____ minutes. If you arrive late for an appointment, we still have to end the meeting _____ minutes after it was scheduled to begin. The charge to you for these shortened meetings will be for the full amount. You will not be charged for a session if you cannot keep it and let me know at least 24 hours in advance. You will be charged if you fail to keep a scheduled appointment or do not notify me 24 hours ahead of time.

COSTS. The charge for each of these _____-minute meetings is $_____. This amount is the same if all of you attend the meeting together or if only some or one attends. If we agree in advance to have meetings that are longer or shorter than _____ minutes, the charge will be based on the amount of time we are together. For example, if you have a 25-minute session, the charge will be half that of a 50-minute session.

METHOD OF PAYMENT. You may pay by cash, credit card (VISA or Mastercard), check, or money order. You may pay me or my secretary directly at the time of each visit. If this is not convenient, we can discuss other possibilities, such as monthly billing. If your bill has not been paid before the end of the month, you will be sent a statement itemizing the charges and showing the total balance due. This amount should be paid within 10 days after the month begins. The statement will be sent to the one parent or guardian who initiated these sessions; that person will be totally responsible for payments, no matter what agreements exist between that parent and other parents or guardians. If you are having any financial problems that keep you from paying in this way, let's discuss it. We can make special arrangements if necessary.

INSURANCE. Your health insurance may help to pay these charges. You should find out by contacting your insurance company or agent as soon as possible. If they will help you pay my fees, please obtain the proper forms from them and give them to me. I will complete my portion of the form and return it to *you,* not to your insurance company. After that, it is your responsibility to submit the forms to your company. Ask them to send the money to you and not to me.

Your payment to me should be made on time even if your insurance company delays in reimbursing you. Many health insurance companies generally do not reimburse expenses they consider to be unrelated to health. That means some companies do not pay for things like family therapy. Some companies will reimburse you only when your physician has referred you to me and is involved in your treatment. It is important that you find out about these things from your insurance company if you plan on getting reimbursed.

CONFIDENTIALITY. My profession and my professional ethics require me to keep everything discussed in these meetings in the strictest of confidence. I have no intention of giving information about you to anyone unless you ask me to. I have no objection, however, to your revealing anything you want to anyone you want about our meetings.

I will audiotape or video-record some of our sessions only with your permission. If you permit me to record a session, you may have a copy of the tape if you supply a blank cassette. I keep a written record of our contacts. These notes help me stick to our goals. It also helps us get started where we left off last time. These notes are confidential, but I believe they are your property as well as mine. You may read these notes whenever you want, and you may have a copy.

There is one possible exception to the principle of confidentiality. It applies to me and all other mental health professionals in this state. In some very rare circumstances, I could be called upon (subpoenaed) to testify about you in court. This could happen if there was reason to believe I knew of certain types of criminal wrongdoing. Also, if you indicate to me seriously that you intend to harm someone, I may be required to take action to prevent that harm from occurring, including alerting the authorities and/or warning the person who is being threatened. My colleagues and I are also required to report any suspected child abuse. In such situations, my records about you could also be reviewed in court. If the law ever required me to do this, I would try to discuss with you beforehand any testimony I might be compelled to present. Again, the likelihood of any of this happening is extremely rare, but you deserve to be informed of the possibility.

EMERGENCY MEETINGS. I will try to be available to you as much as possible. The telephone numbers on the front of this letter are attached to 24-hour answering machines, and I monitor them closely. I will try to return your calls promptly. If I am away from town during vacations or professional meetings, I will let you know how to reach me by long-distance telephone. Or I will have a qualified professional return your call. Your case record will be available to that professional, unless you indicate otherwise. If you feel the need for help and cannot reach me or the other professional, please contact your family doctor.

STOPPING OUR SESSIONS. We should agree together when it is time for our meetings to end and for therapy to stop. We can do this in two ways. If you prefer, we can specify as we get started when our last session will be. Then, when the time comes, we will stop, unless we make a new agreement and set new goals. If we end this way, our last meeting will include a final summation and discussion about things to do in the future. Of course, we can resume sessions after that if you want. The second way we might stop is to decide as we go along. We might decide together to stop because we have reached our goals. Or we might decide we are not going to reach them. This is a possibility, because I cannot guarantee that we will reach all of the goals we establish together.

You may tell me your family wishes to stop, for whatever reason at any time. I'd prefer it if you came in for one final session after that so we can have a summing up and discussion about the future. If you stop coming without letting me know in advance, I cannot assume responsibility after that.

MY BACKGROUND. I have been in private practice in this office since _____. Before that, I worked at _____. I am also on the faculty of _____, where I teach courses in _____. My profession is social work, and I specialize in _____. My academic degrees are _____ from _____ University. I have been licensed in this state since _____ and am a member of the following professional associations: _____.

OUR AGREEMENT. You are the boss, and I am working in your interests. You can determine what your goals are, and my role is to help you reach them. I may show you how to define your goals or show you what the consequences of reaching these goals might be, but you have the last word on this. On the back of this letter, we will list the goals we hope to achieve in our work together. We both agree they can be changed at any time. If we change goals, we agree to restate them on another letter like this one.

SIGNATURE. We the undersigned have read this statement, understand it, and agree with its terms. We will comply with all the points in this letter on our personal and professional honor. It is understood that our relationship may be discontinued whenever these terms are not fulfilled by either of us.

_____   _____

      (signature and date)   (signature and date)

SAMPLE CONTRACT FOR CLIENTS IN GROUP THERAPY

LETTER OF AGREEMENT

Hello. I hope your time in our therapy group is worthwhile. I'm giving you this letter now to answer some questions you may have about the group and your role in it. It will tell you what you can expect from the group and what is to be expected of you in the group.

Please go over this carefully. Feel free to ask me anything about it before you start in the group. If you have a question about this agreement letter after you start group, it's better to bring the question up in the group itself.

At the end of this letter, there is a place for us to sign our names. Signing means we agree with all the points in this letter. There is also space for us to write down the goals we hope to accomplish with the help of the group. The group can help us review these goals as we go along. We can change them anytime we want if you and I and the group all agree. Now, let's discuss what you and I should understand and do to make our meetings worthwhile.

SEE YOUR DOCTOR. Before you start the group, please get a physical examination from your personal physician. This is important to make sure that none of the problems you face are the result of physical health difficulties. Because I am not a physician, I cannot know if you have physical health conditions that might affect these problems. Please tell your family doctor, as soon as possible, that you will be entering a therapy group. It is also important that I am informed about any work your doctor is doing with you. I especially need to know about any medications or health problems you may have. Please ask your doctor to send me this information.

I think information about your participation in group therapy should be included in your doctor's medical record. Therefore, unless you say otherwise, I'll write to your doctor to describe your progress. These letters can be included in your medical chart if your doctor wants. You will be given a copy of these letters before they are sent. That way, any possible corrections or things you feel should be left out or added can be done before it is sent.

BASIC GROUP RULES. To get the most out of group, four basic rules should be respected. First, everything you say to group members should be truthful. You can talk about any subject you want in group, and you will not be required to talk about anything you do not want to talk about. However, when you talk, it should be honest. Second, you should attend all sessions and be there on time. When members miss group time, the others have to spend their time explaining what was learned previously, and this reduces the effectiveness of the process. Third, you should respect the privacy and confidentiality of the other group members. Do not tell others what any member of the group has revealed to you. And fourth, confine your relationship with other group members to the group setting. Do not attempt to see or contact other members outside of the group, even after you have stopped therapy. If a group member or former group member tries to contact you, politely remind them about this rule, and discuss it in group. All these rules exist for very good reasons, and the group can discuss these reasons further, if you want.

TIME OF GROUP SESSIONS. Each group therapy session will begin at _____ and will last _____ minutes. The group members and I are almost never late for the beginning of these sessions. If ever I cannot be there on time, I'll try to let you and the other members know in advance, even if the delay is just a few minutes. If I cause a late start, we will still be together for the full _____ minutes. If you arrive late for a group session and it has already begun, you should quietly enter the meeting room and find a chair. Usually, it is better not to ask the group to bring you up to date when you arrive late; it will disrupt their exchange of ideas and communication, and you'll learn soon enough about what has happened anyway.

NONGROUP PROFESSIONAL SESSIONS. Once you have started group, it is better not to telephone me or seek individual appointments with me. Nearly everything you would want to talk about could be discussed with me and the group. If, however, you feel it is absolutely necessary to arrange a private meeting, you may discuss that in group; otherwise you may call me for an appointment. I will not tell the group or others about the meeting but will probably encourage you to do so.

EMERGENCY MEETINGS. I will try to be available as much as possible. The telephone numbers on the front of this letter are attached to 24-hour answering machines, and I monitor them closely from wherever I am. I will try to return your calls promptly. If I am away from town during vacations or professional meetings, I will let you know how to reach me by long-distance telephone. Or I will have a qualified professional in the area return your call. Your case record will be available to that professional, unless you indicate otherwise. If you feel the need for help and cannot reach me or the other professional, please contact your family doctor.

ENDING GROUP THERAPY SESSIONS. When you feel it is time for your participation in group therapy to end, there is an effective and healthy procedure. First, review your goals and decide whether you have reached them. Second, tell the group at least two weeks before you stop. Third, during your remaining sessions discuss with the group the reasons for your decision, your gains, and what work remains to be done. Fourth, after you stop, honor the agreement to not contact other group members; however, you may, of course, contact me privately anytime thereafter. Do not simply stop coming to group. This will reduce the gains you have made and may impede the work of other group members.

COSTS. Your charge for each of the _____-minute group meetings is $_____. You'll be charged this amount whether or not you are late or absent the entire session. You will be charged even if you let the group know well in advance of your planned absence. This is because the position in the group is kept open for you, whether or not you are there for a given session. If the group or I make any exceptions to the fee charging system, we'll discuss it in group.

METHOD OF PAYMENT. You may pay by cash, credit card (VISA or Mastercard), check, or money order. You may pay me or my secretary directly at the time of each session. If this is not convenient, we can discuss other possibilities, such as monthly billing. If your bill has not been paid before the end of the month, you will be sent a statement itemizing the charges and showing the total balance due. This amount should be paid within 10 days after the month begins. If you are having any financial problems that keep you from paying in this way, let's discuss it. We can make special arrangements if necessary.

INSURANCE. Your health insurance may help to pay these charges. You should find out by contacting your insurance company or agent as soon as possible. If they will help you pay my fees, please obtain the proper forms from them and give them to me. I will complete my portion of the form and return it to *you*, not to your insurance company. After that, it is your responsibility to submit the forms to your company. Ask them to send the money to you and not to me.

Your payment to me should be made on time even if your insurance company delays in reimbursing you. Many health insurance companies generally do not reimburse expenses they consider to be unrelated to health. That means some companies do not pay for things like marriage counseling, family relationship therapy, and vocational and educational counseling. Some companies will reimburse you only when your physician has referred you to me and is involved in your treatment. It is important that you find out about these things from your insurance company if you plan on getting reimbursed.

CONFIDENTIALITY. My profession and my professional ethics require me to keep everything you discuss here in the strictest of confidence. I have no intention of giving information about you to anyone unless you ask me to. You may disclose to others anything you want about yourself or about these meetings as long as you do not reveal personal information about the other group members. There is one possible exception to the principles of confidentiality. It applies to me and all other mental health professionals in this state. In some very rare circumstances, I could be called upon (subpoenaed) to testify about you in court. This could happen if there was reason to believe I knew of certain types of criminal wrongdoing. Also, if you indicate to me seriously that you intend to harm someone, I may be required to take action to prevent that harm from occurring, including alerting the authorities and/or warning the person who is being threatened. My colleagues and I are also required to report any suspected child abuse. In such situations, my records about you could also be reviewed in court. If the law ever required me to do this, I would try to discuss with you beforehand any testimony I might be compelled to present. Again, the likelihood of any of this happening is extremely rare, but you deserve to be informed of the possibility.

MY BACKGROUND. I have been in private practice in this office since _____. Before that, I worked at _____. I am also on the faculty of _____, where I teach courses in _____. My profession is social work, and I specialize in _____. My academic degrees are _____ from _____ University. I have been licensed in this state since _____ and am a member of the following professional associations: _____.

OUR AGREEMENT. You are the boss, and I am working in your interests. You can determine what your goals are, and my role is to help you reach them. I may show you how to define your goals or show you what the consequences of reaching these goals might be, but you have the last word on this. On the back of this letter, we will list the goals we hope to achieve in our work together. We both agree they can be changed at any time. If we change goals, we agree to restate them in another letter like this one.

SIGNATURE. We the undersigned have read this statement, understand it, and agree with its terms. We will comply with all the points in this letter on our personal and professional honor. It is understood that our relationship may be discontinued whenever these terms are not fulfilled by either of us.

_____	_____
(signature and date)	(signature and date)

APPENDIX B: STATE BOARDS REGULATING SOCIAL WORK

State	Board Address
Alabama	Alabama State Board of Social Work Examiners 100 Commerce St., #403 Montgomery, AL 36104
Alaska	Board of Clinical Social Work Examiners Division of Occupational Licensing Department of Commerce and Economic Development P.O. Box D Juneau, AK 99811-0800
Arizona	Board of Behavioral Health Examiners 1624 W. Adams #100A Phoenix, AZ 85007
Arkansas	Social Work Licensing Board P.O. Box 250381 Hillcrest Station Little Rock, AR 72225
California	Board of Behavioral Science Examiners Department of Consumer Affairs 1021 O St., Room A-198 Sacramento, CA 95814
Colorado	Colorado State Board of Social Work Examiners 1560 Broadway, Suite 1340 Denver, CO 80202
Connecticut	Department of Health Services Division of Medical Quality Assurance Social Work Certification 150 Washington St. Hartford, CT 06106
Delaware	Board of Social Work Examiners Division of Professional Regulation Margaret O'Neill Building P.O. Box 1401 Dover, DE 19903

District of Columbia   DC Board of Social Work
                            Department of Consumer and Regulatory Affairs
                            Occupational and Professional Licensing
                               Administration
                            614 H St., NW, Room 923
                            Washington, DC 20001

Florida   Board of Clinical Social Work
                            Marriage and Family Therapy, Mental Health
                               Counseling
                            1940 N. Monroe St.
                            Tallahassee, FL 32399-0750

Florida   Certified Master Social Work Certificate
                            1940 N. Monroe St.
                            Tallahassee, FL 32399-0750

Georgia   Georgia Composite Board of Professional
                               Counselors, Social Workers, and Marriage and
                               Family Therapists
                            166 Pryor St., SW
                            Atlanta, GA 30303

Idaho   Bureau of Occupational Licensing
                            Board of Social Work Examiners
                            2417 Bank Dr., #312
                            Boise, ID 83705

Illinois   Social Workers Examining and Disciplinary Board
                            Department of Professional Regulation
                            320 West Washington St.
                            Springfield, IL 62786

Iowa   Board of Social Work Examiners
                            Department of Public Health
                            Lucas State Office Bldg.
                            Des Moines, IA 50319

Kansas   Behavioral Sciences Regulatory Board
                            Landon State Office Bldg.
                            900 Jackson, Room 855
                            Topeka, KS 66612

Kentucky   State Board of Examiners of Social Work
                            P.O. Box 456
                            Frankfort, KY 40602

Louisiana   Louisiana State Board of Certified Social Work
                               Examiners
                            P.O. Box 345
                            Prairieville, LA 70769

Maine   State Board of Social Work Licensing
                            Department of Business and Financial Regulation
                            State House Station #35
                            Augusta, ME 04333

Maryland	State Board of Social Work Examiners
	4201 Patterson Ave.
	Baltimore, MD 21215-2299

Maryland · State Board of Social Work Examiners · 4201 Patterson Ave. · Baltimore, MD 21215-2299

Massachusetts · Board of Registration of Social Workers · 100 Cambridge St. · Boston, MA 02202

Michigan · Board of Examiners of Social Workers · P.O. Box 30018 · Lansing, MI 48909

Minnesota · Board of Social Work · 2700 University Ave., West · Suite 225 · St. Paul, MN 55114

Mississippi · State Board of Health · Social Work Advisory Council · P.O. Box 1700 · Jackson, MS 39215-1700

Missouri · Advisory Committee for Licensed Clinical Social Workers · Division of Professional Registration · P.O. Box 162 · 3605 Missouri Blvd. · Jefferson City, MO 65102

Montana · Board of Social Work Examiners and Professional Counselors · 111 N. Jackson, Arcade Building · Helena, MT 59620-0407

Nebraska · Board of Examiners in Social Work · Bureau of Examining Boards · P.O. Box 95007 · Lincoln, NE 68509

Nevada · Board of Examiners of Social Workers · University of Nevada–Reno · Business Bldg., Room 523D · P.O. Box 9779 · Reno, NV 89507

New Hampshire · Board of Examiners of Psychologists · Box 457 · 105 Pleasant St. · Concord, NH 03001

New Mexico · Board of Social Work Examiners · P.O. Box 25101 · Santa Fe, NM 87504

New York	State Board for Social Work
	State Education Department
	Cultural Education Center
	Room 3041
	Albany, NY 12230

New York
State Board for Social Work
State Education Department
Cultural Education Center
Room 3041
Albany, NY 12230

North Carolina
Certification Board for Social Work
P.O. Box 1043
Asheboro, NC 27204

North Dakota
Board of Social Work Examiners
P.O. Box 6145
Bismarck, ND 58502

Ohio
Counselor and Social Worker Board
77 S. High St., 16th Floor
Columbus, OH 43266-0340

Oklahoma
State Board of Licensed Social Workers
4145 NW 61st Terrace
Oklahoma City, OK 73112

Oregon
State Board of Clinical Social Workers
835 Summer St., NE
Salem, OR 97310

Pennsylvania
State Board of Social Work Examiners
P.O. Box 2649
Harrisburg, PA 17105-2649

Puerto Rico
Board of Examiners of Social Work
Box 3271
San Juan, PR 00904

Rhode Island
Department of Human Services
Board of Registration of Social Workers
600 New London Ave.
Cranston, RI 02920

South Carolina
Board of Social Work Examiners
P.O. Box 1083
Columbia, SC 29202

South Dakota
Department of Commerce and Consumer Affairs
Board of Social Work Examiners
P.O. Box 654
Spearfish, SD 57783-0654

Tennessee
Board of Social Worker Certification and Licensing
Department of Health and Environment
283 Plus Park Blvd.
Nashville, TN 37247-1010

Texas
Council for Social Work Certification 550-W
Texas Department of Human Services
P.O. Box 149030
Austin, TX 78714-9030

Utah	Division of Occupational and Professional Licensing P.O. Box 45802 160 East 300 South Salt Lake City, UT 84145-0801
Vermont	State of Vermont Secretary of State State Office Bldg. Montpelier, VT 05602
Virginia	Virginia Board of Social Work Department of Health Professions 1601 Rolling Hills Dr. Richmond, VA 23229-5005
Virgin Islands	Board of Social Work Licensure P.O. Box 3852 St. Thomas, VI 00801
Washington	Social Work Certification Advisory Committee Department of Health Professional Licensing Service 1300 SE Quince St. Olympia, WA 98504
West Virginia	Board of Social Work Examiners P.O. Box 5477 Charleston, WV 25311
Wyoming	Professional Licensing Board P.O. Box 591 Cheyenne, WY 82003

APPENDIX C:
NASW CHAPTER OFFICES

ALABAMA
100 Commerce St., Suite 407
Montgomery, AL 36104

ALASKA
8923 Tanis Dr.
Juneau, AK 99801

ARIZONA
610 W. Broadway, Suite 218
Tempe, AZ 85281

ARKANSAS
1123 South University, Suite 1010
Little Rock, AR 72204

CALIFORNIA
1016 23rd St.
Sacramento, CA 95816

CALIFORNIA—L.A. Branch Office
6030 Wilshire Blvd., Suite 202
Los Angeles, CA 90036-3617

COLORADO
6000 E. Evans, Bldg. 1, Suite 121
Denver, CO 80222

CONNECTICUT
1800 Silas Deane Hwy., Suite 20–21
Rocky Hill, CT 06067

DELAWARE
3301 Green St.
Claymont, DE 19703

DISTRICT OF COLUMBIA
(Metropolitan Area)
2025 Eye St., NW, Suite 105
Washington, DC 20006

FLORIDA
345 South Magnolia Dr., No. 14B
Tallahassee, FL 32301

GEORGIA
3166 Maple Dr., NE, Suite 124
Atlanta, GA 30305

HAWAII
200 N. Vineyard St., Suite 20
Honolulu, HI 96817

IDAHO
200 North 4th St.
Boise, ID 83702

ILLINOIS
180 N. Michigan Ave., Suite 400
Chicago, IL 60601

INDIANA
1100 W. 42nd St., Suite 316
Indianapolis, IN 46208

INTERNATIONAL
147th Postal Unit, Box 224
APO, NY 09102

IOWA
4211 Grand Ave.
Des Moines, IA 50312

KANSAS
817 West Sixth St.
Topeka, KS 66603

KENTUCKY
P.O. Box 1211
Frankfort, KY 40602

LOUISIANA
LSU School of Social Work
311 Huey Long Field House
Baton Rouge, LA 70803

MAINE
P.O. Box 5065
Augusta, ME 04332

MARYLAND
5710 Executive Dr., Suite 105
Baltimore, MD 21228

MASSACHUSETTS
14 Beacon St., Suite 409
Boston, MA 02108

MICHIGAN
230 N. Washington Sq., Suite 212
Lansing, MI 48933

MINNESOTA
480 Concordia Ave.
St. Paul, MN 55103

MISSISSIPPI
P.O. Box 4228
Jackson, MD 39216

MISSOURI
Parkade Center, Suite 138
601 Business Loop 70 West
Columbia, MO 65203

MONTANA
9440 Hodgeman Canyon
Bozeman, MT 59715

NEBRASKA
c/o Aspen Exeuctive Services
1701 S. 17th St., Suite 1-E
Lincoln, NE 68502

NEVADA
P.O. Box 50352
Henderson, NY 89016

NEW HAMPSHIRE
25 Walker St.
Concord, NH 03301

NEW JERSEY
110 West State St.
Trenton, NJ 08608

NEW MEXICO
1503 University Blvd., NE
Albuquerque, NM 87102

NEW YORK CITY
545 8th Ave., 6th Floor
New York, NY 10018

NEW YORK STATE
225 Lark St.
Albany, NY 12210

NORTH CAROLINA
P.O. Box 12082
715 West Johnson St., Suite 204
Raleigh, NC 27605

NORTH DAKOTA
P.O. Box 1775
Bismarck, ND 58502-1775

OHIO
40 West Long St., Suite 203
Columbus, OH 43215

OKLAHOMA
P.O. Box 2609
Norman, OK 73070

OREGON
109 N.E. 50th Ave.
Portland, OR 97213

PENNSYLVANIA
#2 Shore Drive Office Center
2001 North Front St., Suite 122
Harrisburg, PA 17102

PUERTO RICO
D3 Via Bernardo
Monte Alvernia
Rio Piedras, PR 00927

RHODE ISLAND
345 Blackstone Blvd.
Providence, RI 02906

SOUTH CAROLINA
P.O. Box 5008
Columbia, SC 29250

SOUTH DAKOTA
4961 Sheridan Lake Rd.
Rapid City, SD 57702

TENNESSEE
2704 12th Ave., South
Nashville, TN 37204

TEXAS
810 West 11th St.
Austin, TX 78701

UTAH
University of Utah
Graduate School of Social Work
Salt Lake City, UT 84112

VERMONT
P.O. Box 147
Woodstock, VT 05091

VIRGINIA
1500 Forest Ave., Suite 224
Richmond, VA 23288

VIRGIN ISLANDS
P.O. Box 5247, Sunny Isle
Christiansted, St. Croix,
U.S. Virgin Islands 00820

WASHINGTON
2366 Eastlake Ave., East, Suite 236
Seattle, WA 98102

WEST VIRGINIA
1608 Virginia St., East
Charleston, WV 25311

WISCONSIN
14 Mifflin St., Suite 2
Madison, WI 53703

WYOMING
3904 Dillon Ave.
Cheyenne, WY 82001

INDEX

ABOUT THE AUTHOR

ROBERT L. BARKER opened his full-time private practice in 1970 in Washington, D.C. His practice specialty was in marital and family therapy and group psychotherapy. The practice began as a partnership with a psychiatrist, and it eventually expanded to include another psychiatrist, a psychologist, and another social worker. He later joined the faculty at The Catholic University of America. His MSW is from the University of Washington, and his DSW is from Columbia University. He is the founder of the *Journal of Independent Social Work* and author of 16 books, including *Treating Couples in Crisis* (Free Press, 1984), *The Green-Eyed Marriage* (Free Press, 1987), *The Business of Psychotherapy* (Columbia University Press, 1982), *Forensic Social Work* (Haworth Press, 1991), and the second edition of *The Social Work Dictionary* (NASW Press, 1991).

Look on Internet process
of obtaining ACSW & QCSW

Cronley
Menlove
Wagner
Schwab
Piccurdo
Terry
Stefan

→Wagner